Credit
Analysis

WILEY PROFESSIONAL BANKING AND FINANCE SERIES
EDWARD I. ALTMAN, Editor

THE STOCK MARKET, 4TH EDITION
    Richard J. Teweles and Edward S. Bradley
TAX SHELTERED FINANCING THROUGH THE R & D LIMITED
PARTNERSHIP
    James K. La Fleur
CORPORATE FINANCIAL DISTRESS: A COMPLETE GUIDE TO
PREDICTING, AVOIDING, AND DEALING WITH BANKRUPTCY
    Edward I. Altman
CREDIT ANALYSIS: A COMPLETE GUIDE
    Roger H. Hale

Credit
Analysis
A Complete Guide

ROGER H. HALE

A Wiley-Interscience Publication

JOHN WILEY & SONS

New York • Chichester • Brisbane • Toronto • Singapore

Library of Congress Cataloging in Publication Data:

Hale, Roger H.
    Credit analysis.

    (Wiley professional banking and finance series)
    "A Wiley-Interscience publication."
    Includes bibliographical references and index.
    1. Bank loans—Handbooks, manuals, etc. 2. Credit—
Handbooks, manuals, etc. 3. Credit bureaus—Handbooks,
manuals, etc. I. Title. II. Series.
HG1641.H255 1983   658.8′8   83-10217
ISBN 0-471-88725-0

Printed in the United States of America

10 9 8 7 6 5 4 3 2 1

Series Preface

The worlds of banking and finance have changed dramatically during the past few years, and no doubt this turbulence will continue through the 1980s. We have established the Wiley Professional Banking and Finance Series to aid in characterizing this dynamic environment and to further the understanding of the emerging structures, issues, and content for the professional financial community.

We envision three types of books in this series. First, we are commissioning distinguished experts in a broad range of fields to assemble a number of authorities to write specific primers on related topics. For example, some of the early handbook-type volumes in the series concentrate on the Stock Market, Investment Banking, and Financial Depository Institutions. A second type of book attempts to combine text material with appropriate empirical and case studies written by practitioners in relevant fields. An early example is a forthcoming volume on The Management of Cash and Other Short-Term Assets. Finally, we are encouraging definitive, authoritative works on specialized subjects for practitioners and theorists.

It is a distinct pleasure and honor for me to assist John Wiley & Sons, Inc. in this important endeavor. In addition to banking and financial practitioners, we think business students and faculty will benefit from this series. Most of all, though, we hope this series will become a primary source in the 1980s for the members of the professional financial community to refer to theories and data and to integrate important aspects of the central changes in our financial world.

EDWARD I. ALTMAN

Professor of Finance
New York University
Schools of Business

Preface

This is a book about credit: It is not about accounting or about law relating to banking. The reason is that there seems to be a genuine lack of published material on credit, and this book is intended to fill that gap. Because credit decisions are the reflection of personal judgment about a borrower's ability to repay, it ought to be possible to write in general terms about this subject without relating the material just to the business environment of one country. For, after all, business risks are of the same type although not of the same magnitude all over the world. The aim is, therefore, to assist bankers and credit analysts to make credit decisions by writing about a universal form of credit analysis. As a result of its approach to the study of risk, this book should also be valuable to long-term lenders and bond market investors, as well as to those who are undertaking a business school program with special emphasis on finance.

The idea for this book came one wet weekend in the Philippines, where I was working for two months to start up an Asian credit training program. It was clear that there was keen interest from foreign bankers to learn the U.S. bank credit analysis system so as to apply this within their own countries. However, most available material was not written for such an audience and was primarily oriented toward the U.S. domestic banking scene. Further, it was frequently full of jargon and not suitable for people for whom English is a second language. Accordingly, as I had had the privilege of teaching credit to trainees from more than 20 countries over the previous three years, and as I had learned the U.S. system after several years in a British bank, it seemed appropriate to attempt the task of writing a general guidebook that could be applied in any country. Furthermore, in order to make it a practical book, problems and case studies have been included to illustrate the points made.

All the views expressed in this book are my own rather than any expression of the policy of the major New York bank for which I work. However, I would like to thank many colleagues for their ideas and constructive criticism. I would also like to thank Stauffer Chemical Company and Northern Engineering Industries Limited for permission to use their financial statements as examples.

One word of warning: References will be made frequently to Generally Accepted Accounting Principles (GAAP) as issued by the U.S. Financial Accounting Standards Board. Readers should become familiar with U.S. accounting principles in order to get the best out of this book.

ROGER H. HALE

Oldwick, New Jersey
August 1983

Contents

CHAPTER 1   WHAT IS CREDIT ANALYSIS?   1

CHAPTER 2   EXAMINING THE EVIDENCE   11

CHAPTER 3   CASHFLOW ANALYSIS   39

CHAPTER 4   CORPORATE STRUCTURE   65

CHAPTER 5   USING FINANCIAL RATIOS   79

CHAPTER 6   FINANCIAL CONDITION   103

CHAPTER 7   EVALUATION OF INDUSTRY AND MANAGEMENT   121

CHAPTER 8   CORPORATE COLLAPSE   135

CHAPTER 9   TERM LOANS   151

CHAPTER 10   ANALYSIS OF COMMERCIAL BANKS   167

CHAPTER 11   HOW TO WRITE A CREDIT ANALYSIS   199

CHAPTER 12   EIGHTEEN CREDIT PROBLEMS   213

APPENDIX 1   CASE STUDIES   219

APPENDIX 2   SOLUTION TO NORTHERN ENGINEERING INDUSTRIES PROBLEM   281

APPENDIX 3   GLOSSARY OF FINANCIAL TERMS   285

INDEX   301

1 What Is Credit Analysis?

If a pawnbroker lends money against a gold watch, he does not need credit analysis. He needs instead to know the value of the watch. But if a banker lends money either to a person or to a corporation, the banker needs credit analysis to help determine the risks involved with the loan and the likelihood of repayment.

If credit is, as the English philosopher John Locke wrote in the seventeenth century, "nothing but the expectation of a sum of money within some limited time,"[1] then credit analysis is the process of inquiry prior to making the decision to lend. In this inquiry, the banker today does his best to replace emotional feelings, such as hopes and fears, with reasoned arguments based upon a careful study of a borrower's strengths and weaknesses.

The fundamentals of modern credit analysis are twofold: First is the examination of the nature of the borrower's business in the context of its industry, and second is the analysis of cash flow. The purpose of the former is to understand the comparative market position of the firm, the pressures of competition, the risk and reward structure of the industry, the barriers to entry, the degree of technological change, and so on. The purpose of cashflow analysis, on the other hand, is to disentangle from financial statements based on historical accounting principles the actual movements of cash in terms of its sources and uses. Once these past sources and uses have been examined, a reasonable estimate can be made as to future sources and uses, and this can be combined with the understanding of the borrower already gained to permit a judgment to be made as to the borrower's credit worthiness.

It was not always so. In the old days, bankers relied extensively on secured lending, which, as I have suggested, requires only a good valuation of the security being offered rather than a knowledge of credit. Then, too, financial statements, standards of disclosure of information, and the amount of market information which is generally available have all changed radically in the past 50 years, especially in industrialized countries. As a result, a much

---

[1]Quoted in *A Dictionary of the English Language,* Samuel Johnson, London, 1773.

more detailed comparison is now possible based on financial ratio calculations, but at the same time, the reader must also be warned that financial
analysis is only part of the process.

In the old days, too, money was traditionally available from banks for
only short periods of up to a year and usually was related to seasonal borrowings. As a result, early textbooks on banking, besides spending many
chapters describing the legal requirements of secured loans, usually concentrated on the seasonal borrower. In such cases, most attention was paid
to the balance sheet and in particular to the working capital of the firm. To
quote an example from a 1924 textbook, "It is necessary for the credit man
to 'shade the assets,' or to write off a certain percentage merely as a pre-
cautionary measure. The important factor is not the applicant's opinion as
to the value of his assets, which the listed valuation all too frequently represents, but the actual value that will ultimately be realised from them."

At that time, the main concern was working capital. Was there enough?
How would it change if conditions changed? How much would be left if the
assets were written down? The emphasis thus was placed upon the ability
of a company to repay its debts if liquidation were to occur. As A. S. Dewing
observed: "Bankers have proverbially been interested in statements of
the net worth of a business at liquidation—as if the fundamental value of a
working horse were its value for fertilizer."[2] Unfortunately, this tended to
concentrate the analyst's mind on the balance sheet and not on the income
statements. Therefore, the analyst was looking at a static situation, not a
dynamic one. At best, three years of balance sheets would be compared,
but too little emphasis would be placed on the income statements, which
are the bridge connecting each static situation. And cashflow was not really
discussed at all.

One limitation of this approach was that it was not possible to know
whether working capital was adequate. Some financial analysts claimed that,
if current assets were double the figure of current liabilities, thus giving a
current ratio of two to one, this could be taken to mean that working capital
was adequate. They argued that, in case of bankruptcy, falling prices, or
inflated figures, the book value of current assets could shrink by 50% in
liquidation, and current creditors, provided there were no long-term creditors,
would still receive payment of their obligation in full.

Such an approach has several weaknesses. First, it pays no regard to the
quality of the assets. Current assets such as short-term investments which
are readily marketable without further cost or work being undertaken have
quite a different quality from assets such as work in progress or partly finished
goods for which no market may exist. Companies often fail because their
products fail. In these circumstances, the value of their inventories will bear
no relation to recorded values. If the products failed to sell when the firm

---

[2]*The Financial Policy of Corporations*, 5th ed., Vol. 2, A. S. Dewing, Copyright © 1953 Ronald
Press. Reprinted by permission of John Wiley & Sons, Inc.

was a going concern, then how much more likely is it that they will fail to sell when the firm is, as they say, a "gone" concern.

Second, the approach pays no regard to the nature of the liabilities. Some liabilities are much more current than others. One person to whom the liability is owed may have very strong bargaining power. Another may have a pressing need for payment and cannot wait. While the government is often a creditor of a firm—for taxes due or social security payments—and has strong bargaining power, it seldom exercises this by putting firms into liquidation. However, a supplier of goods—especially one that is bigger than the firm, has been extending credit for large amounts, and is the sole supplier available—can have a great deal of power. One might say that such liabilities are the most current of all in that if they are not settled regularly, the supplies of goods will cease. But these situations are rare. It is nearly always the banks, not the suppliers, who put firms into liquidation. Indeed, as one witty and experienced banker once remarked, "The principal asset of many insolvent firms is the forbearance of their creditors."

CASHFLOW ANALYSIS

Working capital analysis and the current ratio, then, were the core of the old system. But they were often found to be insufficient. The depression of the 1930s, the rapid expansion of nearly all types of business in the 1945–1955 period, and increased international trade and competition brought about a searching reappraisal of all types of business practices. Many creditors found that they suffered losses even when they lent to businesses with "adequate" working capital. Demand for credit was changing also. Whereas short-term lending had been the order of the day in the 1930s and 1940s, with the emergence of the 1950s, demand for longer term funds from banks began to appear. This happened first in the United States, and then as American banks moved overseas, taking their term lending techniques with them, it was found that business firms in most other countries had needs for bank credit of longer than one year.

To quote A. S. Dewing again,

> The Banker has come to understand that the basis of credit is the presumption that earning power will continue, it is not based on the amount of working capital nor on the liquidity of any kind of capital as such. Ultimately he has come to recognise that such a loan can be paid except through other borrowings only over the comparatively long period during which the earnings can accumulate. Whatever may have been the tradition of banking, the basis of value upon which the credit of the corporation must ultimately rest, is the earning power.[3]

[3]*The Financial Policy of Corporations,* 5th ed., Vol. 1, A. S. Dewing, Copyright © 1953 Ronald Press. Reprinted by permission of John Wiley & Sons, Inc.

This was indeed an improvement upon the static balance sheet analysis. From this approach grew more reliance upon debt service coverage ratios and the total amount of long-term debt in relation to the overall long-term sources of funds available to the firm (that is, equity). Debt service coverage ratios compare a firm's available income with the demands of interest payments and capital requirements. Although they are useful ratios, they suffer from comparing two things which are not of like nature. Interest payments need to be made in cash, and income is based on accounting principles that are not related to cash movements. With the emergence of the 1950s, cashflow first became more important in the short-term analysis of bankers. It was given strong emphasis in the 1953 textbook *Introduction to Business Finance*.[4] The authors B. B. Howard and M. Upton made this statement:

> It should be clear that the real problem in judging a business's short term financial position is to ascertain as closely as possible the future cash generating ability of the business in relation to the claims upon that cash that will have to be met in the near future. . . . It matters not what conditions prevail at a given time; the important thing is whether the business in performing its regular operating functions can continue to generate cash in sufficient quantity and in satisfactory time to meet all operating and financial obligations.

It was another decade before long-term capital markets also reflected the cashflow approach. In a classic *Harvard Business Review* article of 1962,[5] Donaldson discussed the viewpoint of the corporate treasurer in looking at the debt capacity of the firm. Pointing out the inadequacies of traditional debt capacity decision rules for purposes of internal debt policy, Donaldson stated that the basic question to be answered in the appraisal of the magnitude of risk associated with long-term debt could be posed with deceptive simplicity: "What are the chances of the business running out of cash in the foreseeable future?" Donaldson highlighted the fact that debt service coverage ratios related to accounting income, not cash, and that debt had to be serviced with cash. His new approach based the maximum debt capacity on what management can estimate to be the "maximum adverse limits of recession behavior covering each factor affecting cashflow." In other words, this approach required management to make worst-case projections to see what cashflows would still be available for servicing long-term debt.

> Suppose a company has been assuming, as many do, that it can safely incur longterm debt up to a maximum of 30% of capitalization. This rule can be translated into its equivalent of dollars of annual debt servicing charges and directly compared with the results of the recession cashflow analysis. In view

---

[4]B. B. Howard and M. Upton. *Introduction to Business Finance.* New York: McGraw-Hill, 1953, p. 135. Reproduced with permission.

[5]Reprinted by permission of *Harvard Business Review.* Excerpt from "New Framework for Corporate Debt Policy" by Gordon Donaldson (March/April 1962), Copyright © 1962 by the President and Fellows of Harvard College. All rights reserved.

of the fact that the rule probably has been derived from external sources, it is likely that the annual debt servicing which it permits either exceeds or falls short of the amount of cashflow indicated by the internal analysis.

In view of the approximate nature of the analysis however, this is not likely to cause a change in debt policy unless the amount of the variation is substantial."[6]

These views are now widely accepted as the proper basis for assessing the solvency of corporations. A balance sheet by itself does not provide this sort of information because it says nothing about cash-generating ability. Most of the cash which a company will receive over the next 12 months is not represented by balance sheet assets as of the date of that balance sheet, just as most of the obligations to be paid are not shown as liabilities since they have not at that time come into existence. Such obligations are, for instance, the regular payments to suppliers and employees and the purchase of capital equipment.

In the same way, sales are the basic source of cashflow, and a balance sheet tells little about sales. The former notion that current assets are the source from which current liabilities are paid is not very useful. Current liabilities are not paid with current assets—they are paid with cash. It is the cash conversion cycle that demands the analyst's attention. This cycle is the process of buying goods, converting them, adding value, selling them, and collecting the proceeds of sale. In the course of this cycle, current assets are constantly being created and replaced. (This will be discussed further in Chapter 6.)

Cashflow from operations is the phrase chosen by analysts to cover the cash resulting from normal sales of goods in any period, less the cash paid out to settle operating liabilities in that period. As will be seen, this cashflow is not the same as profit, nor is it necessary or likely that the operating cash outflow in any one period is related to the same set of goods and services that caused cash to flow in. Cashflow from operations under normal conditions provides the banker's source of repayment. In this, we include seasonal loans, where short-term debt is repaid by the reduction in the level of current assets (inventory and accounts receivable) at the end of the season, as inventories are reduced and accounts receivable are collected. To find a company's cashflow from operations, it is necessary to have two balance sheets and an income statement for that period. How to use these is explained in Chapter 3.

Earlier, reference was made to the earning power of the corporation. Now we are saying that cashflow is more important than earnings. This deserves some explanation. There is not necessarily a contradiction here. In the long run, companies that do not have the ability to generate earnings will die, either by dissolution or through being acquired by another company. In the long run, too, a dollar has been or is expected to be received at some time during the life of the enterprise for each dollar of revenue recognized by accounting principles during a given period, and a dollar either has been or will be paid out at some time for every dollar of expense matched with that revenue. However, because of the leads and lags between cash payments and the definition of a cash payment as an expense, the amount of cash generated by a company in a short period of time, such as a year, will equal accounting profit only by accident. And furthermore, while monetary profits for the actual lifetime of the firm must equal its net cashflows over the same period, profitable firms, as will be seen later, can have large cash outflows over extended periods of time as a result of the need to build up inventories for future growth. Indeed, some levels of sales growth are unsustainable without negative cashflows, even for very profitable firms. In the short-term, therefore, cashflows are more important than earnings. The principal reason is that earnings can be manipulated by management's choice of accounting policies, whereas cashflow cannot be changed by any accounting policy. Examples of these policies are discussed in the section on the nature of accounting principles in Chapter 2.

Identifying Risks

After recognizing the importance of cashflow in the analysis of credit, the next feature to study is the degree and type of risks affecting that cashflow. Bear in mind that, in statistics, risk is measured by the probability of certain outcomes. Probability itself represents the extent to which an outcome can be predicted on the basis of observations of historic results and their distribution around a mean or average figure. It is an accepted principle that the more certain a future cashflow is, the greater the funds that can be borrowed against it. Indeed, the basis for modern investment analysis involves the discounting of future cashflows so as to make capital budgeting decisions and recognizes that more risky future cashflows require higher rates of discount. It follows, therefore, that as analysts you should try to list and quantify the risks affecting the firms you are studying.

Business risks are very diverse. You need more than an organized approach to judge which risks are important in any situation. You also need good judgment. The following list simply presents one way of looking at business risks, but the suggested questions regarding risk are certainly not exhaustive. It is based on the four major functional disciplines of business— namely, production, marketing, personnel, and finance—plus the influence of government.

Production.   Does the business have one or many sources for supplies of materials? What is the effect of changes in the cost of power and fuel? What is the main element in production costs? Capital? Labor? Is there rapid technological change? How costly is it to innovate? How dependent is the business on other firms? What are the effects of research and development? What is the effect of volume changes on the cost structure? What risks affect the location of the plant?

Marketing. What factors affect industry sales? Are sales highly variable? Is demand price elastic? Is income elastic? What are substitute products? Are imports significant? What are the competitors' strategies? What are the barriers to entry of new competitors? What changes in customer needs could happen? Are buyers more powerful than suppliers? What is a source of strength in this market? How vulnerable is it? What is the risk of losing a major customer?

Personnel. What causes labor turnover? What causes productivity increases? What is the motivation of employees? What is the risk of strikes? When will labor contracts expire? How dependent is the firm on certain key individuals?

Finance. How vulnerable is the firm to interest rates? How much access to outside capital does it have? How dependent is it on a single large project? How diversified are revenue sources? How vulnerable is it to customer credit losses?

Government Action. In what ways could the government or its agencies affect the firm? Monopoly or antitrust regulation? Economic policy? Protection from imports? Export subsidiaries? Government contracts? State-owned competitors? Tax on output? Excise duty? Licensing of new products? License to do business?

In thinking about such risks, you would do well to try and quantify the degree of probability of the events which affect cashflow.

Comparative Analysis

All businesses face risks. Every member of an industry faces risks, although obviously the successful members have overcome these risks better than the unsuccessful. To judge the credit worthiness of a company, you have to look at it in the context of its industry through the process of comparative analysis. This is similar to the way a doctor must compare a patient's medical test results against the results for a healthy person so as to judge the patient's current state of health. In credit analysis, it is normal to use financial ratios to compare companies within the same industry. Choosing and using financial ratios is discussed in Chapter 5. For the moment, however, it will be sufficient to introduce an alternative to simple financial ratios to illustrate how it is possible to compare members of the same industry by rating each of them on what analysts consider to be key strengths or key elements within that industry. For example, let's look at the worldwide heavy equipment industry. Table 1.1 shows the key elements chosen by experienced industry analysts.

Table 1.1   Variables in Industry Analysis

Marketing Variables	*Production Variables*
Product quality	Capacity
Product line comparison	Operating leverage
Price	Degree of integration
End sales financing	Automation
Dealer network	Sourcing
Advertising	Economies of scale
Market share	Labor relations
Financial Variables	*Strategic Variables*
Size of assets	Research
Profitability	Management
Debt capacity	Government support
Access to capital markets	Marketing strategy
Ownership	
Capital spending requirements	
Characteristics of banking group	
Foreign exchange effects	

After listing the features, the analysts assigned numerical ratings to each feature for each company according to its perceived strength, adjusting each rating for how accurate they thought their perception to be. Variables were also given different weightings according to their perceived importance. Companies then emerged with a credit score, and for portfolio analysis purposes, a bank is able to compare the extent of its exposure to each member of the industry against the perceived strength of that member.

Comparative analysis also includes comparing the latest financial results of a company with its own track record, using a form of "spread sheet" described in Chapter 2. This is sometimes called horizontal analysis, because the comparison with prior years' performance is made by looking horizontally across the columns for each year. By contrast, vertical analysis is the process of determining what caused changes in the current year's results. This is discussed further in the following chapters.

CREDIT ANALYSIS WITHIN THE LENDING FUNCTION

There was a time a few years back when competition between banks for lending to businesses was less severe than today. Bank marketing departments did not exist, and bankers did not go out to call on prospects. Companies were expected to prepare their own loan applications, and generally they chose to stay loyal to those banks which had been with them for some years. Indeed, if a company approached a bank with whom it had had no previous relationship, it was generally assumed that this must be a poor credit risk, since why else would it want to leave its existing bank?

In our increasingly competitive environment, however, all that has changed, and it is now the bankers who call on the customers rather than vice versa. The lending process has therefore developed into a four-stage affair: (1) the development of new business; (2) the process of credit evaluation, including an annual review of the borrower; (3) the pricing and structuring of the loan or line of credit; and (4) the obtaining of repayment. Regrettably, the fourth stage can deteriorate into work-out and even charge-off. *Work out* is the process whereby, because the borrower has failed significantly with its repayment plans, the lender is obliged to work out the problem by some kind of restructuring, renegotiation, or even ultimately liquidation of the company. *Charge-off* is the term used to designate amounts written off as uncollectible—that is, bad loans. Obviously, no bank wants bad loans, but in the nature of things, every bank has them. If it does not, it is likely that it is too risk averse and is possibly contracting in size. Credit analysis is intended to keep the number of bad loans to a minimum and to highlight a potential problem early enough to enable the lender to seek early repayment or withdrawal from the credit. Getting out of problem loans is the supreme test of the bank lending officer, and to this extent, every bank officer should maintain his or her credit skills.

From time to time, there is debate about whether a lending institution should be organized with two separate functions—namely, a business development group and a credit department. The business development group, consisting of account officers, is charged with the responsibility of marketing and selling financial services, including credit products, while the credit department performs analyses and decides which borrowers are acceptable. The alternative structure is one without a credit department but where each officer accepts responsibility for his or her lending decisions, including performing the credit analysis (or at least supervising and reviewing it).

Both structures have their weaknesses. The two-function approach tends to generate fierce conflict between those who want to develop new business (that is, sell loans) and those who want to keep risk acceptable. In prosperous times, the marketing people have the dominant organizational position, but in recessions, the credit department becomes more powerful. Besides this conflict, there are also other problems: The business development group usually does not consider itself responsible for asset quality, may well be judged for its performance on increasing loan volume, tends to have more organizational influence, especially in growth-oriented institutions, and feels superior to the credit department.

On the other hand, the delegated responsibility approach, where account officers accept the need for quality as well as volume in their loan portfolios, has the weakness that its success depends on having experienced account officers. Without them—the seasoned lenders—credit policy can become very weak, especially if the credit decision process is structured so that too much authority is delegated to junior officers. Some U.S. banks experienced severe problems in the early 1980s in part because the credit function was poorly structured within the organization. Having said that, however, I must add that there is no golden rule, other than that the corporate strategy of the lending institution should determine its credit decision-making structure.

2 Examining the Evidence

I keep six honest serving men,
(They taught me all I knew):
Their names are What and Why and When
And How and Where and Who.

RUDYARD KIPLING

In order to complete financial analysis successfully and thoroughly, you must begin by examining the evidence as if you were a detective. This does not, of course, mean believing that you are examining the scene of a crime, but you might say that it is dangerous to accept evidence at face value, and tests must be performed on what is found in order to establish its usefulness.

The principal evidence available to the analyst is always the company's financial statements or Annual Report and Accounts—and, therefore, it is to these that we turn first.

FINANCIAL STATEMENTS

It must be stated at once that there is absolutely no substitute for reading the company's Annual Report from cover to cover, including and indeed paying especially close attention to items in small print. A typical public company's Annual Report, of course, contains considerably more than financial statements, including generally such items as a Chairman's statement, a historical record of five or more years, pictures of happy employees or the company's gleaming products, charts, graphs, and various other information, much of which will be useful to the analyst in learning about nonfinancial aspects of the company.

On the other hand, privately controlled companies, which are not obliged to disclose information to the same extent as publicly owned companies, will be much more discreet and generally limit themselves to the minimum disclosure required by the laws of the country of residence. This semisecrecy is sometimes seen as common sense on the grounds that "what you don't tell can't hurt you," but often it is also considered wise for a company not to give competitors and critics any ammunition that they could use against the company.

Frequently, whether dealing with public or private companies, you will be looking for certain information and will find it is not disclosed in the financial statements available. Rightly, you will ask yourself "I wonder why not," and it is the answer to this question that will help you understand the company. There are several very successful firms that probably attribute part of their success to a policy of nondisclosure, among which the best-known are Michelin and Hallmark Cards, and thus in no way should the absence of information be considered by itself a credit weakness. You must be satisfied that the reason for disclosure or nondisclosure of information is a legitimate one, and to this end, you must always consider for whom the financial statements were produced. This is particularly true in countries where strict accounting standards are unknown; here, rumor has it, there are often three sets of books kept by the bookkeeper—one for the tax collector, one for the banker, and one for the actual owners of the business.

WHERE TO START

Given a public company's Annual Report, you might wonder where to start. A good place is often the Auditor's Opinion, followed by the page disclosing the company's principal accounting policies. Bearing in mind that no management would use anything except management accounting for making decisions in running the business, you should at once recognize that these figures are being produced by management for others to read and are based on financial accounting principles, not management accounting principles. It is appropriate, therefore, at the outset to see first whether management has been given a clean report by the outside auditors, one of whose jobs it is to check that the figures "present fairly" the results for the year, and then to determine whether the accounting principles employed seem reasonable for the kind of industry being examined.

Next, it is sensible to get a simple profile of the company by turning to the balance sheet to answer three questions: How large? How profitable? How solvent? Proper measures of size, profitability, and solvency are discussed in Chapter 5, but suffice it to say at this point that a rapidly growing, profitable but rather insolvent company may have good reasons to choose accounting principles that are different from those chosen by a large, steady but highly solvent company. The most obvious reason that comes to mind is that the former will be more conscious of presenting itself to investors in a highly attractive form because of its probable need for new equity capital. In other words, it will want to make its profits look as good as possible.

THE AUDITOR'S OPINION

It has already been stated that one of the auditor's tasks is to see that the financial statements present fairly the financial position. The auditor has other tasks as well, but contrary to popular belief, these do not normally

FINANCIAL REPORT

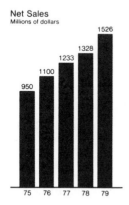

Net Sales
Millions of dollars

950 1100 1233 1328 1526
75   76   77   78   79

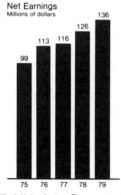

Net Earnings
Millions of dollars

99 113 116 126 136
75   76   77   78   79

Statement of management responsibility for financial statements

The accompanying financial statements of Stauffer Chemical Company and subsidiaries for the years ended December 31, 1979 and 1978, were prepared by management in conformity with generally accepted accounting principles.

The Company is responsible for the integrity and objectivity of its financial statements. In preparing these financial statements, management makes informed judgments and estimates of the expected effects of events and transactions that are currently being accounted for.

The Company maintains systems of internal accounting controls which are designed to provide reasonable assurance that assets are safeguarded and records reflect in all material respects the transactions of the Company, in accordance with management's authorizations. These systems include formal policies and procedures, organizational structures that provide an appropriate division of responsibility, careful selection and training of qualified personnel, and an extensive program of internal audits and appropriate management follow-up. The Company believes its systems provide reasonable assurance that assets are safeguarded and that its records are reliable.

The Board of Directors, through its Operating and Audit Committees, monitors the financial and accounting administration of the Company, including the review of the activities of both the internal auditors and the independent public accountants, the review and discussion of periodic financial statements, and the evaluation and adoption of budgets.

Deloitte Haskins & Sells, Certified Public Accountants, have examined the accompanying financial statements and their opinion is included herein. Their examination includes a review of the systems of internal accounting control and appropriate tests of transactions. The auditors met with members of the Audit Committee to discuss the results of their examination, and were afforded an opportunity to present their opinions in the absence of management personnel with respect to various financial matters.

Exhibit 2.1 Statement of Management Responsibility for Financial Statements (Stauffer Chemical Company 1979 Annual Report, p. 23). Reprinted by permission.

include preparation of the statements, which is in fact done by the company's own staff (see Exhibit 2.1). Auditors are members of independent outside firms of accountants, who meet certain prescribed professional standards and have received a certificate or license to practice in the country or state of the client company. Although they perform the audit for a commercial fee which the company pays, it is important to note that it is their responsibility, not that of management, to decide how thorough a job is required, and thus companies cannot really negotiate the extent of auditing by insisting on a maximum fee payable.

AUDITORS' OPINION

Deloitte
Haskins + Sells
Certified Public Accountants
44 Montgomery Street
San Francisco, California

To the Stockholders of Stauffer Chemical Company:

We have examined the consolidated balance sheets of Stauffer Chemical Company and subsidiaries as of December 31, 1979 and 1978, and the related statements of consolidated earnings, consolidated stockholders' equity, and changes in consolidated financial position for the years then ended. Our examinations were made in accordance with generally accepted auditing standards and, accordingly, included such tests of the accounting records and such other auditing procedures as we considered necessary in the circumstances.

In our opinion, such consolidated financial statements present fairly the financial position of Stauffer Chemical Company and subsidiaries at December 31, 1979 and 1978, and the results of their operations and the changes in their financial position for the years then ended, in conformity with generally accepted accounting principles consistently applied during the period except for the change, with which we concur, in 1979 in the method of accounting for certain interest costs as described in the notes to financial statements.

Deloitte Haskins + Sells

February 19, 1980

Exhibit 2.2   Auditor's Opinion (Stauffer Chemical Company 1979 Annual Report, p. 34). Reprinted by permission.

All companies whose shares are listed on an organized stock exchange, and indeed many other companies too, have their financial statements audited, but it is suspected that few readers of these statements are aware of the exact limitations of an auditor's opinion. First of all, it is widely and incorrectly referred to as an Auditor's Certificate. It is in fact seldom a certificate. For instance, careful examination of the words used in the Typical U.S. auditor's opinion shown in Exhibit 2.2 will assure the reader that nothing has been certified as true or existing. All that is clear is that the auditors have conducted certain examinations of records and tests such as they considered necessary and that their opinion is that the three specified statements perform a definite function within a set of definite rules. There are four significant points to make here:

1.   *The three statements which are audited are the balance sheet, the income statement, and the statement of changes in financial position.*   The auditors do not comment on any other financial information that may be included in the annual report, although of course the notes to the three audited statements are covered by the opinion. It is conceivable therefore that some innocent readers of company reports believe the Chairman's remarks to have been verified by the auditors. This is understandably seldom the case.

2.   *Fairness.*   The words *present fairly* are used by design. There is a world of difference between presenting fairly and presenting accurately. Indeed, accounting often involves such judgments and estimates that accuracy, in the sense of 100% certainty, is impossible. Whereas a clock can be made accurate by reference to Greenwich mean time, accounting results cannot have such accuracy, since there are no absolute standards.

3.   *GAAP.*   What standards do exist for U.S. firms are known as Generally Accepted Accounting Principles, or GAAP. At the time of writing,

GAAP is expressed in a handbook of professional standards that runs to more than 2,000 pages. Even so, not all the accounting practices which are generally accepted by accounting firms are discussed in this volume, and not all practices can be verified by reference to these rules. Furthermore, GAAP sometimes changes more rapidly than the professional standards book can document. In countries where what is generally accepted is frequently not published in a handbook at all, it is that much more difficult to know the accepted standards.

Another drawback arises from the fact that what is a generally accepted reporting method in accounting practice may not be acceptable to a banker. Accounting cannot record all the assets or liabilities of a firm, since some have no definable monetary value. However, the banker regards certain unrecorded liabilities as very significant. For example, at the present time, U.S. balance sheets under GAAP do not show pension fund shortfall (that is, the actuarially computed value of vested benefits less the actuarially computed value of pension funds), although these are very significant. In the case of the Chrysler Corporation in 1978, for instance, this figure exceeded $1 billion, or more than one-third of its tangible net worth at that time.

4. *Consistency.* This means only that what was done last year has been done this year, not that the principles are themselves internally consistent, nor even that one subsidiary uses the same principles as another subsidiary. It does mean, however, that the figures are comparable one year with another.

QUALIFIED OPINIONS

No company likes a qualified opinion, neither does a banker or an investor. However, there are variations in the degree of qualification. If the opinion is stated "subject to . . ." some unresolved matter, that should be viewed differently from one that is stated "except for. . . ." The former (for example, "subject to the outcome of litigation") is used when there is an event outside the company's control that will affect certain recorded values of assets or liabilities. The latter (for example, "except for the change . . . in the method of accounting for certain interest costs," see Exhibit 2.2) is used where the auditor has to qualify an opinion either for a change in accounting policy that affects consistency (with which the auditor concurs or does not concur), or where GAAP is not followed (which is rare), or where a fair presentation is not made (which is even rarer). Before making such an opinion, the auditor will discuss the situation with the management of the company, and very often management will prefer to change the statements. This is especially true of statements that go to the U.S. Securities and Exchange Commission (namely, Form 10K), since that body will not accept any statements that are not in conformity with GAAP.[1]

---

[1] It should be observed that, in annual reports, U.S. companies may give shareholders less or even different financial information from that included in Form 10K.

WHO ARE THE AUDITORS?

Unfortunately for the banker, but fortunately for the accounting profession, not all practicing accountants belong to the largest and most respected auditing firms. Nor are these large firms, sometimes known as "The Big Eight," infallible, as many actions for negligence have shown. It falls to the banker, therefore, in whatever city he is, to know the reliability of the local accounting firms, and especially their integrity and independence. Small firms with large corporate clients are generally thought to be vulnerable to pressure from their clients which may erode their independence.

As an analyst, you should note whether the auditors have been changed. A change may not signify anything, but it could indicate that corporate management had a dispute over accounting policies with the previous auditors and sought a more congenial auditor.

Finally, a quick check of the date of the opinion will be worth the effort. The longer accounts take to prepare compared with the previous year, the more likely it is that there were unusual or complex transactions, or possible disagreements with auditors. Late accounts seldom contain good news.

SUMMARY OF SIGNIFICANT ACCOUNTING POLICIES

Consolidation

The consolidated financial statements include those of the Company and its subsidiaries. Investments in associated companies (20 to 50 per cent owned) are stated at cost plus equity in undistributed earnings since acquisition. All significant intercompany transactions and balances have been eliminated.

Marketable Securities

Marketable securities are stated at the lower of aggregate cost or market. Carrying value approximated market at December 31, 1979 and 1978.

Inventories

Inventories are stated at the lower of cost or market. Cost for domestic inventories is generally determined using the last-in, first-out method (LIFO). Cost for other inventories is determined using the average cost method.

Property, Plant and Equipment

Property, plant and equipment is stated at cost, which includes interest for fixed assets constructed during 1979. (See "Accounting Change" in accompanying notes.) Renewals and improvements are added to property. Maintenance and repairs are charged to income.

Depreciation is computed over the estimated useful lives of depreciable assets principally using the straight-line method. The estimated useful lives applied to principal properties vary from three to sixty years.

Any profit or loss related to the disposal or retirement of property is included in income.

Intangibles Arising from Business Acquisitions

Intangibles are amortized over periods up to forty years using the straight-line method, except for intangibles of $7 million acquired prior to November 1, 1970, which are not being amortized.

Income Taxes

The provision for income taxes is based on income reported for financial statement purposes rather than amounts currently payable under tax laws. Deferred taxes are provided for significant timing differences. Investment tax credits are reflected as a reduction of the provision for income taxes in the year the credits are available for tax purposes.

Earnings per Share

Earnings per common share is based on the weighted average number of shares of common stock outstanding. The computation excludes outstanding stock options, as their dilutive effect is not material.

Exhibit 2.3 Summary of Significant Accounting Policies (Stauffer Chemical Company 1979 Annual Report, p. 24). Reprinted by permission.

THE NATURE OF ACCOUNTING PRINCIPLES

After the auditor's opinion, a good next page to read is that setting out the summary of significant accounting principles (see Exhibit 2.3).

Although this is not a book on accounting, it will be important at this point to review some basic choices in accounting principles within GAAP that are available to management in presenting financial statements. In countries where accounting principles are less sophisticated than in the United States, it will pay to check through the list to see which ones are permissible and can thus be expected to influence the figures.

Skeptics have also described the list as "ways in which companies can make their income look good." It will be demonstrated later that the cashflow approach is the best for credit analysis, since changes in accounting principles cannot affect cashflow, except insofar as the current tax charge is greater or less.

Inventory

Inventory may be carried at last in first out (LIFO), first in first out (FIFO), or average cost. It is possible for a company to have some inventories at LIFO and some at FIFO. Different subsidiaries may have different policies. It is normal practice for a company to disclose the effect of inventory valuation in the notes to the financial statements.

Example 2.1.   Stauffer Chemical Company reported in 1980 in the notes to their financial statement as follows: "Inventories stated using LIFO amounted to approximately 75 percent of total inventories at December 31, 1979 and 80 percent at December 31, 1978. If inventories stated at LIFO had been stated using the average cost method they would have been greater by approximately $100,300,000 at December 31, 1979 and $66,700,000 at December 31, 1978."

Actual inventories at December 31, 1979 were $318 million. Hence, the degree of undervaluation was on the order of 25–32%, depending on calculation basis. If the higher valuation had been used, cost of goods sold would have been lower (but it is not possible to estimate the amount) and thus trading profits would have been higher. On the other hand, cashflow would not have been affected (other than through the tax charge), as it is based on cash receipts less cash expenses for the period. In this case, the amount of cash spent on purchases of inventory and on manufacturing costs is unaffected by the method of inventory valuation.

Example 2.2.   A brewing company carries its beer barrels in inventory at the lower of cost or market value. Market value is taken to be the cash deposit paid by the brewery's customers, which is refundable when they return the empty barrels. Suppose there are 10,000 barrels on hand, the cost of each barrel is $20, and the deposit charged is $5. Barrels are then carried at $5 each, making $50,000. If the deposit level is raised to $8, there will be a revaluation of inventory, giving rise to a pretax gain of $30,000, which will show up as extraordinary income. The cashflow effect of the revaluation will be none, although, of course, cash received and paid out for barrels will be greater. None of this, however, will affect income—that is, operating cash flow. Even if barrels are (illegally) retained by purchasers, this will give rise to an inventory write-off or noncash expense.

Fixed Assets and Depreciation

Any systematic and rational method of depreciation may be used. One must not forget that depreciation charges involve at least two estimates—namely, length of life and scrap value—and both of these are open to optimistic or pessimistic approaches. Neither, of course, affects cash flow (other than through current tax expense) since depreciation is noncash expense. Only purchases and sales of assets affect cash, and these are nonoperating items.

Changes in the method of depreciation or in the length of life of assets or the scrap value of those assets will significantly affect a firm's income. This is especially true for firms that are expanding. Normally, U.S. management can choose between straight-line depreciation or accelerated depreciation. Both methods will, of course, provide the same total expense over the life of the asset. However, because straight-line expense is lower in the early years, an expanding firm's income will appear greater if this method rather than accelerated depreciation is used.

Example 2.3. Suppose a company buys an asset worth $15,000 in 19X1, two of these in 19X2, 3 in 19X3, 4 in 19X4, 5 in 19X5. Accelerated depreciation will be, let's say, on the basis of $5,000 in 19X1, $4,000 in 19X2, $3,000 in 19X3, $2,000 in 19X4, and $1,000 in 19X5. This is the sum of the year's digits method with a five-year life. Annual depreciation charges will be as follows:

Year	Straight-Line	Accelerated
19X1	$3,000	$5,000
19X2	$6,000	$9,000 ($5,000 + $4,000)
19X3	$9,000	$12,000 ($5,000 + $4,000 + $3,000)
19X4	$12,000	$14,000 ($5,000 + $4,000 + $3,000 + $2,000)
19X5	$15,000	$15,000 ($5,000 + $4,000 + $3,000 + $2,000 + $1,000)
19X6	$15,000	$15,000

As a result, an expanding firm will prefer to show income after straight-line depreciation, as this will improve its position.

Notice how misleading it is to speak of cashflow as net income plus depreciation. This is discussed further in Chapter 3. For the present, it is enough to show that, if this firm in 19X2 had an income of $20,000 before depreciation and taxes, but after deducting every other expense, cashflow on a straight-line basis would be:

Income	$20,000
Depreciation	(6,000)
	14,000
Tax at 50%	(7,000)
	7,000
Cashflow	13,000

However, on an accelerated basis, cashflow would be:

Income	$20,000
Less depreciation	(9,000)
	11,000
Less tax at 50%	(5,500)
Cashflow	14,500

How convenient life would be if companies could increase their cashflow by changing their depreciation policy. What has happened is indeed a lower tax charge, but whether cashflow has changed cannot be known without examining the degree to which cash payments have been made for taxes payable as well as for all revenue and expense items. This is discussed further in Chapter 3. Suffice it to say for the moment that cashflow is *not* net income plus depreciation, because this overlooks the effect of cash received or paid as a result of changes in the level of operating (working) assets and operating liabilities.

In some countries, fixed assets revaluation is practiced in such a way that, where professional outside valuers provide a market value substantially in excess of current recorded value for property, this new value is adopted, giving rise to an increase in owner's equity. Once again, this is noncash income and is normally shown in the reserve movements.

In many countries, costs of installation and development of properties are capitalized. (For example, interest expense on construction may be capitalized in the United States—see FASB No. 34.) This improves income but does not affect cashflow.

Revenue Recognition

The principle of revenue recognition probably gives rise to the greatest range in variation of reported income (see also Appendix to Chapter 10). It would be much easier for students of accounting if the phrase "revenue recognition" were replaced by "taking the profit" or some such words. After all, it is this question of recording the profit on a transaction which is at issue, and the issue essentially involves two things: timing and estimates.

Revenue on long-term contracts may normally be recognized on a completed contract basis or on a percentage of completion method. Under the former, no revenue or expense is shown until the contract is finished; under the latter, revenue is included proportionately with the percentage estimate of the total costs on the contract which have been incurred during that accounting period. The amount of cash received under the contract does not affect reported profits. Thus, we have both a timing question (Should no profit be shown in a period when no contracts are completed?) and an estimates question (Is it safe to report profit on a contract where only 15% of costs have been incurred and where our estimate of the remaining 85% may be very unreliable?).

Example 2.4.   Far East shipyards had three contracts on hand during 19X9. The relevant details are as follows:

Ship Kristabel: Commenced in 19X7: Finished March 31, 19X9

Local contract price	$10,000,000
Cost of work in 19X7–19X8	8,400,000
Cost of work in 19X9	2,150,000
Percentage completed in 19X9	20%
Cash received	950,000

Ship Lara: Commenced in 19X8: Finished January 20, 19X9

Local contract price	3,000,000
Cost of work in 19X8	2,800,000
Cost of work in 19X9	390,000
Percentage completed in 19X9	5%
Cash received in 19X9	None

Ship Melina: Commenced May 1, 19X9

Total contract price	4,000,000
Cost of work in 19X9	1,250,000
Percentage completed	80%
Cash received	4,000,000

Assume there is $300,000 of unallocated central overhead. The completed contract method indicates a loss for the year of ($10,000,000 − $10,550,000)

+ ($3,000,000 − $3,190,000) + $300,000—or a loss of $1,040,000. On the other hand, the percentage of completion shows a profit of $1,260,000; this is (20% × 10,000,000) − $2,150,000 + (5% × $3,000,000) − $390,000 + (80% × $4,000,000) − $1,250,000 − $300,000)—Hence $1,260,000. Readers will note that the latter may be a "truer" picture if in fact, on contracts begun after April 19X9, price negotiation favored the shipyard and if in fact 80% is an accurate estimate of costs on the Melina. Also note the wide variation in reported income under the two different methods.

Other Examples

There are several other examples where the choice of accounting principle can affect reported net income. These include but are not limited to:

Cash discounts on sales may be recorded at the time of sale or at the time of collection.

Inventory costs may include storage costs, holding costs, and costs of acquiring inventories in addition to the normal purchase cost of goods.

Oil and gas exploration cost may be expensed, or it may be capitalized.

Intangible assets may be amortized over short or long lives.

Investment tax credits may be treated on the flow-through or deferred method.

Some subsidiaries may not be consolidated if they are regarded as significantly different from the parent company or "if the presentation of financial information concerning them would be more informative if made separately,"[2] and thus they are not considered when reporting the parent company's net income. This is typical of financing subsidiaries of manufacturing companies. In Germany, foreign subsidiaries are not consolidated at all but are carried on an equity basis. Although income would not necessarily be affected by the principles of consolidation, it could be very distorted if the equity method is not used.

The acquisition of companies can be treated on a pooling or purchase basis.

Pension liabilities may be calculated using a variety of different assumptions—for instance, the interest rate which is assumed to apply to the fund's earning assets. The related pension expense may be on either of two different conceptual bases. In 1981 in the case of General Motors Corporation, there was a change in the rate assumed which affected reported net earnings by several million dollars.

Various choices are available for recognizing revenue on purchasing or leasing operations.

[2]GAAP Handbook.

Various expenses relating to assets under construction may or may not be capitalized.

Warranty costs may be accrued at time of sale or expensed as incurred. Similarly, although estimated future losses should be provided for, in practice if the loss cannot be reasonably estimated, no provision is made.

(For a special instance of this, see Manville Corporation's statements in 1980 and 1981.)

SPREADING FINANCIAL STATEMENTS

Armed with the knowledge of the limitations of audited figures, you can now proceed to the financial statements themselves. Companies are not obliged to present these in a rigidly defined format, and indeed under different national accounting systems, assets will sometimes be presented on the right hand side, sometimes on the left, and sometimes above or below the other side of the balance sheet.

As a result, bankers have developed a technique to transform this information into a standard pattern for the purpose of credit analysis. This technique is usually known as "spreading the figures." An example of a spread sheet is shown as Exhibit 2.4, but it is common practice for each bank to have variations based on local needs. (Another example is shown in the Appendix to this chapter.) Spread sheets are particularly useful in comparing a series of historical figures. They also impose a discipline on the analyst when calculating financial ratios. For example, the ratio earnings before interest and taxes/total assets is generally considered a very valuable ratio in showing the pretax rate of return generated by businesses in using assets.

Many analysts tend to start spreading the figures before reading the notes and the accounting policies. This is an unwise practice, since it can lead to classifying items incorrectly. For example, marketable securities are usually shown as current assets by companies and also by analysts on their spread sheets. On the other hand, some marketable securities may be described as "quoted investments." This may represent a long-term relationship between the subject company and another business. Most companies show this as a long-term asset, which should also be the credit analyst's approach, but occasionally such an investment might be shown by the company as a current asset, in which case the analyst should reclassify it.

Notes on Spreading Stauffer

For a good understanding of spreading, let's now work through the example shown as Exhibit 2.4 following the notes below:

1. *Balance Sheet* (Exhibit 2.5).   No technical difficulties. Note only that some items have been combined on the bank spread sheet (for example, trade receivables and notes receivable) on the assumption that there is

NAME: _____

STAUFFER CHEMICAL COMPANY

DATE →

(000'S OMITTED)

STATEMENT BASIS:
[X] CONSOLIDATED
[ ] CO. ALONE

LINE	INCOME STATEMENT	31/Dec/78	31/Dec/79	
1	NET SALES	1,328|114	1,526|160	
2	COST OF GOODS SOLD	(848|041)	(1,013|594)	
3	DEPRECIATION	(78|340)	(93|064)	
4	GROSS PROFIT	401|733	419|502	
5	OPERATING EXPENSES	135|883	161|866	
6	OPERATING PROFIT	265|080	257|636	
7	R&D	33|562	36|963	
8	INTEREST	37|923	31|839	
9	Other Expenses (Income)	6|432	(3|730)	Consider here the
10	OTHER INCOME Interest Dividends	12|044	10|277	effects of accounting
11	NET INCOME BEFORE TAXES	212|841	202|791	changes
12	Minority Interest	10|206	16|555	
13	INCOME TAXES — CURRENT	48|464	24|418	
14	— DEFERRED	24|346	36|657	
15	NET INCOME	116|961	125|161	
16	Equity Earnings of Associates	9|054	10|800	
17	PREFERRED DIVIDENDS			
18	COMMON DIVIDENDS	42|600	47|132	
19	OTHER AFTER TAX DEDUCTIONS			
20				
21	ADDITION TO RETAINED EARNINGS	83|355	88|829	

Exhibit 2.4 Spread Sheet for Balance Sheet and Income Statement

NAME: __STAUFFER CHEMICAL COMPANY__

DATE ⟶

(000'S OMITTED)

LINE	ASSETS		31/Dec/78	31/Dec/79		
22	CASH		24,996	24,712		
23	MARKETABLE SECURITIES		64,011	31,191		
24	ACCOUNTS RECEIVABLE — NET		260,506	308,562		
25	INVENTORY		278,313	318,743		
26	OTHER CURRENT ASSETS		14,434	15,489		
27	TOTAL CURRENT ASSETS		642,260	698,697		
28	FIXED ASSETS, GROSS					
29	(DEPRECIATION)					
30	FIXED ASSETS — NET		903,246	1,040,542		
31	INVESTMENTS AND ADVANCES		40,384	41,412		
32	OTHER ASSETS		50,066	66,215		
33	INTANGIBLES		31,273	29,368		
34	TOTAL		1,667,229	1,876,234		

	LIABILITIES		
35	NOTES PAYABLE	135,841	196,699
36	CURRENT PORTION — LONG TERM DEBT	13,599	9,145
37	CURRENT PORTION — SUB. DEBT		
38	ACCOUNTS PAYABLE	97,106	116,857
39	ACCRUED LIABILITIES	22,456	23,950
40	ACCRUED TAXES	21,483	25,343
41	OTHER	31,239	41,658
42	TOTAL CURRENT LIABILITIES	321,724	413,652
43	SENIOR LONG TERM DEBT	415,868	390,899
44	TOTAL UNSUBORDINATED LIABILITIES	737,592	804,551
45	SUBORDINATED DEBT		
46	TOTAL LIABILITIES		
47	DEFERRED TAXES	108,289	146,105
48	OTHER RESERVES		
49	MINORITY INTEREST	60,011	74,433
50	PREFERRED STOCK		
51	COMMON STOCK	55,757	55,856
52	CAPITAL SURPLUS	95,936	96,703
53	RETAINED EARNINGS	617,628	706,457
54	(TREASURY STOCK)	(7,984)	(7,871)
55	TOTAL	1,667,229	1,876,234

Exhibit 2.4 (Continued)

25

56	WORKING CAPITAL		320|536	285|045
57	CURRENT RATIO		2.0x	1.69x
58	TNW + SUBORDINATED DEBT		730|064	821|777
59	TOTAL UNSUB. LIAB. / CAPITAL BASE		1.01x	0.98x
60	CAPITALIZED LEASES		None	None
61	SOURCE OF FIGURES		. A/R	A/R
62	AUDITED/NON-AUDITED		Aud.	Aud.

Exhibit 2.4 (*Continued*)

little real difference. This could be wrong; for instance, notes receivable might include funds arising from the sale of fixed assets. Without further information, one cannot say.

2. *Balance Sheet Ratios.* Note the drop in the current ratio and the drop in working capital. Tangible net worth (which is defined in the Glossary) has risen, but not enough to offset the rise in liabilities. At this stage, the analyst could expect to find later as an explanation of the change in working capital either a sharp drop in income from operations or a shortfall in capital expenditures compared with long-term sources of cash.

3. *Income Statement* (Exhibit 2.6). Note the considerable reclassifying of items on Exhibit 2.4. Depreciation was found from the notes to the balance sheet and has been taken out of Cost of Goods Sold. Research and Development (R&D) is shown after Operating Profit, since it is not related to sales volume, and Interest is excluded from Operating Expense, as it is a result of a financing decision, not an operating decision. The objective is to get a "clean" figure for Operating Profit (line 6) to compare with other companies in the same industry. Note also that Equity in Earnings of Associates (line 16) has been placed net of taxes below the Net Income line to show that it is noncash income and not connected with this company's operating profits.

DEALING WITH UNAUDITED STATEMENTS

If you have annual audited statements available to you, then the occasional unaudited statement between annual audits is acceptable. But bankers very often have to deal with totally unaudited statements drawn up by management. It is natural to wonder about their reliability given what you know about the nature of the auditing process. The only way that I can suggest using them with any degree of confidence is to perform for yourself some of the functions that the auditors perform. This may mean on occasion a physical inspection of the plant, inventory, and books of account. It almost certainly means asking management to spell out the basic accounting principles which have been used, paying particular attention to inventory valuation methods and the basis for recognizing revenue.

Which figures are likely to be the most reliable in unaudited statements? In general, liabilities will be fairly reliably stated since management has no reason to understate these and they can be checked in part by calls to other known lending institutions. Credit from suppliers is not so easy to check, so this figure may need to be taken on trust. Owner's equity should be treated as a residual number and left aside for the moment. Next you should examine assets, and these will be the hardest to check. In particular, inventory valuations are suspect, since they provide the easiest place to conceal the truth (see Chapter 6). Accounts receivable could be checked against an ageing

CONSOLIDATED BALANCE SHEET

Stauffer Chemical Company and Subsidiaries

ASSETS December 31	1979 (Dollars in thousands)	1978
Current Assets Cash	$ 24,712	$ 24,996
Marketable Securities	31,191	64,011
Receivables:		
Trade — Net of Allowance for Doubtful Receivables (1979 — $2,963; 1978 — $2,554)	266,726	234,411
Notes and Other	41,836	26,095
Inventories:		
Finished Products and Work in Progress	226,195	196,261
Raw Materials and Supplies	92,548	82,052
Prepaid Expenses	15,489	14,434
Total Current Assets	**698,697**	**642,260**
Property, Plant and Equipment Land	27,011	26,901
Buildings, Machinery and Equipment — Net of Accumulated Depreciation (1979 — $600,925; 1978 — $527,852)	1,002,741	863,136
Mineral Deposits — Net of Accumulated Depletion	10,790	13,209
Property, Plant and Equipment — Net	**1,040,542**	**903,246**
Investments and Other Assets Investments and Advances — Associated Companies	41,412	40,384
Intangibles Arising from Business Acquisitions	29,368	31,273
Other Assets	66,215	50,066
Total Investments and Other Assets	**136,995**	**121,723**
Total	**$1,876,234**	**$1,667,229**

See information on page 24 and notes to financial statements on pages 30 through 34.

Exhibit 2.5 Consolidated Balance Sheet, Stauffer Chemical Company and Subsidiaries

statement (see Chapter 6) to see if any uncollected accounts need to be written off. If the preceding year's financial statements have been audited or otherwise checked, it will be possible to check fixed assets against last year's figure. Beware of revaluations of fixed assets, and ask the borrower about depreciation policies. Also, in unaudited statements, it is safest to assume that any intangible assets have no value. Now it is possible to adjust owner's equity for any changes in asset values that you may feel necessary.

Next, examine carefully the income statement. Sales are more likely than expenses to be overstated, especially if revenue recognition methods are

LIABILITIES AND STOCKHOLDERS' EQUITY	December 31	1979	1978
		(Dollars in thousands)	
Current Liabilities Notes Payable		$ 196,699	$ 135,841
Accounts Payable		116,857	97,106
Income Taxes Payable		17,899	15,121
Accrued Interest		11,636	11,312
Accrued Payroll		12,314	11,144
Other Taxes Payable		7,444	6,362
Other Liabilities		41,658	31,239
Long-Term Debt Due within One Year		9,145	13,599
Total Current Liabilities		**413,652**	**321,724**
Long-Term Debt		**390,899**	**415,868**
Deferred Income Taxes		**146,105**	**108,289**
Minority Interest in Subsidiaries		**74,433**	**60,011**
Stockholders' Equity Common Stock, $1.25 Par — 70,000,000 Shares Authorized; Issued (1979 — 44,685,172; 1978 — 44,605,492); Outstanding (1979 — 43,882,583; 1978 — 43,791,426)		55,856	55,757
Other Capital		96,703	95,936
Retained Earnings		706,457	617,628
Reacquired Common Shares — at Cost (1979 — 802,589; 1978 — 814,066)		(7,871)	(7,984)
Stockholders' Equity — Net		**851,145**	**761,337**
Total		**$1,876,234**	**$1,667,229**

(Stauffer Chemical Company 1979 Annual Report, pp. 26–27). Reprinted by permission.

being used that might be considered "creative accounting" (see Chapter 8). Watch out for shipments to customers on consignment which are treated as sales but which may be returned unsold later. Also, if you find items on the balance sheet such as "unbilled accounts receivable," then you should carefully inquire into when revenue is recognized, since such an item suggests that a profit has been recorded on items that have not even been invoiced to the customer. Since invoices invariably accompany deliveries, you can assume that this means there is inventory in the warehouse which is treated as sold even though it has been neither delivered nor invoiced to the customer.

STATEMENT OF CONSOLIDATED EARNINGS

Stauffer Chemical Company and Subsidiaries

	Year ended December 31	1979 (Dollars in thousands, except per-share amounts)	1978
Revenues	Net Sales	$1,526,160	$1,328,114
	Interest and Dividends	10,227	12,044
	Total Revenues	**1,536,387**	**1,340,158**
Cost and Expenses	Cost of Goods Sold	1,106,658	926,381
	Selling, General and Administrative	161,866	135,883
	Research and Development	36,963	33,562
	Interest	31,839	37,923
	Other Expense (Income) — Net	(3,730)	6,432
	Minority Interest	16,555	10,206
	Total Cost and Expenses	**1,350,151**	**1,150,387**
Earnings before Provision for Income Taxes		186,236	189,771
Provision for Income Taxes		61,075	72,810
Earnings from Consolidated Operations		125,161	116,961
Equity in Earnings of Associated Companies		10,800	9,054
Net Earnings		$ 135,961	$ 126,015
Earnings per Common Share		$ 3.10	$ 2.88

See information on page 24 and notes to financial statements on pages 30 through 34.

Exhibit 2.6 Statement of Consolidated Earnings, Stauffer Chemical Company and Subsidiaries (Stauffer Chemical Company 1979 Annual Report, p. 25). Reprinted by permission.

It is not likely that expenses have been understated. Borrowers may be using these financial statements as tax returns, so they will tend to be depressing income with a view to reducing taxes payable. Expenses might be overstated, but this would be to the lender's advantage since it would mean that income and cashflow were understated.

I cannot stress too strongly that knowledge of local practice as to how unaudited statements are made and used must be your guide in looking at them. In the United States, bankers tend to dismiss these statements as worthless, and they are right to do so since it is common knowledge that U.S. lenders expect audited statements. However, in many countries unaudited statements or tax returns are all that are available. They are better than nothing!

PROBLEMS

The end-of-chapter problems give you an opportunity to apply the material covered in each chapter. You will have to do additional research to solve some of the more advanced problems.

1. Why would a banker want to know why a borrower has changed auditors?
2. What would be likely to cause financial statements to be later than usual in being signed off by the accounting firm?
3. What is the meaning of *consistent* in the auditor's opinion?
4. What disciplines are applied in your country to auditing firms that provide financial statements?
5. In a country where the local currency has just been devalued against the U.S. dollar, a company which has long-term debt in U.S. dollars has adjusted its reported liability to reflect the increased amount payable in local currency. It has also adjusted upward the amount of the fixed asset (a factory) financed by this debt. Do you think this is reasonable? Why?
6. Changes in foreign exchange rates affect the value of all assets and liabilities of foreign subsidiaries, but parent companies do not always have to make adjustments for every change when preparing consolidated balance sheets.
   a. What choices are available to them in your country?
   b. How do movements in foreign exchange rates affect the parent company's cashflow? Is a loss shown on revaluing foreign subsidiaries a cash expense?
7. A manufacturing company which you are examining has an unconsolidated financing subsidiary. This subsidiary borrows from banks and other lenders to finance a portfolio of accounts receivable which arise from sales of products made by the parent company. The subsidiary gives its lenders the comfort of a support agreement from its parent which undertakes to maintain the subsidiary in a solvent condition. There are no other assets except cash, and no liabilities apart from banks and some currently payable taxes. Explain why such a company's debt should or should not be included as part of the consolidated parent company's debt for the purpose of ratio calculation.
8. Audited financial statements are offered to you as a lender, but the most recent ones are two years old. What would you do and why?
9. Give reasons why companies switch from FIFO to LIFO.

APPENDIX
ALTERNATIVE FORM OF SPREAD SHEET, INCORPORATING RATIOS AND CASHFLOWS

The simple form of spread sheet shown as Exhibit 2.4 has its limitations. A more useful form is shown in Exhibit 2.7, which includes ratio calculation and a cashflow analysis.

NOTES TO SPREAD SHEET

Comparative statement of financial condition:

Lines   1–8.   Net Sales, Net Income, and certain key ratios.

Lines   9–22.   Assets.

Lines 23–44.   Liabilities and net worth.

Lines 45–53.   State these numbers if available. Contingent Liabilities will probably not be on the balance sheet but in the notes, as will lease rentals.

Cashflow and ratio analysis:

Lines 54–68.   Income statement items.

Lines 69–84.   Calculation of cashflow from operations, as described in Chapter 3.

Lines 86–91.   Sources of cash, other than operations.

Lines 92–98.   Uses of cash, other than operations.

Lines 100–103. Useful ratios.

COMPARATIVE STATEMENT OF FINANCIAL CONDITION

NAME	SAMPLE COMPANY	ADDRESS			
AUDITOR	PRICE WATERHOUSE				
SOURCE — AUDIT OR DIRECT	AUDIT	AUDIT			
STATE IF QUALIFIED	NO	NO			
DATE (DAY/MO./YR.)	31 March 19X1	31 March 19X2			

		AMOUNTS IN		MILLIONS	CURRENCY	US$
LINE	DESCRIPTION	AMOUNT	AMOUNT	AMOUNT	AMOUNT	AMOUNT
1	NET SALES	719.8	770.2			
2	NET INCOME	19.8	16.7			
3	WORKING CAPITAL	135.5	128.3			
4	CURRENT RATIO	3.10x	2.77x			
5	QUICK ASSET RATIO	1.45x	1.27x			
6	TANGIBLE NET WORTH	201.1	210.5			
7	TOTAL LIABIL./TANG. NET WORTH	0.84x	0.79x			
8	TOTAL DEBT./TANG. NET WORTH	0.52x	0.46x			
9	CASH	9.8	4.6			
10	MARKETABLE SECURITIES	13.0	11.2			
11	RECEIVABLES/DEBTORS	68.7	76.5			
12	INVENTORY/STOCKS	104.8	106.3			
13						
14						
15	PREPAID EXPENSES	2.5	3.0			
16	TOTAL CURRENT ASSETS	198.8	201.6			
17	NET FIXED ASSETS	158.2	163.5			
18	INV. & ADV. SUBS & AFFILIATES	12.7	12.6			
19						
20						
21	INTANGIBLES	25.2	23.7			
22	TOTAL ASSETS	394.9	401.4			

ASSETS

Exhibit 2.7 Alternative Spread Sheets.

#			Col 1	Col 2
23		SHORT-TERM DEBT	6.6	12.8
24		ACCOUNTS PAYABLE/CREDITORS	48.6	54.2
25		ACCRUALS		
26		INCOME TAXES	8.1	5.7
27				
28				
29		TOTAL CURRENT LIABILITIES	63.3	72.7
30				
31				
32		TOTAL LONG-TERM SENIOR DEBT	97.8	53.3
33				
34				
35		TOTAL Subordinated long-term Debt		
36		Deferred Tax	7.5	5.6
37		OTHER L.T. Liability	—	5.6
38		TOTAL L.T. Liabilities & Reserves	105.3	94.5
39		PREFERRED STOCK/SHARES	19.5	18.5
40		COMMON STOCK/Ordinary Shares	45.0	47.3
41		CAPITAL SURPLUS/Capital Reserves		
42		EARNED SURPLUS/Retained Earnings	164.0	170.6
43			(2.2)	(2.2)
44		TOTAL LIABILITIES & Net Worth	394.9	401.4
45		LEASE RENTALS		
46		CONTINGENT LIABILITIES		
47	Inventory	FINISHED GOODS		
48		WORK IN PROCESS		
49		RAW MATERIALS, ETC.		
50		LAND AND BUILDINGS		
51	Fixed	MACHINERY, Equipment, etc.		
52	Assets	GROSS FIXED ASSETS	279.8	285.8
53		DEPRECIATION RESERVE	121.6	122.3

LIABILITIES

CASH FLOW
RATIO ANALYSIS
NAME

SAMPLE COMPANY

		DATE	31 March 19X1		31 March 19X2					
		No. OF MONTHS	12		12					
LINE	DESCRIPTION		AMOUNT	%	AMOUNT	%	AMOUNT	%	AMOUNT	%
54	NET SALES (GROWTH RATE)		719.8		770.2	7.0				
55	COST OF GOODS SOLD (% OF SALES)		531.9	73.9	573.4	74.4				
56	GROSS OPERATING PROFIT (% OF SALES)		187.9	26.1	196.8	25.6				
57	SELLING, GEN., ADMIN. EXP. (% OF SALES)		128.1	17.8	134.7	17.5				
58	Operating Profit (% of Sales)		59.8	8.3	62.1	8.1				
59	DEPRECIATION (% AVG. GROSS PLANT)		13.5		14.4	5.1				
60	OTHER NON-CASH CHARGES									
61	OTHER INCOME (% OF SALES)									
62	OTHER EXPENSE (% OF SALES)									
63	Profit before Int. & Other Fixed Chgs. (% of Sales)		46.3	6.4	47.7	6.2				
64	INT. & OTHER FIXED CHGS: (% Avg. Debt)		6.9		7.3	7.3				
65	Profit Before Income Tax (% of Sales)		39.4	5.5	40.4	5.2				
66	INCOME TAX (% PRE-TAX PROFIT)		19.6	49.7	19.0	47.0				
67	EXTRAORDINARY CHARGES				5.1					
68	NET INCOME (% OF SALES)		19.8	2.8	16.3	2.1				

Exhibit 2.7   (Continued)

69	NET-OPERATING CASH GENERATION	NET INCOME			16.3								
70		DEPRECIATION			14.4								
71		OTHER NON-CASH CHARGES			7.1								
72		**GROSS FUNDS FROM OPERATIONS**			37.8								
73		LESS CHANGES IN NET WORKING ASSETS											
74													
75		(INC.)/DEC. IN ACCOUNTS RECEIVABLE — %		9.5	(7.8)	9.9							
76		(INC.)/DEC. INVENTORY INV./COST OF GOODS SOLD — %		19.7	(1.5)	18.5							
77		(INC.)/DEC. PREPAID EXPENSES PPD. EXPS./COST OF GOODS SOLD — %			(0.5)								
78													
79													
80		INC./(DEC.) ACCTS. PAYABLE ACCTS: PAY./COST OF GOODS SOLD — %		9.1	5.6	9.5							
81		INC./(DEC.) TAXES PAYABLE TAXES PAY./PREV. INC. TAX — %			(4.3)								
82		INC./(DEC.) ACCRUALS ACCRUALS/TOTAL OPER. EXP. — %											
83		Sub-Total: Change in NWA			(8.5)								
84		**TOTAL (LINE 72 + 83) CASH FROM OPS**			29.3								
85	NON-OPERATING CASH GENERATION	SALE OF EQUITY			1.3								
86		INC. LONG-TERM DEBT											
87		INC. SHT.-TERM DEBT (and Bills Dis.)			6.2								
88		SALE OF ASSETS											
89		SALE OF MARKETABLE SECURITIES											
90													
91		**TOTAL**			7.5								

92	NON-OPERATING CASH NEEDS	CAPITAL EXPEND. — GROSS SALES /GROSS PLANT (LAND, BLDG., EQUIP)	257.3	19.7	264.5
93		DIVIDENDS PAID (Payout Ratio)		9.7	59.5
94		RED. LONG-TERM DEBT		14.5	
95		RED. SHORT-TERM DEBT (and bills dis.)			
96		INV. & ADV. SUBS'. AND AFFIL.		(0.1)	
97					
98		TOTAL		43.8	
99		NET INC./(DEC.) IN CASH AND MARKETABLE SECURITIES (LINE 84 + 91 MINUS LINE 98)		(7.0)	
100	Analytical Ratios	NET PROFIT/NET WORTH	9.8		7.9
101		EBIT/Total Assets	14.8		15.0
102		DEBT SERVICE COVERAGE			
103		NWA/Sales			

Exhibit 2.7 (Continued)

3 Cashflow Analysis

This chapter explains how to perform a cashflow analysis and how to find cash from operations. Bearing in mind that companies normally provide financial statements based on accrual accounting, together with a statement of changes in working capital (that misleading document sometimes called the funds flow statement), you must once again put on your detective's hat. Your main task will be to distinguish first between cash and noncash revenues and expenses, and then to distinguish between operating and nonoperating items.

Cashflow analysis is necessary because of the flexibility in accounting policies and because financial statements are prepared from the point of view of recording income and presenting information to investors. Modern credit analysis is based on a return to business fundamentals (see Chapter 1). No banker was ever repaid out of accrual income—hence the concentration on cashflow. Further, a cashflow statement is intended to provide some basis for estimating the future ability of the business to generate cash—hence the emphasis on repeatable operating performance and the exclusion of "once and for all" gains and losses.

While income and profitability is important, solvency (that is, the ability to pay one's debts) is of vital short-term interest to the banker. In fact, as will be seen in Chapter 5, there is strong evidence that cashflow/total liabilities is one of the most important financial ratios in predicting future problem credits.

Our purpose will therefore be to make a summary statement of sources and uses of cash for the year under review so that the following questions can be answered:

1. Did the business generate positive cash flows after allowing for the effects of changes in the working accounts?
2. How was capital expenditure financed?
3. What use was made of debt raised?

Some simple cashflow examples now follow. Later in the chapter, a more difficult cashflow is shown.

NET WORKING ASSETS

Before beginning, it is necessary to introduce one new concept. While importance has traditionally been given to working capital, it is now considered necessary to refine this, since there are often items included in current assets or current liabilities which are not related to normal operations. For instance, the payment of dividends is a result of financial decision making, and although dividends payable is a current liability, it is not regarded as a working account. So, too, maturing long-term debt items are not considered as working accounts.

Thus, a new net current item called net working assets (NWA) is used as a substitute for working capital. This can be defined as those items (assets or liabilities) which move with the level of sales, in particular accounts receivable, accounts payable, and inventories (including work in progress). It does not include cash or short-term debt, as the objective of this exercise is to find the cash or lack of it resulting from the ordinary process of buying raw materials, manufacturing these into products, selling them, and collecting the proceeds. The result of this process or cycle is called cash from operations.

Example 3.1.   Let's begin with the simplest example, drawn from a story on management training once told to me by a successful businessman in retail ladies' fashion. According to Maurice, management training for his shop managers involved giving them a stall in a street market and $200. "Go away," he used to say, "and run that stall in the market. Buy dresses for $1 and sell for $3. But bring me more cash at the end of the week than you started with, and no dresses!" The point to be learned is this: Net working assets consists here of only one thing—namely, the inventory of dresses. Suppose sales of dresses during the week were $3,000 (all cash) and purchases were $1,400. If at the end of the week the trainee has 400 unsold dresses at $1 each (cash price), his profit, of which he will be very proud, is clearly:

Sales	$3,000
Less purchases	(1,400)
Less closing inventory	(400)
= Cost of goods sold	1,000
Profit	$2,000

His cash from operations (that is, the cash he has left to give back to Maurice) is, however, only $1,600 plus the $200 that he began with. The difference between the profit of $2,000 and the $1,600 cash generated represents the amount of unsold dresses—the one thing Maurice did not want because who knows what those dresses will fetch next week?

Example 3.2. Alan runs an engineering job shop that performs subcontracts for various local firms. He employs eight people and always has a lot of work going on. Three months' figures are available, disclosing the following information:

Beginning Balances: February 1, 19X0 Ending Balances: April 30, 19X0

Inventories	$ 960	$ 1,430
Work in progress	1,425	1,960
Accounts receivable	2,400	4,175
Accounts payable	(853)	(1,042)
Accrued expenses	(460)	(745)
Net working assets	3,472	5,778
Cash	250	350
Plant and machines	6,400	6,000
Total net assets	10,122	12,128

Three months to April 30:		
Sales	$4,000	
Cost of goods sold	(1,500)	
Depreciation	(400)	
Other Expenses	(94)	
Profit before tax	2,006	

Cash from operations, however, is not so easily found, and we must first perform a simple transaction analysis, recording the sales and expenses as follows:

	Assets			
	Cash	Net Working Assets	Plant	Liabilities and Owner's Equity
February 1, 19X0	$ 250	$ 3,472	$6,400	$ 10,122
1. Sales		+4,000		+4,000
2. Cost of goods sold		(1,500)		(1,500)
3. Depreciation			(400)	(400)
4. Other expenses		(94)		(94)
5. Cash from operations	+100	(100)		
April 30, 19X0	350	5,778	6,000	12,128

Explanation:

Line 1. Notice that any change in assets is matched by a change on the side of Liabilities and Owner's Equity. Sales were on account, so they must have increased accounts receivable (that is, made net working assets increase).

Line 2. Cost of goods sold makes inventory and work in progress decrease. Hence, net working assets decrease.

Line 3. Depreciation is a noncash expense; it makes plant go down, and thus does not affect net working assets.

Line 4. Other expenses are going to make accrued expenses increase. Hence, net working assets go down.

Line 5. Since we do not know exactly what cash collections or what payments in cash were made, we have to deduce the net figure. Sales make accounts receivable go up (net working assets goes up); expenses incurred (lines 2 and 4) make net working assets go down. Hence, cash collections decrease net working assets, and cash paid to settle liabilities increases net working assets since it reduces the liability. Thus, the balancing figure, which is cash from operations, will be the net of these payments and collections. This turns out to be $100—very different from profits of $2,006!

Note also that we could have found cash from operations by taking net income, adding back noncash charges (in this case only depreciation of $400), and subtracting the change in net working assets. Thus, $2,006 + $400 − ($5,778 − $3,472) = $100. Observe that the popular notion of cashflow being net income plus depreciation is true *only* if there is no change from beginning to ending net working assets. Given that net working assets normally rise with inflation and business activity, this assumption will generally be true only by accident.

Compare this result with the effect on working capital. Beginning balance for working capital was $3,472 + $250 = $3,722 and ending balance is $6,128. Under the conventional approach this is a good sign—working capital has gone up nearly 70%. But beware! There is no provision for current taxes, and even a small change in ability to collect receivables will make this business into one where profits are good but cash decreases. Thus, with Alan's Engineering Company, we have a strong expansion but a shortage of cash and an increasing lack of solvency. Any shortfall in the recorded value of work in progress compared with its salable value will impair this solvency even further.

Sometimes a business goes through a period of rapid growth and high profitability and also experiences a mounting need for cash. Such an example is Wonderdrug Company, which has, let's say, discovered a cure for the common cold. Sales were growing 40% in 19X0 and 19X1. What is likely to happen to cash from operations? How can this growth be financed? Is a pretax profit margin of about 16% going to be enough to generate internal cash for expansion? How do we show capital expenditure in a cashflow analysis?

Before working through the example, let's make one more definition clear. Cash from operations is the cash resulting from buying, manufacturing, selling, and collecting the proceeds; there is also another term, Funds from Operations (FFO). This is an accrual accounting concept—it is not the same as cash from operations and is defined as: sales (accounting basis) minus cost of goods sold and other cash-related operating expenses (accounting basis), or net income plus noncash expenses. In order to find cash from operations, it is necessary to find funds from operations and then add or subtract the change in net working assets.

Example 3.3. We are now ready to perform the 19X9 transaction analysis for Wonderdrug Company using data shown in Exhibit 3.1.

Exhibit 3.1   Wonderdrug Company (in thousands of dollars)

	19X8	19X9	19X0
Cash	$ 9	$ 15	$ 25
Inventory	210	295	436
Accounts Receivable	240	336	470
Net Plant	400	525	650
	859	1,171	1,581
Accounts Payable	126	177	247
Accrued Expenses	100	143	201
Short-Term Debt	83	181	353
Owner's Equity	550	670	780
	859	1,171	1,581
Sales	1,714	2,400	3,360
Cost of Goods Sold	1,028	1,440	2,016
Selling General and Administrative Expense	257	360	420
Depreciation	88	125	175
Research and Development	100	136	190
Earnings before Taxes	241	339	559
Taxes	(120)	(169)	(279)
Net Income	121	170	280
Dividends	50	50	70
Retained Earnings	70	120	110
Net Working Assets	224	311	458
Working Capital	150	145	130
Capital Expenditure	224	250	300

First set out the beginning and ending balances. Then enter items from the income statement under each column—for example, sales increases owner's equity and also increases accounts receivable; cost of goods sold decreases owner's equity and increases accrued expenses (which means it decreases net working assets).

To perform the 19X9 transaction analysis for Wonderdrug Company we use the figures shown in Exhibit 3.1:

	Cash	Net Working Assets	Plant	Short-Term Debt	Owner's Equity
December 31, 19X8	$ 9	$ 224	$ 400	$ 83	$ 550
Sales		2,400			2,400
Cost of goods sold		(1,440)			(1,440)
Selling general and administrative expense		(360)			(360)
Depreciation			(125)		(125)
Research and development		(136)			(136)
Taxes		(169)			(169)
Dividends	(50)				(50)
New short-term debt	98			98	
New plant	(250)		250		
Cash from operations	208	(208)			
December 31, 19X9	15	311	525	181	670

Sources and Uses of Cash 19X9

Cash from operations	$208	Buy plant	$250
New debt	98	Pay dividends	50
	306		300
		Increase in cash	6
			306

Only two new points are introduced here: capital expenditure and dividends paid. By convention, all capital expenditure is treated as being made for cash. The reason is that accounts payable are for trade purchases unless the company tells you otherwise. Dividends too are paid in cash. In the absence of a dividends payable liability, these are also put through the cash column.

Observations

Although net working assets expanded from 224 to 331 (+38%), funds from operations was strong at 295, thanks to the substantial profitability of sales. Thus, cash from operations was positive at 208. However, because of the 40% sales growth, a substantial amount of capital expenditure was required. Cash from operations less dividends paid provided 158 toward capital expenditure, and the remainder had to be financed by new debt of 98. This would have decreased working capital substantially but for the strong profit performance. In fact, working capital falls by 5, while net working assets increase by 87.

It might appear that the increase in new working assets is being financed by debt, but this would be a wrong interpretation. As cash from operations is positive, the absence of capital expenditure would have meant that no new debt was required. Here a short-term source of cash is being used to finance a long-term need (capital expenditure) under the guise of financing higher inventories and receivables. If growth continues at 40% with corresponding increases in capital expenditure, this debt will never be repaid.

Net Working Assets/Sales

Notice that a useful ratio to calculate is net working assets/sales. This indicates whether the terms of trade (credit given and credit taken) have changed and whether inventories are in about the same proportion to sales as in the previous year. Here for 19X9 the net working assets/sales ratio is 13.0%, which compares favorably with 13.1% in 19X8. If inventories expanded without an equal increase in accounts payable or accrued liabilities, the net working assets/sales ratio would increase—or in fact get worse from the point of view of cash, as higher ending net working assets means less cash from operations. Wonderdrug is fortunate, perhaps because of the high added value in production, that its net working assets/sales ratio is only 13%. Many other companies have net working assets/sales ratios around 20%. This favorable ratio explains why growth at 40% produces less strain on Wonderdrug than one would expect.

Assume the same sales growth, but a 20% net working assets/sales ratio:

Beginning net working assets (20% of 19X8 sales of 1,714)	$342.8
Ending net working assets (20% of 19X9 sales of 2,400)	480.0
19X9 increase in net working assets	137.2

Immediately it is clear that cash from operations would be 295 − 137.2 = 157.8 instead of 208, leading to a new debt requirement of 148.2 in place of 98. In the following year, the effect would be:

Beginning net working assets   480.0
Ending net working assets (20% of 3,360)   672.0

19X0 increase in NWA   192.0

This will lead to cash from operations of 455 − 192.0 = 263 and new debt of 217, producing total debt at the end of 19X0 of 83 + 148.2 + 217 = 448.2. By this point, working capital has nearly disappeared and anything wrong with inventory will severely impair solvency. Hence, rapid growth even with good profitability can be risky for a lender.

Another approach to Wonderdrug's current asset/current liability situation parallels the net working assets/sales ratio. This involves calculating the number of days represented by receivables, payables, and inventory figures.

Thus for 19X9, number of days of inventory on hand at December 31, 19X9 is:

$$\frac{\text{Inventory}}{\text{Cost of goods sold}} \times 365$$

That is,

$$\frac{295}{1,440} \times 365 = 74.78 \text{ days}$$

Number of days of receivables on hand is:

$$\frac{\text{Receivables}}{\text{Sales}} \times 365$$

That is,

$$\frac{336}{2,400} \times 365 = 51.1 \text{ days}$$

while payables are:

$$\frac{\text{Payables}}{\text{Costs of goods sold}} \times 365$$

That is,

$$\frac{177}{1,440} \times 365 = 44.8 \text{ days}$$

The cash cycle is therefore said to be: Inventory (days) + accounts receivable (days) − payables (days):

$$74.78 + 51.1 - 44.8 = 81.08 \text{ days}$$

This can be compared to the 19X8 figures, which turn out to be:

$$74.56 + 50.98 - 44.73 = 80.81 \text{ days}$$

The net working assets/sales method is considered superior to the current asset/current liability approach, as it will include such items as accrued expenses, prepayment, and other current assets or liabilities related to operations.

In general, the analyst is advised to check any variation in the net working assets/sales ratio by seeing what changes there are in days of inventory, days of payables, or days of receivables. These points are discussed further in Chapter 6.

NONOPERATING ITEMS

Nonoperating items are those revenues or expenses that are not related to day-to-day business transactions. Obviously, sales and purchases of goods are operating items. The payment of current taxes is also considered part of the normal cycle of operations. However, capital expenditure, dividend payments, acquisitions, and raising of new capital are definitely nonoperating items. We have to exclude these carefully in constructing a cashflow analysis because we want to find cash from operations—that is, the cash generated in the day-to-day cycle of the business that we can reasonably expect (other things being equal) to be repeated next year.

Because nonoperating items are not directly related to the level of sales, they are considered to be more subject to management control than are operating items. Capital expenditure, for instance, can usually be postponed. Dividend payments can be reduced or omitted. But the regular process of buying goods, manufacturing, paying for purchases, selling goods, and collecting the proceeds of sales is the life blood of the business—hence, our interest in cash from operations, as that is the source of repayment toward which the banker most regularly looks.

HOW TO COMPLETE A TRANSACTION ANALYSIS

There are many nonoperating items besides capital expenditure and dividends. Rather than giving a comprehensive list of these, it will be more constructive to work through an example. The way in which this is done is called a transaction analysis, since it emphasizes treating each transaction separately so as to find its effect upon cash. What you do is use published financial statements, together with the associated notes. By using the beginning balance sheet, the income statement, and the ending balance sheet, you can convert accrual accounting information into cashflow information. How this is done is now explained using an actual example.

CONSOLIDATED BALANCE SHEET

Stauffer Chemical Company and Subsidiaries

ASSETS	December 31	1979	1978
		(Dollars in thousands)	
Current Assets	Cash	$ 24,712	$ 24,996
	Marketable Securities	31,191	64,011
	Receivables:		
	Trade — Net of Allowance for Doubtful Receivables (1979 — $2,963; 1978 — $2,554)	266,726	234,411
	Notes and Other	41,836	26,095
	Inventories:		
	Finished Products and Work in Progress	226,195	196,261
	Raw Materials and Supplies	92,548	82,052
	Prepaid Expenses	15,489	14,434
	Total Current Assets	**698,697**	**642,260**
Property, Plant and Equipment	Land	27,011	26,901
	Buildings, Machinery and Equipment — Net of Accumulated Depreciation (1979 — $600,925; 1978 — $527,852)	1,002,741	863,136
	Mineral Deposits — Net of Accumulated Depletion	10,790	13,209
	Property, Plant and Equipment — Net	**1,040,542**	**903,246**
Investments and Other Assets	Investments and Advances — Associated Companies	41,412	40,384
	Intangibles Arising from Business Acquisitions	29,368	31,273
	Other Assets	66,215	50,066
	Total Investments and Other Assets	**136,995**	**121,723**
	Total	**$1,876,234**	**$1,667,229**

See information on page 24 and notes to financial statements on pages 30 through 34.

Exhibit 3.2 Consolidated Balance Sheet and Statement of Consolidated Earnings, Stauffer Chemical Company and Subsidiaries (Stauffer Chemical Company 1979 Annual Report, pp. 25, 26, 27). Reprinted by permission.

Example 3.4.   Balance sheets, income statement, Statement-of-Changes in Consolidated Financial Position, and notes relating to Stauffer Chemical Company's 1979 annual results are shown as Exhibits 3.2 and 3.3. First, set out the balances as shown in Exhibit 3.4, with assets on the left and liabilities

LIABILITIES AND STOCKHOLDERS' EQUITY	December 31	1979	1978
		(Dollars in thousands)	
Current Liabilities Notes Payable		$ 196,699	$ 135,841
Accounts Payable		116,857	97,106
Income Taxes Payable		17,899	15,121
Accrued Interest		11,636	11,312
Accrued Payroll		12,314	11,144
Other Taxes Payable		7,444	6,362
Other Liabilities		41,658	31,239
Long-Term Debt Due within One Year		9,145	13,599
Total Current Liabilities		**413,652**	**321,724**
Long-Term Debt		**390,899**	**415,868**
Deferred Income Taxes		**146,105**	**108,289**
Minority Interest in Subsidiaries		**74,433**	**60,011**
Stockholders' Equity Common Stock, $1.25 Par — 70,000,000 Shares Authorized; Issued (1979 — 44,685,172; 1978 — 44,605,492); Outstanding (1979 — 43,882,583; 1978 — 43,791,426)		55,856	55,757
Other Capital		96,703	95,936
Retained Earnings		706,457	617,628
Reacquired Common Shares — at Cost (1979 — 802,589; 1978 — 814,066)		(7,871)	(7,984)
Stockholders' Equity — Net		**851,145**	**761,337**
Total		**$1,876,234**	**$1,667,229**

Exhibit 3.2   *(Continued)*

STATEMENT OF CONSOLIDATED EARNINGS

Stauffer Chemical Company and Subsidiaries

	Year ended December 31		1979	1978
			(Dollars in thousands, except per-share amounts)	
Revenues	Net Sales		$1,526,160	$1,328,114
	Interest and Dividends		10,227	12,044
		Total Revenues	**1,536,387**	**1,340,158**
Cost and Expenses	Cost of Goods Sold		1,106,658	926,381
	Selling, General and Administrative		161,866	135,883
	Research and Development		36,963	33,562
	Interest		31,839	37,923
	Other Expense (Income) — Net		(3,730)	6,432
	Minority Interest		16,555	10,206
		Total Cost and Expenses	**1,350,151**	**1,150,387**
Earnings before Provision for Income Taxes			**186,236**	**189,771**
Provision for Income Taxes			**61,075**	**72,810**
Earnings from Consolidated Operations			**125,161**	**116,961**
Equity in Earnings of Associated Companies			**10,800**	**9,054**
Net Earnings			**$ 135,961**	**$ 126,015**
Earnings per Common Share			**$ 3.10**	**$ 2.88**

See information on page 24 and notes to financial statements on pages 30 through 34.

Exhibit 3.2 *(Continued)*

Stauffer Chemical Company and Subsidiaries

	Year ended December 31	1979	1978
		(Dollars in thousands)	
Source of	Operations:		
Working Capital	Net Earnings	$135,961	$126,015
	Depreciation	93,064	78,340
	Deferred Income Taxes	37,816	23,689
	Other — Net	18,645	4,616
	Provided from Operations	**285,486**	**232,660**
	Issuance of Long-Term Debt	9,475	9,736
	Issuance of Common Stock	979	1,353
	Property Disposals	6,125	5,474
	Total Source	**302,065**	**249,223**
Application of	Capital Expenditures	239,303	201,196
Working Capital	Dividends Paid	47,132	42,660
	Reduction of Long-Term Debt	34,444	10,867
	Acquisition — Net Non-Current Assets		18,715
	Other — Net	16,677	7,431
	Total Application	**337,556**	**280,869**
Decrease in			
Working Capital		**$ (35,491)**	**$ (31,646)**
Change in	Cash and Marketable Securities	$ (33,104)	$ (7,777)
Working Capital	Receivables	48,056	48,300
by Component	Inventories	40,430	44,614
	Prepaid Fxpenses	1,055	1,517
	Notes Payable	(60,858)	(112,451)
	Accounts Payable	(19,751)	(7,470)
	Income Taxes Payable	(2,778)	15,501
	Other Current Liabilities	(8,541)	(13,880)
	Decrease in Working Capital	**$ (35,491)**	**$ (31,646)**

See information on page 24 and notes to financial statements on pages 30 through 34.

Exhibit 3.3 Funds Flow Statement and Notes (Stauffer Chemical Company 1979
Annual Report, pp. 28–34). Reprinted by permission.

NOTES TO FINANCIAL STATEMENTS

Stock Split

In May, 1979, the stockholders approved an increase in authorized shares of common stock from 30,000,000 shares to 70,000,000 shares, a two-for-one stock split, and a reduction in par value from $2.50 to $1.25 per share. Common stock data in the accompanying consolidated financial statements and notes to financial statements have been restated for the two-for-one stock split.

Accounting Change

During the fourth quarter of 1979, the Company adopted Financial Accounting Standards Board Statement No. 34, "Capitalization of Interest Cost," which requires that interest be added to the cost of qualifying assets. Interest cost during 1979 was $44,454,000, of which $12,615,000 was capitalized. The effect of capitalizing such interest was to increase net earnings by $6,417,000 or $.15 per share. Previously reported results for the first three quarters of 1979 have been restated as follows:

	As Previously Reported		Accounting Change		As Restated	
	Net Earnings	Per Share	Net Earnings	Per Share	Net Earnings	Per Share
	(Net earnings in thousands)					
Quarter Ended:						
March 31	$61,253	$1.40	$ 949	$.02	$62,202	$1.42
June 30	23,597	.54	1,356	.03	24,953	.57
September 30	11,013	.25	1,867	.05	12,880	.30

Inventories

Inventories stated using LIFO amounted to approximately 75 per cent of total inventories at December 31, 1979, and 80 per cent at December 31, 1978. If inventories stated at LIFO had been stated using the average cost method they would have been greater by approximately $100,300,000 at December 31, 1979, and $66,700,000 at December 31, 1978.

Income Taxes

The provision for income taxes includes the following:

	1979	1978
	(Dollars in thousands)	
Current:		
Federal	$ 12,886	$ 34,866
State	7,094	8,227
Foreign	4,438	5,371
	24,418	48,464
Deferred:		
Depreciation	27,041	24,665
Capitalized interest	6,090	
Other	3,526	(319)
	36,657	24,346
Total	**$ 61,075**	**$ 72,810**

A reconciliation of the provision for income taxes and the effective tax rate with the amount computed by applying the federal statutory income tax rate follows:

	1979		1978	
	Amount	Rate	Amount	Rate
	(Dollars in thousands)			
Income taxes computed at statutory rate	$85,669	46%	$91,090	48%
State tax, net of federal income tax	3,831	2	4,278	2
Investment tax credits	(19,685)	(10)	(16,395)	(9)
Percentage depletion	(7,858)	(4)	(7,334)	(4)
Lower foreign tax rates	(10,473)	(6)	(2,956)	(2)
Minority interest	7,615	4	4,899	3
Other — net	1,976	1	(772)	
Provision and effective tax rate	**$61,075**	**33%**	**$72,810**	**38%**

The net amount of prepaid income taxes related to current timing differences, included in prepaid expenses, was $9,800,000 at December 31, 1979 and $8,700,000 at December 31, 1978.

Deferred taxes have not been provided on undistributed earnings of consolidated domestic and foreign subsidiaries as such earnings will be required in the subsidiaries' operations. The cumulative amount of these earnings on which United States taxes have not been provided was $124,800,000 at December 31, 1979. Under current federal income tax laws, dividend exclusions and foreign tax credits would be available to reduce substantially the federal income taxes which might otherwise result from distributions of such undistributed accumulated earnings. The estimated income taxes payable on these earnings, if distributed, would be $17,900,000 at December 31, 1979.

Exhibit 3.3 *(Continued)*

Notes Payable

	1979	1978
	(Dollars in thousands)	
Commercial paper	$178,170	$ 67,998
Other notes payable	18,529	67,843
Total	**$196,699**	**$135,841**
Average interest rate at year-end	13%	10%
Maximum aggregate notes payable outstanding at any month-end during the year	$196,699	$135,841
Average month-end notes payable outstanding during the year	$ 93,846	$ 37,113
Weighted average interest rate for the year	11%	8%

The Company had unused short-term bank lines of credit amounting to $54,700,000 at December 31, 1979.

Long-Term Debt

	1979	1978
	(Dollars in thousands)	
8.85% debentures due 2001 ($8,000,000 to be retired annually under sinking fund commencing 1987)	$125,000	$125,000
8⅛% notes due 1986	75,000	75,000
8⅛% debentures due 1996 ($4,000,000 to be retired annually under sinking fund commencing 1982)	53,990	60,000
5% to 8% industrial development and pollution control revenue bonds payable 1985 to 2008	67,950	62,250
9¾% to 13% notes due 1981 to 1985	13,552	31,704
7½% notes due 1997 ($1,625,000 to be retired annually commencing 1983)	25,000	25,000
7.3% to 9.4% notes due 1981 to 1983	8,130	14,746
4½% sinking fund debentures due 1989 ($1,750,000 retired annually under sinking fund)	12,223	12,953
Other notes payable through 1991	10,054	9,215
Total	**$390,899**	**$415,868**

The aggregate maturities and sinking fund requirements (stated in thousands) on long-term debt for the next five years are as follows: 1980, $9,145; 1981, $10,477; 1982, $7,315; 1983, $9,670; and 1984, $11,399.

The Company has revolving credit agreements with groups of major domestic and foreign banks totalling $150,000,000 at December 31, 1979. The domestic agreement provides for borrowings up to $100,000,000 through December 31, 1982, at which time outstanding borrowings may be converted into a four-year term loan. The foreign revolving credit agreement provides for borrowings up to $50,000,000 through March 1, 1984. At December 31, 1979 there were no borrowings under either agreement.

Under the Company's most restrictive debt agreement, approximately $172,000,000 would have been available at December 31, 1979 for dividends and reacquisitions of capital stock.

Stock Option Plans

Options under all plans are granted at the market price of the shares on the dates of the grants. Transactions during 1978 and 1979 for such plans are as follows:

Options outstanding, December 31, 1977 (at per-share prices from $6.59 to $23.72) of which 668,552 shares were exercisable	**1,440,572**
Changes in options during 1978: Exercised (at per-share prices from $6.59 to $17.53)	(133,800)
Lapsed or cancelled	(19,760)
Options outstanding, December 31, 1978 (at per-share prices from $6.59 to $23.72) of which 834,412 shares were exercisable	**1,287,012**
Changes in options during 1979: Granted	216,400
Exercised (at per-share prices from $6.59 to $17.53)	(129,040)
Lapsed or cancelled	(34,200)
Options outstanding, December 31, 1979 (at per-share prices from $6.59 to $23.72) of which 900,712 shares were exercisable	**1,340,172**

The number of shares available for granting additional options was 892,884 at December 31, 1978 and 700,484 at December 31, 1979.

Pension Plans

The Company has several pension plans covering substantially all employees. The total cost of these plans, including amortization of prior service cost was $14,000,000 for 1979 and $13,800,000 for 1978. The policy of the Company is to fund pension cost accrued. As of December 31, 1979, the actuarially-computed vested benefits were fully funded. Unfunded prior service costs approximated $39,000,000 at December 31, 1979, and are being amortized principally over 40 years from the dates such costs were established.

Exhibit 3.3 *(Continued)*

NOTES TO FINANCIAL STATEMENTS

BUSINESS SEGMENTS

The Company operates in three domestic industries, Agricultural, Chemicals, and Plastics, as well as in the foreign area. The Agricultural Chemicals and Fertilizer and Mining divisions and Seeds compose the Agricultural industry. The Chemicals industry includes the Industrial Chemicals, Specialty Chemicals, Food Ingredients and Chemical Systems divisions. Information concerning the Company's operating industries is shown below:

NET SALES TO UNAFFILIATED CUSTOMERS	1979	1978	1977	1976
		(Dollars in thousands)		
U.S. Group				
Domestic				
Agricultural	$ 352,127	$ 284,469	$ 254,514	$ 223,850
Chemicals	747,034	687,541	648,451	584,376
Plastics	156,236	142,269	152,244	126,980
	1,255,397	1,114,279	1,055,209	935,206
Export				
Agricultural	32,418	22,354	36,510	54,946
Chemicals	65,854	49,640	43,797	37,625
Plastics	4,033	4,112	5,516	9,364
	102,305	76,106	85,823	101,935
Transfers between U.S. Segments — at cost				
Agricultural	9,696	9,012	11,737	11,056
Chemicals	29,995	23,610	23,774	25,304
Eliminations	(39,691)	(32,622)	(35,511)	(36,360)
Transfers to Foreign Group — at market				
Agricultural	6,936	3,556	4,701	5,097
Chemicals	16,262	10,640	8,960	8,786
Plastics	1,443	1,367	1,865	1,750
	24,641	15,563	15,526	15,633
Total U.S. Group Sales				
Agricultural	401,177	319,391	307,462	294,949
Chemicals	859,145	771,431	724,982	656,091
Plastics	161,712	147,748	159,625	138,094
Eliminations	(39,691)	(32,622)	(35,511)	(36,360)
	1,382,343	1,205,948	1,156,558	1,052,774
Foreign Group	168,458	137,729	91,728	62,859
Eliminations	(24,641)	(15,563)	(15,526)	(15,633)
Total Net Sales	$1,526,160	$1,328,114	$1,232,760	$1,100,000

OPERATING INCOME	1979	1978	1977	1976
U.S. Group				
Agricultural	$ 107,407	$ 89,332	$ 76,474	$ 78,360
Chemicals	160,481	159,717	154,469	145,470
Plastics	(33,081)	4,253	13,096	15,645
	234,807	253,302	244,039	239,475
Foreign Group	36,714	30,638	15,910	8,345
Total Operating Income	271,521	283,940	259,949	247,820
Interest Expense	(31,839)	(37,923)	(35,198)	(30,968)
Foreign Currency Losses	(3,616)	(5,803)	(6,677)	(4,154)
Interest and Dividend Income	10,227	12,044	10,612	10,458
Corporate Expenses	(50,848)	(51,652)	(42,046)	(40,630)
Other Unallocated (Expense) Income — Net	(9,209)	(10,835)	844	(386)
Earnings before Provision for Income Taxes	$ 186,236	$ 189,771	$ 187,484	$ 182,140

Exhibit 3.3   *(Continued)*

DEPRECIATION EXPENSE		1979		1978		1977		1976
				(Dollars in thousands)				
U.S. Group								
Agricultural		$ 21,649	$	19,040	$	16,287	$	14,640
Chemicals		48,843		41,159		33,438		23,543
Plastics		11,442		8,168		7,214		3,863
		81,934		68,367		56,939		42,046
Foreign Group		6,540		5,902		3,941		693
Total Identifiable Depreciation Expense		88,474		74,269		60,880		42,739
Corporate Assets		4,590		4,071		3,169		2,751
Total Depreciation Expense		$ 93,064	$	78,340	$	64,049	$	45,490

CAPITAL EXPENDITURES

U.S. Group								
Agricultural		$ 25,690	$	21,877	$	29,632	$	39,351
Chemicals		153,414		109,309		99,411		71,718
Plastics		25,493		38,489		33,097		26,448
		204,597		169,675		162,140		137,517
Foreign Group		7,335		8,215		14,420		42,015
Total Identifiable Capital Expenditures		211,932		177,890		176,560		179,532
Corporate Assets		27,371		23,306		16,876		19,243
Total Capital Expenditures		$ 239,303	$	201,196	$	193,436	$	198,775

ASSETS

U.S. Group								
Agricultural		$ 430,364	$	387,997	$	337,411	$	329,859
Chemicals		761,939		632,807		528,649		446,587
Plastics		216,515		207,067		159,310		119,749
		1,408,818		1,227,871		1,025,370		896,195
Foreign Group		197,662		177,506		152,926		108,062
Eliminations		(29,766)		(22,882)		(22,823)		(18,443)
Total Identifiable Assets		1,576,714		1,382,495		1,155,473		985,814
Cash and Marketable Securities		55,903		89,007		96,784		122,448
Investments and Advances — Associated Companies		41,412		40,384		34,348		30,568
Corporate Assets		202,205		155,343		142,939		129,671
Total Assets		$1,876,234		$1,667,229		$1,429,544		$1,268,501

Exhibit 3.3 *(Continued)*

NOTES TO FINANCIAL STATEMENTS

Leases

The Company's operations include leases of office and warehouse facilities and transportation, manufacturing, data processing and office equipment. The bulk of the Company's leases are operating leases. Capital leases are not significant. The office and warehouse leases expire over the next 20 years, the transportation and manufacturing equipment leases during the next 25 years and the data processing and office equipment leases over the next 5 years. In most cases, management expects that such leases will be renewed or replaced by other leases.

Approximately one-third of the above leases permit the Company to (a) purchase the property, generally at its fair value at the end of the initial lease term, or (b) renew the lease at various rental value options for periods of 1 to 20 years. Portions of office facilities are sublet under leases expiring during the next 14 years.

Rental expense was $17,100,000 for 1979 and $13,300,000 for 1978, net of sublease revenues of $3,600,000 in both years and transportation equipment mileage credits of $3,700,000 in 1979 and $3,900,000 in 1978. Contingent rental payments, escalation charges and restrictions imposed by lease agreements are not significant. Minimum rental commitments before mileage credits under non-cancellable leases at December 31, 1979 are as follows:

	Real Estate Rentals	Real Estate Subleases	Transportation Equipment	Other	Total
	(Dollars in thousands)				
1980	$ 6,000	$ (3,500)	$ 9,800	$2,600	$14,900
1981	5,500	(3,500)	9,400	2,300	13,700
1982	4,800	(3,400)	8,500	1,600	11,500
1983	4,700	(3,100)	7,500	900	10,000
1984	4,200	(3,000)	6,300	500	8,000
Remainder	27,100	(25,400)	34,600	1,600	37,900
	$52,300	$(41,900)	$76,100	$9,500	$96,000

Supplementary Earnings Statement Information

	1979	1978
	(Dollars in thousands)	
Inventories entering into the computation of cost of goods sold:		
Beginning of year	$278,313	$233,699
End of year	$318,743	$278,313
Maintenance and repairs	$ 83,877	$ 73,985
Taxes, other than income taxes:		
Property	$ 12,744	$ 12,462
Payroll	17,945	15,264
Other	3,884	3,192
Total	**$ 34,573**	**$ 30,918**
Interest incurred on long-term debt	$ 34,245	$ 34,421

Commitments

Unexpended appropriations for the construction of additional facilities approximated $129,000,000 at December 31, 1979. Portions of these appropriations are covered by firm commitments.

Replacement Cost Information

Unaudited replacement cost information for the two years ended December 31, 1979 and 1978, is included in the Company's Form 10-K to be filed with the Securities and Exchange Commission.

Exhibit 3.3   *(Continued)*

STATEMENT OF CONSOLIDATED STOCKHOLDERS' EQUITY

Stauffer Chemical Company and Subsidiaries

		1979	1978
		(Dollars in thousands)	
Common Stock	**Balance at Beginning of Year**	$ 55,757	$ 55,649
	Issuance of Common Shares Under Employee Plans		
	(1979 — 91,157 shares including 11,477 reacquired;		
	1978 — 117,200 shares including 31,090 reacquired)	99	108
	Balance at End of Year	$ 55,856	$ 55,757
Other Capital	**Balance at Beginning of Year**	$ 95,936	$ 94,996
	Issuance of Common Shares Under Employee Plans	767	940
	Balance at End of Year	$ 96,703	$ 95,936
Retained Earnings	**Balance at Beginning of Year**	$617,628	$534,273
	Net Earnings	135,961	126,015
	Cash Dividends (Per Share: 1979 — $1.075;		
	1978 — $.975)	(47,132)	(42,660)
	Balance at End of Year	$706,457	$617,628
Reacquired Stock	**Balance at Beginning of Year**	$ (7,984)	$ (8,289)
	Issuance of Common Shares Under Employee Plans	113	305
	Balance at End of Year	$ (7,871)	$ (7,984)
	Total Stockholders' Equity, December 31	$851,145	$761,337

See information on page 24 and notes to financial statements on pages 30 through 34.

Exhibit 3.3 *(Continued)*

Exhibit 3.4   Stauffer Chemical Company: Transaction Analysis for 1979

Line		Cash	NWA	Market- able Securities	Property, Plant & Equipment	Investment and Advances
1	31 December 78	$24,996	$412,208	$64,011	$903,246	$40,384
2	Net Sales		+1,526,160			
3	Interest and Dividends	+10,227				
4	Cost of Goods Sold/Depreciation		(1,013,594)		(93,204)	
5	SG & A		(161,866)			
6	Research and Development		(36,963)			
7	Interest		(31,839)			
8	Other income	+3,730				
9	Minority Interest					
10	Provision for Taxes		(23,259)			
11	Associates Earnings					+10,800
12	New Owner's Equity	+979				
13	Pay Minority Dividends	(2,133)				
14	Cash Dividends	(47,132)				
15	New Long-Term Debt	+9,475				
16	Current Portion LTD					
17	Pay Cur. portion LTD	(13,599)				
18	Repay Long-Term Debt	(25,299)				
19	New Short-Term Debt	+60,858				
20	Capital Expenditure	(239,303)	+1,905		+236,485	
21	Amortize Intangibles					
22	Sell Fixed Assets	+6,125			(6,125)	
23	Div. from Associates	+9,772				(9,772)
24	Sell Marketable Securities		+32,820		(32,820)	
25	Net Other Assets Minus Liabilities	(2,912)				
26	Cash from Operations	+196,108	(196,108)			
		24,712	476,644	31,191	1,040,542	41,412

Intangibles	Other	Short-Term Debt	Current Portion of Long-Term Debt	Other Liabilities	Long-Term Debt	Deferred Taxes	Minority Interest	Owner's Equity
$31,273	$50,066	$135,841	$13,599	$31,239	$415,868	$108,289	$60,011	$761,337
								+1,526,160
								+10,227
								(1,106,658)
								(161,866)
								(36,963)
								(31,839)
							+16,555	+3,730
								(16,555)
						+37,816		(61,075)
								+10,800
								+979
							(2,133)	
								(47,132)
					+9,475			
			+9,145		(9,145)			
			(13,599)					
					(25,299)			
		+60,858						
	+2,818							
(1,905)								
	+13,331			+10,419				
29,368	66,215	196,699	9,145	41,658	390,899	146,105	74,433	851,145

with owner's equity on the right. Now work through the available information. Remember that each line of the analysis must balance. Any increase in an asset must be balanced by an equal decrease in another asset or by an increase in a liability or in the owner's equity.

There are several useful rules to remember:

1. If the item might correctly be called nonoperating, or if you are unsure at this point, do not make an entry in the net working assets column. Make an entry instead in the cash column. For example, dividends received by a company are not part of its operating income. They will therefore be an increase to cash and an increase to owner's equity.

2. If you cannot completely understand a transaction while working through the information, leave it until later. By then, you may have more information that relates to it.

3. If there is a conflict of information, especially in relation to the precise numbers involved, between the Statement of Changes in Consolidated Financial Position and the income statement, balance sheet, or the notes to either of these, always prefer the numbers recorded in the latter. Auditing standards are never applied as strictly to the Statement of Changes as to the other statements. In fact, management often presents the Statement of Changes in an unaudited form. (Statement of Changes is sometimes called Funds Flow Statement, or Statement of Changes in Working Capital. There is no strict rule as to its name.)

In performing a transaction analysis, you should follow a set routine for recording information. First work through all the information contained in the income statement (Exhibit 3.2). Then work through the note showing changes in owner's equity (Exhibit 3.3). The owner's equity column should now balance. Now use the Statement of Changes in Consolidated Financial Position (Exhibit 3.3) to help you balance each column, working across from right to left. It will be necessary to make assumptions because companies do not always disclose enough information.

In practice, different analysts make different assumptions. The quality of your cashflow analysis depends on how reasonable your assumptions are. You are encouraged to work through this example on paper.

STEP 1.   Enter beginning and ending balances for the year from balance sheet on your work sheet. Check that assets equal liabilities plus owner's equity. (NWA stands for Net Working Assets)

STEP 2.   Work through the income statement. Note the following:

Line 3.   Interest and Dividends received are nonoperating items for a manufacturing company. They are shown in the cash column. For a complete picture, tax on this income should be calculated, deducted from $10,227, and deducted from $23,259 in line 10.

Line 4.   Depreciation of $93,204 was disclosed in a note and is included in the Cost of Goods Sold figure. It is assumed that other assets are not depreciated. (This may be unrealistic, but see line 25.)

Line 7.   It is assumed that all interest is cash related. Some interest could be amortization of bond discount but examination of the note on Long-Term Debt suggests not.

Line 8.   Other Income is nonoperating income by definition.

Line 9.   Minority Interest represents the share of minorities in Stauffer's consolidated income, and therefore, it is a nonoperating and noncash expense.

Line 10.   Reference to the note on Income Taxes confirms the split between current and deferred taxes shown in the statement of changes in consolidated financial position.

Line 11.   Equity in Earnings of Associates represents the Stauffer Company's share of their profits. It is accordingly a noncash revenue and a nonoperating item. Dividends from Associates appear on line 23.

STEP 3.   From the note on Owner's Equity we check the information in the Statement of Changes as to new stock issued (line 12).

STEP 4.   Work from the right, using the Statement of Changes and notes to the accounts.

Line 13.   Minority Interest could decrease if Stauffer purchased additional shares in those subsidiaries. However, payment of dividends to Minorities seems more probable. Minority Interest now balances.

Line 14.   From the Statement of Changes. Owner's Equity now balances.

Line 15.   From the Statement of Changes.

Lines 16 and 17.   Current Portion of Long-Term Debt by definition is that part due for payment within 12 months.

Line 18.   With line 16 equals $34,444—see Statement of Changes. Paying debt decreases cash. Long-Term Debt now balances.

Line 19.   By definition, New Short-Term Debt increases cash. The notes confirm that this is new commercial paper. However, as short-term debt is included in working capital, this does not show up on the Statement of Changes as a source of cash, only as net change.

Line 20.   Sometimes it is necessary to leave a column until more information is available. Accordingly Other Liabilities and Other Assets for the moment are left on one side. From the Statement of Changes sheet, we know that Property Disposals were $6,125. In this case (and normally), this is net book value, as gains or losses on disposal are included in income according to the company's policies. We also know that Depreciation was $93,204. To balance the Plant, Property, and Equipment column, we need $263,485. Accordingly, of the $239,303 Capital Expenditure shown in the Statement of Changes, $236,485 is assumed to be plant and $2,818 to be an increase in other assets.

Line 21. It is normal to amortize intangibles, so the expense of $1,905 must be already included in Selling, General, and Administrative Expense in line 5. We assumed that all these were cash expenses, but this one is not. It is therefore added back to net working assets since it is a noncash expense and was wrongly included in $161,866 in line 5. No acquisition took place during 1979, so there could not have been an increase in this asset.

Line 22. From the Statement of Changes. As we do not know gain or loss on sales, we can assume cash received was net book value. If the amount of gain or loss was known, an adjustment would be made.

Line 23. See line 11.

Line 24. Marketable securities must have been sold.

Line 25. Only Other Assets and Other Liabilities remain unexplained. Unfortunately, there is nothing here to help us determine the nature of these items. The analyst has accordingly "plugged" the numbers by a net decrease to cash of $2,912. Given more information, this deficiency in the analysis could be remedied. However, it is not likely to affect cash from operations and is not considered material given the cash from operations of $196,108 (line 26). This is a typical example of the need to make assumptions.

We are now ready to construct the sources and uses of cash statement from the cash column of our transaction analysis.

Sources and Uses of Cash
Stauffer Chemical Company, 1979
(in millions of dollars)

Sources		Uses	
Cash from Operations	$196	Capital Expenditure	$239
Other Income	24	Pay Dividends	47
New Equity	1	Pay Minorities	2
New Long-Term Debt	9	Repay Long-Term Debt	39
New Short-Term Debt	61	Purchase Other Assets (Net)	3
Sale of Assets	6		
Sale of Marketable Securities	33		
	330		330

Observations

Funds from operations was $260 million and the increase in net working assets was $64 million, hence cash from operations was $196 million. Net working assets/sales ratio was 31% in 1978 and 31.2% in 1979, indicating a stable situation in regard to terms of trade. After deducting cost of dividends, cash from operations plus other income covered $173 million of the $236 million net new capital investment. Sale of marketable securities of $33 million and net new debt of $31 million made up the shortfall. There was a shift from long- to short-term debt, probably due to a rise in long-term interest rates combined with severe restrictions in long-term debt markets. Note that cash from operations was greater than reported net income of $136 million, mainly because of the size of depreciation and deferred taxes.

SUMMARY

Cash from operations represents the normal source of repayment of debt. It can be calculated from the changes in the net working assets. Nonoperating items and nonrecurring items are carefully excluded so that the cash flow analysis shows sources and uses of cash to enable conclusions to be drawn about the year being examined.

Negative cash from operations is normally a serious indication of financial problems unless accompanied by strong and profitable growth. If more than one out of the three most recent years show negative cash from operations, then this is strong evidence of a deteriorating situation. Further, in a study published in 1968 (see Chapter 8), Beaver found that cashflow/total liabilities was the single most significant ratio in predicting a company's likelihood of future collapse.[1] This was confirmed by another article on cashflow analysis and the final years of the W. T. Grant Company, which showed that negative cashflows were a much better leading indicator of financial weakness than were traditional ratios.[2] Accordingly, positive cash from operations is an important requirement for normal lending.

PROBLEMS

1. Perform a transaction analysis, and obtain a sources and uses of cash for Wonderdrug for 19X0.
2. Why is nonoperating income and expense excluded from cash from operations?

[1]W. H. Beaver, "Financial Ratios as Predictors of Failure,"*Journal of Accounting Research,* 4 (1968): Supplement.
[2]James A. Largay and Clyde P. Strickney, "Cash Flows, Ratio Analysis, and the W. T. Grant Bankruptcy," Amos Tuck School of Business Administration, no. 180 (1980).

3. Suppose a company includes in its operating income a gain on a sale of trade investments. Where would this be shown on the transaction analysis sheet?

4. Suppose a company shows a loss on the sale of a subsidiary. You are able to trace the disposal of fixed assets associated with this sale, and also the reduction of long-term debt associated with this sale. What other asset or liability might change as a result of this sale?

4 Corporate Structure

Those who are not lawyers, accountants, or bankers are usually unaware of the complex corporate structure of large businesses. They think of Ford or British Steel as just one big company. If they are a bit better informed, they recognize that the word *group* is frequently used about a business organization. And rightly so, for a business organization is generally a group of separate companies, with a parent company and subsidiaries. This chapter is about the effects of corporate structure on consolidated financial statements. It is also about how bankers decide which member of the group will be the borrower.

First, we will review accounting practice under GAAP as it affects consolidations. A consolidated statement presents the results and balance sheets of a family of companies as if they were the results of one company. Thus, it largely ignores the legal separation of the entities in the group. A consolidated corporation has no legal existence by itself; it is just an accounting convenience. Consider for a moment a company with two subsidiaries. Let's call the parent "DADCO" and the subsidiaries "Charley" and "George." DADCO makes no sales, nor does it purchase goods. Charley and George do all the manufacturing and selling. DADCO performs only one function: It owns all the shares in Charley and George and receives dividends as owner. During a period, Charley sells 15 apples, including 2 to George, and George sells 20 apples. A consolidated sales statement shows that DADCO sold 33 apples, since intercompany transactions are eliminated.

The first point, therefore, is that inclusion of an item in consolidated statements does not by itself reveal which member of the family it relates to. The second point to remember is that transactions within the family do not count. All that consolidated statements show are transactions, with the rest of the world, and assets, and liabilities vis-á-vis the rest of the world.

Analysts usually face problems when dealing with that part of the consolidated balance sheet representing owner's equity, including the ownership of parts of subsidiaries by persons outside the group (minority interests), together with an intangible asset that sometimes arises on consolidation which does not appear in the balance sheet of either the parent or the subsidiary. In consolidations, the owner's equity shown in the consolidated statement is always that of the parent or top company. The reason is simply that a consolidation replaces an investment item with the actual assets and liabilities comprising that investment (that is, its net asset value). This is best illustrated by an example.

Example 4.1. Once more, DADCO owns Charley and George. DADCO has always paid out in cash to its owners all the dividend income which it has received from Charley and George. DADCO has owner's equity of 100, and its investment in George cost 60 and in Charley 40. Thus, DADCO (by itself) shows:

Owner's Equity 100   Investment 100

This is a very simple balance sheet, with assets at cost.[1] Unfortunately, it tells us nothing about the affairs of the group.

Suppose Charley and George have the following balance sheets:

Charley		George	
Assets	300	Assets	500
Liabilities	270	Liabilities	440
Owner's Equity	30	Owner's Equity	60
	300		500

Using the procedure of expanding the investment item by replacing it with the actual assets and liabilities, we now see the consolidation:

DADCO (Consolidated)

Liabilities	710	Assets	800
Owner's Equity	100	Goodwill	10
	810		810

This assumes there are no intercompany items. "Goodwill" refers to the intangible asset arising on consolidation. Notice that this intangible asset represents the amount by which the cost of Charley (40) exceeded the net assets acquired (which is Charley's owner's equity of 30). Notice also that, if we added Charley and George's equity to that of the parent, we would get a nonsense result. In consolidations, therefore, the investment in the ownership of a subsidiary which would otherwise be shown as investments is replaced by that subsidiary's actual external assets and liabilities. If the recorded cost of the investment is different from the actual net assets, then there will be a gain or loss on consolidation—that is, an asset for the gain and a reserve for the loss.

---

[1]This would also represent investments on an equity accounting basis if dividends received were always equal to Charley and George's net income.

MINORITY INTERESTS

So far we have dealt with 100% owned subsidiaries. What happens with partially owned subsidiaries? The rule in GAAP is that, if more than 50% is owned, they must be consolidated. Once again, let's look at an example.

Example 4.2. Suppose DADCO buys another subsidiary, Fiona, but is only able to obtain 60% of Fiona's shares. The other 40% remain with Fiona's previous owners. On consolidation, this 40% will become a minority interest, since it represents claims by outsiders on the combined equity of the business. These outsiders will on consolidation appear as if they were external liabilities of the group. Of course, they are not really liabilities, since they do not represent money owned in the way in which debt is owed. If the minority interest is large, it may well cause problems in estimating total owner's equity or tangible net worth, especially when constructing ratios of debt to net worth, such as are used in term loan covenants (see Chapter 9).

Fiona has assets of 200 and liabilities of 130, with owner's equity of 70. DADCO's consolidated statements—after it raised 42 in new cash from its own investors to enable it to buy 60% of Fiona for exactly 60% of 70 (that is, 42)—will now be:

Liabilities	840	Assets	1,000
Minority Interest	28	Goodwill	10
Owner's Equity	142		
	1,010		1,010

Notice that goodwill did not change, because 60% of Fiona was acquired for exactly the net asset value.

It will be useful at this point to list ways in which minority interest will change from year to year, since this often will require explanation by analysts. Minority interest increases when the following occurs:

1. Profits earned by a partially owned subsidiary must be shared between the parent and the minority interest. Hence, if Fiona's net income is 200, minority interest will increase by 40% of 200 (80), while owner's equity increases by the rest.
2. If the parent sells some of its shares in a partially owned subsidiary to outsiders. But if the parent reduces its ownership to less than 50%, the subsidiary will become an associated company, and thus there will then be no minority interest.
3. If the subsidiary raises new shares from its owners either in proportions equal to their ownership or even disproportionately.
4. When fixed assets are revalued, resulting in a gain to reserves (owner's equity). Such revaluation is allowed in some countries, though not the United States.

Decreases in minority interest will occur in the following instances:

1. As a result of losses occurring in that subsidiary.
2. As a result of dividends paid to the outside owners. But only if these dividends exceed the outside owners' share of that year's earnings will minority interest decrease at the end of the period because of dividend payments alone.
3. When a subsidiary is sold completely.
4. When a subsidiary becomes an associated company. That is, if a parent sells shares in a subsidiary to such an extent that its ownership falls below 50%, then the parent will not consolidate the subsidiary's figures. Hence, on the consolidated balance sheet, minority interest will decrease, or disappear altogether, if this was the only partially owned subsidiary.

SUBSIDIARIES NOT CONSOLIDATED

It is quite possible for a company to have subsidiaries which are not included in consolidated balance sheets or in consolidated income statements. To be precise, such subsidiaries are not excluded entirely from such figures; they are treated as investments, even though the parent owns 51% or more. In the United States, accounting principles permit companies not to consolidate subsidiaries if the inclusion of such subsidiaries would not present a clear picture:

> Separate statements for a subsidiary or group of subsidiaries would be preferable if the presentation of financial information would be more informative than would the inclusion of such subsidiaries in the consolidation. For example separate statements may be required for a subsidiary which is a bank or insurance company, and may be preferable for a finance company where the parent and other subsidiaries are engaged in manufacturing operations.[2]

In the United Kingdom, the rule is similar.

In other countries, there is wider variation. In Italy, until recently, consolidated statements were not produced at all. In Germany it is still the practice to exclude foreign subsidiaries from the consolidation, irrespective of the size of the subsidiary. This is a convenient practice for very large companies in that often a financing subsidiary can be created to raise funds for the group as a whole; if it is not consolidated, these financial obligations are not shown on the consolidated balance sheet.

As an analyst, you must decide in each case whether nonconsolidated subsidiaries should be added to the consolidation. For instance, if a total liabilities/tangible net worth figure is being constructed, there seems little sense in not including such finance company liabilities because they certainly

---

[2]*Handbook of Accounting Standards.* Published annually by the American Institute of Certified Public Accountants. Taken from Volume III, paragraph 2051.04.

represent claims of outsiders on the business that will have to be satisfied from group cashflow. On the other hand, if the subsidiary is a bank or insurance company that is not related to the parent company and that stands by itself for financing purposes, there may be good reason not to include the subsidiary's liabilities in the calculation. Thus, consideration of the purpose of the ratio and the nature of the subsidiary helps to determine whether to include these figures or not.

DEBT PRIORITY

If asked whether it is better to lend to a parent company or to a subsidiary, most people, I suspect, would answer "the parent"—and in most cases, they would be wrong. This is because of the priority of creditors in bankruptcy laws. Such laws, of course, vary in detail from country to country, but they always place shareholders at the bottom of the list of those with claims against the company.

Let's consider an example. Anyone lending to DADCO, our parent or holding company earlier in this chapter, should know that its assets consist only of shares in Charley, George, and Fiona, its three subsidiaries. Because DADCO is a pure holding company, it does not have operating assets of its own. If DADCO cannot pay, its lenders may take possession of its assets. However, in so doing, the lenders become stockholders in Charley, George, and Fiona. In this way, their claims on the assets—the true operating assets of the group—are inferior to those of creditors and holders of preferred stock in the subsidiaries. It follows, therefore, that in general lenders to the subsidiaries are ahead of lenders to the parent in terms of what is known as "debt priority." This will be illustrated by a more detailed case, which will also demonstrate the need for consolidating statements. Note carefully that a *Consolidating* statement shows each company's figures and how they are added together to make the *Consolidated* statement.

Example 4.3. Bovington Holdings, Inc., owns one subsidiary, Bovington Books. In 19X0 a bank makes a $150,000 three-year term loan to Bovington Holdings on the basis of the following consolidated balance sheet and cashflow statement:

Bovington Holdings, Inc.
Consolidated Balance Sheet, December 31, 19X9

Cash	$ 80	Short-Term Debt	$ 100
Accounts Receivable	150	Accounts Payable	100
Inventory	250	Long-Term Debt	500
Plant (Net)	820	Deferred Tax	75
	1,300	Owner's Equity	525
	$1,300		$1,300

Cashflow Statement

Year to	December, 19X9 (Actual)	19X0 (Projected)	19X1 (Projected)	19X2 (Projected)
Funds from operations	$260	$ 280	$ 310	$ 330
Less increase in net working assets	(80)	(90)	(100)	(100)
Cash from operations	180	190	210	230
Plant purchases	(60)	(240)	(90)	(90)
Repay long-term debt	(70)	(120)	(120)	(120)
New loan	—	150	—	—
Increase in cash	50	(20)	0	20
Ending cash balance	80	60	60	80

As can be seen, the purpose of the loan is to buy a new plant, and repayment will come out of cashflow over three years. Unfortunately, by the end of the first six months, the company had suffered a downturn in demand and is unable to make its first repayment of $25,000. This is what its consolidated balance sheet shows:

Cash	$ 100	Short-Term Debt	$ 100
Accounts Receivable	150	Accounts Payable	100
Inventory	278	Long-Term Debt	650
Plant (Net)	960	Deferred Tax	93
		Owner's Equity	545
	1,488		1,488

Net income of 20 has been earned: Adding back depreciation of 50 and the deferred tax charge of 18, funds from operations is 88; and as net working assets have only increased by 28, cash from operations is 60. Why can't Bovington pay? The answer lies in the consolidating statements:

Bovington Holdings
(Company alone)

Cash	$ 10	Short-Term Debt	100
Equity in Subsidiaries	750	Long-Term Debt	150
Other Assets	10	Equity	520
	770		770

Bovington Books

Cash	$ 90	Accounts Payable	100
Accounts Receivable	150	Long-Term Debt	500
Inventory	278	Deferred Tax	93
Plant (Net)	950	Owner's Equity	775
	1,468		1,468

Bovington Books has the cash alright, but it cannot pay its parent because of restrictions in its own existing long-term debt agreement that limit its payment of dividends, management fees, and loans to the parent. If it could "upstream" the money—that is, pay some more to the parent—there would not be a problem. What happened was that the parent "downstreamed" the money to Bovington Books and now cannot get it back. If the bank lends money to the parent, it will be in no better position, since the lenders to Bovington Books have debt priority.

In this instance, a better route would have been to lend to Bovington Books directly, thus getting nearer to the cashflow, or to have taken a guarantee from Bovington Books for the benefit of the holding Company loan. This would have given the lender a direct claim on the subsidiary's assets.

Moral: Always lend as near as possible to the source of the cashflow from operations on which you have chosen to rely for payment.

Example 4.4. Sometimes a parent company also has operating assets of its own. In that case, loans can safely be made up to some level which will be covered by the parents short-term operating assets. One way of presenting this is to specify that all the parent's ownership of long-term assets, including investments in subsidiaries, must be covered by long-term sources of funds.

Intercon shows the following figures for the parent company alone:

Cash	$ 170	Accounts Payable	$ 300
Inventories	382	Short-Term Debt	650
Receivables	529	Accrued Taxes	420
Plant (Net)	1,423	Long-Term Debt	4,333
Investments in			
Subsidiaries	7,106	Owner's Equity	3,907
	9,610		9,610

Applying the rule suggested, Plant plus Investment (1,423 + 7,106 = 8,529) must be covered by Long-term Debt and owner's Equity (4,333 + 3,907 = 8,240). Thus, in this case, there is no room for additional Short-Term Debt without breaking the rule.

MORE ON CONSOLIDATING STATEMENTS

As we saw in Example 4.3, consolidating statements comprise a set of figures for each member of a group. They enable you to review the financial condition and operating ability of each member, whether subsidiary or parent. You can then separate weak companies from strong: those that have too little capital, those with the heaviest debt, those with weak sales, and those with heavy expenses. You may find that one or more of the subsidiaries is a regular loss maker. Another one could be the "cash cow" of the whole group, which if it were sold, would adversely affect the other members. You can determine the individual capital base of each corporation, whether or not there are preferred stock issues made by subsidiaries, and the extent of intercompany support.

ORGANIZATION CHARTS

Where a group is particularly complex, it will help to produce a chart of corporate relationships. A chart of this kind for the Thomson Brandt Group of France as of 1981 is shown as Exhibit 4.1. All companies whose figures are part of the consolidated balance sheet and profit and loss are shown, with their shareholdings in each other set out as of the date of the chart. Thomson Brandt is one of Europe's largest companies and also has one of the most complicated corporate structures. The chart helps to show who owns whom.

DEBT PRIORITY SCHEDULE

Once you decide to which company your bank is going to lend, a debt priority schedule can be drawn up. This will show how much debt is senior to yours in terms of priority. You will want to know whether the debt is secured or unsecured and whether it is short or long term. First, however, let's review the normal priority of claims on a company's assets. These claims arise when a company is in liquidation and are established by law. In most countries, the order in which claims are settled is the same: First are the preferred creditors; second, the secured creditors; third, the unsecured creditors; and finally, the shareholders.

Included in the preferred creditors group are government agencies with any claims for taxes, social security payments, and so on. These are generally given first priority. After all, governments make the rules in bankruptcy, so they have an advantage over all other kinds of creditors. Next, the employees usually have a limited amount of claims of wages, and there are other preferred claims, such as the liquidation expenses.

Exhibit 4.2 Debt Priority Schedule, Low Leverage (in millions of pounds)

	Long-Term	Short-Term	Total
Parent Company			
Unsecured	£10.0	£ 0.8	£10.8
Secured*	0.4	—	0.4
Subsidiaries			
Secured*	6.2	4.0	10.2
Unsecured*	2.5	36.0	38.5
	19.1	40.8	59.9

Percentage secured	17.6%	
*Prior debt	£49.1	million
Tangible net worth	£420	million
Prior debt/tangible net worth	12%	

Since secured creditors have assets to realize which may cover their portion of the debt, unsecured creditors—in which category banks often find themselves—are those with the least chance of full repayment in the event of corporate collapse. Shareholders, being by definition equity risk takers, are paid with anything left after all other claims, including preferred stock, are settled.

Two interesting examples are shown based on two British companies' figures as they were at the end of 1978. In both cases, a bank was considering lending unsecured to the parent company. Prior debt would thus be all secured loans to the parent and all loans (unsecured and secured) to the subsidiaries.

Exhibit 4.3 Debt Priority Schedule, High Leverage (in millions of pounds)

	Long-Term	Short-Term	Total
Parent Company			
Unsecured	£ 69.9	£ 1.1	£ 71.0
Secured*	—	—	—
Subsidiaries			
Unsecured*	68.7	19.3	88.0
Secured*	4.0	0.9	4.9
	142.6	21.3	163.9

Percentage secured	2.9%	
*Prior debt	£92.9	million
Tangible net worth	£152.3	million
Prior debt/tangible net worth	61%	

Exhibit 4.2 shows a company with very little total debt in relation to tangible net worth; Exhibit 4.3 shows a highly leveraged situation. In Exhibit 4.2, 82% of the debt is ahead of (prior to) the bank's proposed loan to the parent company, whereas in Exhibit 4.3, only 57% is ahead of the bank. It might seem, therefore, that Exhibit 4.3 is more attractive simply on the basis of debt priority. But that would be wrong, since a credit decision must consider not only debt priority but also total leverage, stability of cashflow and many other factors. Notice, for instance, the size of total debt/tangible net worth in Exhibit 4.3 compared with Exhibit 4.2. In the former, debt is 61% of tangible net worth, whereas in the latter, it is only 14.3%. As it happens, Exhibit 4.2 is Thorn Electrical Industries, and Exhibit 4.3 is EMI, which Thorn subsequently acquired by takeover.

PARENT SUPPORT FOR SUBSIDIARIES

In a book on credit analysis, it is important to review the extent to which parent companies support their subsidiaries. Support is sometimes by guarantee and sometimes by what are known as "comfort letters." Another form of parent support can be obtained when a bank requires that parent company loans be subordinated to the bank's own loans and not be repaid before the bank is paid in full. Sometimes the support is not apparent and may in fact not exist.

Comfort letters are frequently used in international situations. Although it is rare for companies with international business to walk away from their subsidiaries in foreign countries, this has happened on one or two unusual occasions.

Banks are often asked to accept something less than legal guarantees for a variety of reasons. Since guarantees are legal instruments and subject to different rules in different countries, it is not appropriate to discuss these rules here. However, in view of the fact that comfort letters are moral obligations (only in very rare cases do they represent legally binding contractual obligations), it seems sensible to consider the extent to which such letters strengthen the case for lending to a subsidiary.

The general principle to bear in mind is that a comfort letter is not a guarantee of payment. If you went into a court of law with such a letter, there would be one very solid reason why the document would be rejected as a basis on which you could claim repayment. This reason is that there is a long established, universally applied principle of law that requires courts to determine what was in the minds of the respective parties to an agreement based on what a reasonable observer would conclude. It is immediately obvious that if a guarantee of payment had been intended by the parent, it would have used a specified form of words, perhaps even a standard bank form, guaranteeing payment. By their very existence, comfort letters are recognized as a different type of arrangement from guarantees. Further, in

English law, for instance, for a binding contract to exist, there must be an intention to create legal relationships between the two parties. This would be hard to prove if the parent argued that the reason it did not issue a guarantee was that it had no such intention, and at the same time it showed that there was a legal contract between the bank and its subsidiary to which it was an uninvolved third party.

Comfort letters should be analyzed in four ways: the reason for the absence of a guarantee, the borrower's own condition, the parent company's relationship to the borrower, and the actual text of the comfort letter. The most common reason for issuing a comfort letter is that competitive pressure among banks permits the parent to use its financial strength to avoid issuing a guarantee. Ever since banks have expanded overseas in search of opportunities with the overseas operations of their multinational customers, the prevalence of comfort letters has increased. Remember that the home country bank in a foreign country dealing with the subsidiary there of one of its large domestic customers is able to take comfort from the fact that it has substantial muscle to apply to the parent at home should there ever be a problem in the overseas branch. Other reasons for issuing comfort letters may be that the parent has a worldwide policy of issuing no guarantees or that it is restricted from doing so by prior existing loan agreements or indentures. Or there could be a tax reason: A guarantee could result in an assumption of what is called "constructive dividends" from the subsidiary. That is to say, there would sometimes be payments from the subsidiary which would be taxed as dividends (even though they were not) if the parent guaranteed the debts of the subsidiary. Another reason might be that the parent would have to obtain exchange control permission in its home country to issue the guarantee but not the comfort letter. Finally, if the parent's loan agreements already contain clauses specifying that a default by any subsidiary is treated as a default by the parent, the presence of a guarantee may be unnecessary if the lender believes in the parent's intention to be financially responsible and to avoid default (and hence renegotiation) of any of its medium-term obligations.

Now as to the borrower's own condition, you should consider the extent to which it is financially able to stand on its own. There is a world of difference between a subsidiary that is in a self-contained marketing situation—not reliant on its parent, neither selling to it, nor buying from it, and probably not having any part of its parent's name as its own name—and the sort of subsidiary which is typically found with weak financial condition, heavily dependent on parent supplies or purchases, and subject to the effects of inter company transfer pricing. The former is probably financially self-supporting, and comfort letters will not even be offered, whereas the latter is completely subject to the will of its parent and requires a strong comfort letter at the very least.

Another point to consider is the degree of economic integration between parent and subsidiary. As a general principle, the more closely the subsidiary is economically integrated, the more reason the parent has to support it.

Perhaps it is an important supplier of parts, or perhaps it represents a key marketing company. In general, you should beware of companies that have no economic importance to the parent, even if they are well integrated with it. Pure sales subsidiaries with no manufacturing capability would be poor credit risks if unsupported by the parent at least by a comfort letter specifying a promise to maintain 100% ownership during the life of the credit facility.

Third, the nature of the parent company's relationship with your bank will need to be analyzed. If as already stated you have substantial influence with the parent, you will be able to exercise much more moral suasion than if this proposed lending relationship with the subsidiary is your only point of contact with the entire group. You should also analyze the parent company's financial condition and watch out for any obstacles to its ability to make good on its moral obligation. These obstacles could include tax problems, exchange control restriction, possible stockholder legal action, or legal restriction in senior debt indentures.

Finally, examine the text of the comfort letter itself. In Exhibit 4.4, we see a very weak form. It contains no promises other than the promise to advise the bank of a change of ownership and really provides extraordinarily little comfort to a lender. On the other hand, Exhibit 4.5 has some statements on which you could rely with reasonable assurance.

The words of this letter quite clearly indicate what the parent will do, short of guaranteeing payment, to ensure that the loan is repaid. Be sure to consider the person signing the letter. What is his or her official rank? The higher the rank, the more you can rely on the letter. Consider also that the

---

Exhibit 4.4   Weak Comfort Letter

Gentlemen:

As previously discussed with you by representatives of the Treasurer's office of LK Industries, Inc. (the "Company"), the Company has caused a wholly owned subsidiary, LK Canada Ltd. to be incorporated on October 15, 19X1. LK Canada is intended to serve the Company's financing, currency transactions, and cash management requirements in Canada, where the Company has a number of operating subsidiaries. It is the Company's intention to maintain its 100% ownership of LK Canada Ltd., unless the Company notifies you to the contrary.

As discussed with you, the Company requests that the credit facility previously made available by you to LK Systems Canada Limited, an operating subsidiary of the Company, in an amount not to exceed 5,000,000 Canadian Dollars, be made available to LK Canada Ltd. on or after November 2, 19X1. This facility may be increased from time to time but in no event should exceed 25,000,000 Canadian Dollars unless otherwise notified by the Treasurer of this Company.

Please let us know should you have any questions in connection with this matter.

Very truly yours,

LK Industries, Inc.

Exhibit 4.5   Strong Comfort Letter

Gentlemen:

We are writing to acknowledge the credit facility of 10 million Canadian dollars that you have offered to extend to our wholly owned subsidiary LK Canada Ltd. We appreciate your willingness to lend and we are aware of the terms of the facility which have been agreed.

It is our intention to continue our interest in LK Canada Ltd. and we will not reduce our ownership in this company while any part of the debt is outstanding to you, or any contingent liability.

Further, we wish to advise you that it is a matter of policy that LK Industries, Inc. will manage its subsidiaries in such a way that they are able to meet their obligations. We will not permit LK Canada Ltd. to pay any dividends as long as any debt of that company is outstanding to you. Further, we will not guarantee any indebtedness of the borrower without first guaranteeing the indebtedness of the borrower to your bank on an equal basis. The individual whose signature appears below is duly authorized to sign such a letter on behalf of LK Industries, Inc.

Very truly yours,

Treasurer

---

presence of such a letter at least constitutes a strong argument that the subsidiary was within its authority in negotiating the loan. You should always be concerned that due authority has been granted for such agreements at both subsidiary and parent level.

Two famous examples illustrate better than general discussion the problem of moral support. It should be pointed out that we have no knowledge as to the extent of any oral backing for the lenders in either case. In the first case, in 1960 Freeport Sulphur had a wholly owned subsidiary, Cuban American Nickel Company, operating in Cuba. The subsidiary was autonomous to the extent that it arranged its own financing, without any formal backing from the parent. It appears, however, that the lenders were relying on the strength of the parent when making their loans, since there were over $93 million in liabilities and only $11 million of equity owned by Freeport, which also held nearly $5 million of subordinated notes. When the subsidiary was confiscated by the Castro government in 1960, the lenders were left with their claims but no assets on which to claim other than those of the parent. After due consideration, the board of directors of Freeport concluded that it was their best business judgment not to rescue the lenders because there were no benefits to accrue to Freeport by so doing. Further, any money paid out would have created no benefit to the parent company's stockholders and would not have been tax deductible.

By contrast, the American Express Company, in another case in the 1960s—the "Great Salad Oil Scandal"—concluded that it was in the best interests of the parent to make up some of the losses incurred by creditors of its warehousing subsidiary. It is not necessary to go into the many legal points affecting their decision; however, factors strongly influencing the board were the worldwide reputation of American Express, which would have otherwise been severely weakened, as well as a favorable tax ruling on whether these amounts were tax deductible.

To sum up, then, on parent support for subsidiaries, you must be sure that all the facts of each case are separately and properly reviewed. While comfort letters are widely used, they are of limited value; for instance, they do not generally cover political intervention or fraudulent mismanagement. You should always consider the exact words used, and the extent to which the subsidiary's credit rating can stand alone. And always consider what would happen if the subsidiary were sold without consulting any of the lenders.

PROBLEMS

1. Why is it important to distinguish carefully between an individual statement and a consolidated statement?
2. What is a direct subsidiary? An indirect subsidiary?
3. Under what conditions of ownership is it usually considered proper to consolidate? Discuss.
4. Explain the meaning and significance of a minority interest in a consolidated balance sheet.
5. Briefly explain the elimination of intercompany profits (1) on intercompany inventories and (2) on intercompany sales of fixed assets.
6. Why might the individual statement of a corporation that is one of a related group of corporations be less reliable and significant than a properly prepared consolidated statement of the group as a whole?
7. Why is it usually desirable to obtain and analyze the individual statements of associates?
8. What considerations should be borne in mind in lending to a holding company?
9. In lending to a subsidiary company, why is a consolidated statement still of interest to the analyst?
10. What arrangements may be made to strengthen a loan to a subsidiary company when part of its financing requirements are supplied by the parent company?
11. Explain fully what is meant by the priority of subsidiary debt as to subsidiary assets.

5 Using Financial Ratios

If you can't make 10% on your money, drink it.
BERNARD M. BARUCH

A ratio compares one thing to another. There are so many lessons to be derived from the apocryphal remark attributed to the famous financier Bernard M. Baruch that it probably deserves a chapter of its own. For the moment, however, this chapter is intended to set out how to use financial ratios for credit analysis. We leave aside the questions of the modern approach to portfolio investment. What Baruch is saying, is that a ratio will tell you not only about profitability but also about whether the effort of an investment is worthwhile. In doing so, he stresses the need for comparison. He could have said, "If you don't make $20,000 a year out of the stock market, forget it." But would Baruch have conveyed his message correctly to a very rich person with millions of dollars to invest for whom $20,000 might be a lower return than leaving his or her money in the bank? By using a ratio, he has, of course, made his point with general application to any individual situation.

Many people have annual medical checkups. At that time their heart, lungs, eyesight, weight, blood pressure, and so on are extensively tested. Some items of data are meaningful by themselves (temperature 98.6°); others, however, are not. For instance, it would be of little value to a doctor to know that a man's weight had increased 20 pounds in twelve months without knowing the actual weight at the start of the period. Similarly, it would generally be of little help to know that a man's weight was 200 pounds without knowing his height and his age. Ratios solve the problem.

Analysts perform something like an annual health checkup on a company when they receive its financial statements. Indeed, it is commonplace to speak of a company's financial health. We also hear references to companies as "the ailing giant of the industry" or perhaps as "the vigorous newcomer to the market." This chapter will outline which ratios may be generally useful for determining financial health without attempting to cover all the possible ratios that could be calculated. Chapter 8 presents a model using financial ratios to predict corporate bankruptcy, together with a review of some other research on the use of ratios. Remember, however, that ratios are only as valid as the numbers on which they are based. Financial ratios are based on audited financial statements (see Chapter 2), and those statements may be unrepresentative of the company's condition at dates other than those of the balance sheet. Window dressing is, regrettably, practiced in December by firms who have no connection with businesses seeking bigger sales at Christmas.

Before using ratios, you should be quite sure of what you are looking for. It is a common weakness in teaching financial analysis to overburden the student with ratios without discussing their purpose. Let's therefore state plainly that a lending banker is looking for answers to the following questions:

1. What is the nature of the industry of the borrower? For example, is this a high risk/high return industry? A stable industry? Or is this industry "dying"?
2. How does the borrower compare with its competitors in terms of profits? In terms of sales? In terms of cost structure? In using assets?
3. What is the borrower's financial condition? What expectations can be made regarding cashflows? How high are the obligations of the firm in relation to its size? Is it solvent?

TYPES OF RATIOS

There are four types of financial ratios:

1. *Profitability Ratios.* These are intended to measure the company's ability to earn profits. Since the term *profitability* may reflect different things to different users of financial ratios, no one indicator is presented here as the sole ratio to be used.
2. *Leverage Ratios.* A company uses debt of various types as well as shareholders' funds. The relative use of these two forms will depend on the company's attitude to risk and return. The most popular, although not necessarily the most perfect ratio, is debt/equity.
3. *Liquidity Ratios (Solvency Ratios).* These ratios are intended to measure the ability of one firm to meet its short-term financial obligations without having to liquidate its long-term assets. Chief among these is the current ratio.
4. *Performance Ratios.* These ratios examine the revenues and expenses of the firm, either to look at cost structure or to relate sales performance to the amount of assets used in creating sales. Generally these ratios concentrate on the efficiency with which assets are used.

Exhibit 5.1 lists some selected financial ratios.

Exhibit 5.1   Selected Financial Ratios

Profitability
Net income/owner's equity   (Return on equity)
Net income/total assets   (Return on assets)
Earnings before interest and taxes/total assets   (Operating efficiency)
Gross profit/total sales   (Gross margin)
Net income/total sales   (Net margin)
Operating income/operating assets   (Excludes investments)
Sales/total assets

Leverage
Total liabilities/owner's equity   (Debt/net worth)
Total liabilities/tangible net worth
Total liabilities/funds from operations   (Debt/cashflow)
Long-term debt/long-term debt plus owner's equity
Earnings before interest
   and taxes/interest expense   (Debt service coverage ratio)

Liquidity
Working capital/total assets
Working capital/current assets
Current assets/current liabilities   (Current ratio)
Net working assets/sales
Cash, marketable securities and receivables/
   current liabilities

WHY PROFITABILITY?

You may well ask why should a credit analyst be concerned with profitability
when cashflow is more important for repayment of loans and less subject to
management manipulation through the use of accounting policies. Consider
the problem that exists, for instance, when assets are revalued (assuming
the national accounting policies permit this). Immediately, owner's equity
is increased by the amount of the revaluation (net of any deferred taxes),
and since there is no change in revenues minus expenses, one profitability
ratio (namely, return on equity) is decreased. What sense does it make to
use such a ratio with such an obvious flaw? The answer must be that the
analyst does not simply use one ratio for profitability and that if there are
obvious distortions, they should be eliminated.

   More importantly, profitability in some form is still used by investors in
judging whether to provide new equity capital to a firm. It is also used by
competitors looking for an attractive new market sector to penetrate either
by direct assault or by acquisition. Management will, once it is attracted to
a new business sector, be accustomed to making capital investment decisions
using measures that are different from those used by external analysts and
unavailable to them (net present value, for instance, which in itself measures

profitability in relation to cost of capital and partly in relation to size of capital). Thus, there are two reasons why analysts should identify these attractive sectors. The first reason is to assess why they are so profitable, and the second is to see if there are sufficient barriers to entry to protect existing firms. On the other hand, very low profitability will tend to make investors reluctant to invest either in existing or in new companies. The result will be a shortage of capital. Given that low profitability leads to a low rate of profits being retained in the firm, the first consequence will be an increase in the amount of debt used to finance asset increases. With such asset increases in monetary terms being practically inevitable today because of the effects of inflation, it will not be long before the company runs out of debt capacity. There typically follows a period of decline brought about by capital shortage, ultimately leading to collapse. Reasons for corporate collapse and the use of financial ratios in predicting this are covered separately in Chapter 8.

It is my firm belief that there is a certain Darwinian process going on in the business world, as in the natural world, that the "fittest" companies survive, while the less fit ones die. Those that do not survive include those that *will* not respond adequately to change, as well as those that cannot. Profitability is a powerful indicator of fitness, indeed probably the best long-run indicator of corporate health. Some of the measures of profitability are discussed in the following sections.

Return on Equity

The traditional measure of profitability has been return on equity, defined as net income after taxes divided by total shareholders' funds. Investors expect to receive dividends and increases in dividends. Companies have to provide these out of net income and at the same time retain enough profits to permit the business assets to grow, or be replaced, which, given inflation, will mean growth in money terms.

There has been much debate in the corporate finance textbooks over the cost of capital to a firm. Some of this discussion—for instance, the intellectually elegant theories of Modigliani and Miller—has no practical application for the credit analyst, since markets are generally imperfect and investors do not leverage themselves to the extent that the theory requires.

Taking a step-by-step approach will be the best way to try and find what return on equity is actually required at any moment. This approach can be applied in any country where long-term government bonds are sold in an open market and where a premium for risk can be estimated.

The important first step is to recognize that the rate of return on equity which investors as a whole expect to receive must be the same as the cost of equity capital to corporations. Because dividends are normally taxed at different rates in different countries, the pretax return to investors must be considered. Since investors as a group receive only dividends on their shares, their return must be in the form of dividends and growth of dividends. When an individual investor sells to another investor in the market, the sale price represents the purchaser's evaluation of future dividends (discounted at some interest rate which will vary with perceived riskiness), and so the seller is simply realizing in cash his right to receive the dividends. Investor hopes to receive a capital gain—the typical investor sees his income as capital gains and dividends—but of course the company pays out only dividends.

The yield on a share is the dividend divided by the market price. It is not difficult to show that, if dividends must grow at a rate of $g\%$ to provide a return of $k\%$ to the investor, then

$$k = \frac{D_0}{P_0} + g$$

where D_0 is today's dividend and P_0 is today's share price. In other words, the total yield must be the current dividend yield plus the growth in dividends.

The next step is to recognize that, in order to provide dividend growth at a specified rate, the company must earn that overall rate k on its owner's equity, and profit will then grow at that rate g to enable dividends to grow at rate g.

Example 5.1. Wonderdrug's dividend yield is 9%. Suppose that investors expect a total pretax return of 12% for this type of company, then dividends should grow at 3% to give them this. Suppose the company's net income and owner's equity position at the start of a five-year period is set at 12 and 100, respectively. Half of net income is paid out in dividends. (This proportion can be varied without making any difference.)

The progression will have to be as follows:

	19X1	19X2	19X3	19X4	19X5
Dividends	6	6.18	6.37	6.56	6.75
Net income	12	12.36	12.73	13.11	13.50
Average equity	100	103.00	106.00	109.27	112.55
Required return on equity	12	12	12	12	12

Assume that equity in 19X1 is exactly at net book value. Then note that if dividends grow at 3% and other factors remain unchanged, the share price will naturally adjust so that it still shows a 9% dividend yield in 19X2. Hence, the share price will have also grown 3% per annum to 103. It is not difficult to reconcile this with the requirement for capital growth. (Readers can verify the figures in the table by calculation.)

The next step is to recognize that equities are more risky than bonds, and therefore investors require a higher return. Taking long-term government bonds to be a good case of risk-free investment, we then have to ask what premium a balanced diversified equity portfolio should provide over and above the yield for government bonds to compensate for increased risk. The final step will be to require a higher premium from a more volatile or risky company and a lower premium from a more stable company.

Example 5.2. The Geraldine Corporation is believed to be a balanced diversified U.S. corporation whose share price moves very closely in line with stock market averages (that is, a beta of one). If U.S. Government bonds yield 10% and the equity risk premium is 4%, then Geraldine's cost of equity should be 14%.

The question generally arises as to what is a reasonable historic return on equity. Some statistics for U.S. industrial sectors are shown in Table 5.1. I suggest that you develop your own table for the industries and countries in which you are interested. These ratios, however, will be useful only for publicly owned companies, where accounting principles are relatively strict.

It follows from the above discussion that, if business cannot consistently earn a rate equal to what investors require by way of dividends and dividend growth, or if the risk-free rate rises to exceptional levels, business will starve for lack of capital (the risk-free alternatives proving too attractive). It is also alarming to reflect that, in figures collected in 1978 by *Management Today,* a leading British business magazine, the largest 200 companies in the United Kingdom (measured by market capitalization) achieved the following return on equity during 1975–1977, a period of 12–20% inflation:

1975	1976	1977
9.1%	11.2%	11.6%

During this period, the long-term rate of interest averaged 13.5%. Readers are left to themselves to wonder how long it would be (if such conditions persisted) before share prices reflected the fact that investment by companies in capital assets produced lower returns than risk free investment in government securities. A final thought: Bernard Baruch's own 10% figure was struck during a time of negligible inflation. What would he want today?

Earnings before Interest and Taxes/Total Assets

Another vitally important profitability ratio is earnings before interest and taxes/total assets. This is usually shortened to EBIT/TA. It represents what the fundamental operations of the business earned as a return on capital invested before any payment for use of that capital either in dividends or in interest. It is also more useful than return on equity in some ways, since it is calculated before the impact of taxation. Because taxes can be varied by government action and by corporate tax-reduction schemes to exploit tax

	1975	1976	1977	1978	1979	1980	1981	Average for 1975–1981
Broadcasting and movies	19.4	21.0	22.2	21.6	22.2	18.0	N/A	20.73
Mining, crude oil	16.3	16.5	12.3	10.1	16.7	21.0	17.6	15.78
Soap, cosmetics	15.6	16.3	16.5	16.7	17.4	16.9	15.8	16.45
Pharmaceuticals	16.2	15.8	16.7	17.6	18.0	17.9	18.0	17.17
Tobacco	13.5	15.5	15.3	15.8	18.4	19.8	19.5	16.82
Beverages	14.2	15.4	12.2	10.5	15.7	15.6	19.2	14.68
Publishing, printing	11.2	14.7	14.8	15.8	17.9	15.9	16.4	15.24
Aerospace	11.9	14.6	14.4	15.6	19.2	16.2	15.0	15.27
Electronics, appliances	11.2	14.1	15.2	14.9	16.3	16.2	14.3	14.60
Chemicals	12.6	14.1	13.0	13.1	15.2	13.9	13.5	13.62
Shipbuilding and transporation equipment	10.8	13.9	15.4	15.9	18.1	14.4	14.4	14.70
Metal products	13.1	13.8	13.9	15.3	16.0	15.3	14.1	14.50
Motor vehicles	5.8	13.8	14.8	15.4	15.7	8.1	7.6	11.60
Industrial and farm equipment	11.9	13.4	13.7	15.2	15.4	13.3	13.9	13.82
Petroleum refining	11.9	13.0	13.1	13.4	19.1	19.4	16.4	15.18
Paper, fiber, and wood	10.8	12.9	12.7	12.9	15.9	12.8	12.0	12.85
Measuring, scientific, photographic equipment	12.6	12.9	14.9	15.0	16.1	17.1	15.6	14.88
Food	13.1	12.8	13.2	13.7	14.4	14.5	14.4	13.72
Toys, sporting goods	N/A	11.9	11.2	10.9	12.1	12.6	9.2	11.32
Glass, concrete, abrasives	8.3	11.9	11.9	13.9	14.0	11.3	9.6	11.55
Office equipment (includes computers)	10.4	11.5	12.7	15.7	15.9	15.1	13.3	13.51
Apparel	4.4	11.2	12.2	15.6	15.6	12.8	16.2	12.57
Textiles	5.4	10.7	8.8	11.2	11.7	8.1	7.8	9.10
Metal manufacturing	8.1	7.8	6.4	10.4	15.6	12.9	12.4	10.51
Rubber, plastic goods	8.8	7.3	11.4	10.7	8.2	5.0	10.4	8.82
All industries	11.6	13.3	13.5	14.3	15.9	14.4	13.8	13.82

Source: Reprinted by permission from *Fortune Magazine,* "The 500 Largest U.S. Industrial Companies," (Annual Survey, 1975, 1976, 1977, 1978, 1979, 1980, 1981). Copyright © Time, Inc. All rights reserved.

Definition: Net income divided by book value of equity and reserves.

incentives (for example, stock relief in the United Kingdom), you need to find out the underlying profitability of the marketing and production parts of the business. After all, tax and financing decisions (that is, choices between debt and equity) are not dependent on the competitive market position or the efficiency of a firm's production, and it is the latter two that you need to know to assess business risk. In constructing the ratio, you should:

1. Include operating income (but not extraordinary income), investment income, and equity income.
2. Exclude the cost of short-term as well as long-term debt.
3. Capitalize any leases as assets, and, if possible, adjust operating income for the interest element in the lease payments.

Notice how it is possible for companies to improve return on equity by increasing their leverage, even though EBIT/TA remains unchanged.

Example 5.3. In 19X8, Hexagon had EBIT of $1,000 on assets of $8,000. There were no interest charges, and there was a tax rate of 50%. EBIT/TA was 12.5%, and the resulting net income was $500. Since owner's equity was $6,000, return on equity $500/$6,000, or 8.33%. (There was $2,000 of non-interest-bearing current liabilities, such as accounts payable.) In 19X9, Hexagon raised additional debt of $3,000 at an average interest cost of 8%. Total assets are now $11,000. EBIT/TA remains constant at 12.5%, producing EBIT of $1,375: After deduction of interest of $240, which is tax deductible, net income after tax is $567.5 and thus return on equity is 9.46%.

Hexagon's return on equity is higher because of leverage. It remains for the market to decide whether the introduction of debt makes the quality of earnings riskier. This depends on a number of variables which are not relevant to this example. If the stock market perceives Hexagon to be riskier than before, the required return on equity may rise to reflect this. As a credit analyst, however, you should be concerned more with any changes in EBIT/TA reflecting *operating* performance, since the loan has to be repaid with cashflow from operations.

LEVERAGE RATIOS

As has already been observed, the addition of debt or leverage improves return on equity for shareholders. Analysts must been keenly interested in the amount of leverage, and there have been a few attempts to devise golden rules as to how much debt a firm can have. For the moment, the suggested rule of thumb is simply to state that high leverage can only be justified by expectation of *reliable* cash flows.

Leverage increases profitability at the bottom line for two reasons: First, interest is tax deductible; second, the cost of debt to a firm is always less than the cost of equity, since lenders assume less risk than investors because they have prior claims on cashflow, both as to servicing their capital, and as to repayment in liquidation. Even if debt costs increase substantially because lenders perceive increased riskiness, the cost of equity in such situations must by definition (greater risk expects greater return) be higher.

Traditionally, debt has been measured by three ratios:

Debt/equity (debt/net worth)
Total liabilities/cash flow
Debt service coverage ratios

Each of these will now be examined in turn.

Debt/Equity (Debt/Net Worth)

There are differences of opinion as to the construction of this ratio. There are also differences of opinion as to its name. Let's deal first with terminology. Frequently, and regrettably, this ratio is referred to as the "debt/worth ratio." *Worth* by itself is not generally accepted as describing owner's equity. *Net worth* is sometimes so accepted, although it is more commonly used in the phrase *tangible net worth,* by which is meant all the owner's equity accounts minus any intangible assets. By reason of general usage, *equity* is usually regarded as meaning "owner's invested funds." So, our first step should be to prefer the phrasing "debt/equity ratio."

Next is a more difficult problem. Are we concerned here with all forms of debt or liability, or only with those forms that carry a financial cost? Does that financial cost mean interest, or does it include opportunity costs, such as the cost of discounts not obtained from suppliers (in which case accounts payable should be included as debt)?

The solution to the problem lies in considering the purpose of this measurement. As usual, the ratio—and indeed the problem—cannot be viewed in isolation. What we want to measure is the amount of total liabilities in relation to owner's equity so that we can see how much the business is built on owner's capital and how much on other people's money.

There's an old saying that OPM + PMA (other people's money plus a positive mental attitude) leads to riches. As a lender, you want to know the extent of the risks born by your bank and other lenders compared with the risks carried by the owners. Other people's money is always fine for the smart operator, but as a member of the "other people" who provide the money, you must be concerned with the extent to which you and other lenders bear the risks and the smart operator gets the rewards.

Following this line of argument, then, it makes sense to compare total liability to owner's equity in calculating the debt/equity ratio, even though some liabilities are noninterest bearing. It is not the cost of using other people's money that concerns us here; it is the amount. It will also be necessary to resolve questions as to whether to include deferred taxes in liabilities and minority interest in equity, and whether to deduct intangibles from owner's equity in order to use tangible net worth as the base. Once again, thinking about how the ratio can be used will help us answer these questions. Remember that a debt/equity ratio helps show by how much the assets could contract in value before the creditors' money is at risk or lost. This is illustrated by an example.

Example 5.4. Here we construct a "liquidation approach" debt/equity ratio. Jack Jones has the following consolidated balance sheet:

Cash	$ 5	Bank Debt	$ 15
Inventory	40	Accrued Liabilities	38
Accounts Receivable	60	Accounts Payable	32
Net Plant	130	Current Taxation	22
Trade Investments	70	Deferred Taxation[1]	27
Intangible Assets	20	Minority Interests	5
		Preferred Stock	45
		Owner's Equity	141
	325		325

All the liabilities are compared to all of the equity interests. The debt/equity ratio is

$$\frac{15 + 38 + 32 + 22 + 27}{5 + 45 + 141} = \frac{134}{191} = 0.70$$

Assets could contract in value from 325 to 134 before creditors were no longer covered by available assets—that is, a reduction in value of 191, or 58.77%. Of course, if this happened, preferred stock and owner's equity would probably be worthless. But we already know that they rank after the claims of creditors in a liquidation. Hence, that is why this is normally called a "liquidation approach" debt/equity ratio (see Chapter 6).

A few observations follow. Note that deferred taxes are treated as liabilities, since in a liquidation these taxes are likely to become currently due and payable. However, when one constructs a debt/equity ratio on a going concern basis, it is a common practice to leave deferred taxes out of both liabilities and equity calculations. Strictly speaking, this cannot be correct. Either deferred taxes are liabilities, or they are owner's reserves. Examination

---

[1]Arising from the fact that Jack Jones used rapid depreciation for tax purposes, but not for financial accounting.

of how the deferred taxes are created and the time span over which they will become due should help resolve the issue.

Note also that intangible assets were not deducted in this construction. This was because we had no information on the nature of these assets. Other practices assume a more conservative approach and deduct intangible assets from owner's equity to get tangible net worth. It seems better to say; "We want to know by how much assets could contract in value." Of course, some will fetch more than book value, some less, and some will have no value at all. But to assume that intangible assets are worthless seems unreasonable, given that we do not know anything about them or the other recorded book values. For instance, are fixed assets at historic cost (less depreciation) based on prices of 20 years ago? If so, market values for land and buildings will be seriously understated.

A final observation: Since minority interests are by definition equity investors in a consolidated business, it seems logical to group them with equity.

The debt/equity ratio is normally used by lenders to limit the risk to which their loans are exposed. Therefore, they require that the proportion of equity to total assets in a business be consistent with the risk level inherent in the assets that have been so financed. As a result, in term loan agreements (see Chapter 9), the debt/equity ratio is of vital importance and is frequently incorporated in the borrower's financial covenants, breach of which would lead to an Event of Default. It is in these situations that the ratio is usually expressed as "total liabilities/tangible net worth."

So the next question must be: How can one assess the risk level inherent in the assets? Only if this can be answered satisfactorily can a judgment be made as to whether a debt/equity ratio is good or bad. And the answer lies in the capacity of the current assets to be converted into cash through the normal course of business operations and, to a lesser extent, in the form of a fallback position the marketability of the fixed assets which could be sold to generate cash if they cannot support a good cash from operations position. That is to say, the risk level of assets is determined by their ability to generate cash on a *reliable basis*.

Once more we return to cashflow, rather than income, as the basis for assessing debt capacity. This time, however, it must be stressed that stability of cashflow is just as important as the amount of cashflow. Debt/equity ratios as they existed in certain U.S. industrial sectors in 1978 are shown in Table 5.2. From this, one may observe that some industries are much more leveraged than others. In theory, one would expect that this would reflect the stability of cash from operations in those industries. While this may be true for utilities, conglomerates, service industries, and tobacco, it seems that the marketability of assets rather than reliability of cashflow supported debt in the airlines industry.

There are definitely flaws in the debt/equity ratio. In summary, these are that it does not measure anything to do with cashflow; that book values of assets in a liquidation are never achieved, so the "asset contraction" ar-

Table 5.2   Debt Ratios of Selected U.S. Industry Sectors as of September 1978

	Percentage Short-Term Debt	Percentage Long-Term Debt	Percentage Equity	Debt/Equity Ratio
Real estate, housing	29.0	39.8	31.2	2.25
Airlines	4.3	54.3	41.4	1.47
Utilities	4.2	47.1	48.7	1.05
Conglomerates	9.4	40.0	50.6	0.97
Food and hotels	2.7	45.6	51.7	0.93
Service industries	9.8	36.8	53.4	0.87
Food retailing	3.8	42.1	54.1	0.85
Tobacco	6.8	34.6	58.6	0.70
Railroads	3.4	37.6	59.0	0.69
Department stores	15.5	25.5	59.0	0.69
Tires	9.1	31.2	59.7	0.69
Metals and mining	3.7	33.6	62.7	0.59
Chemicals	5.4	31.1	63.5	0.57
Steel	2.8	33.5	63.7	0.57
Appliances	9.6	25.3	65.1	0.54
Paper	2.0	30.1	67.9	0.47
Packaging	4.2	26.7	69.1	0.44
Machinery	8.4	21.6	70.0	0.42
Textiles	6.5	23.5	70.0	0.42
Beverages	2.9	21.6	75.5	0.32
Drugs	7.8	15.8	76.4	0.32
All industries	5.5	32.3	62.2	0.61

Source: Business Week, October 16, 1978, based on percentage of invested capital.
Reprinted by permission.

gument is questionable; and that all of a company's liabilities are not shown on balance sheets as debt (for example, contingent liabilities, pensions, and lease commitments). However, since the ratio is so widely used, perhaps I should explain why it is important despite its weaknesses. The main reason is that lenders are keen to limit the total amount of debt that borrowers can undertake, since obviously adding debt to a company increases the claims on a company's cashflow and thus increases the riskiness of existing loans. A secondary reason may be that it is easy to calculate and thus to use as a basis of comparison between companies in the same industry. Remember that ratios are generally usefully calculated only when comparing like with like, and that what we want is a set of ratios that taken together will tell us something about our borrower compared with his competition. Debt/equity ratios will be significant in ranking competitors in an industry, since the financially strongest will usually be the least leveraged, and in being so, a company has more ability to undertake bold moves in strategic terms. Highly leveraged companies, on the other hand, in general have far less room to maneuver since mistakes will be more costly to them in weakening their financial condition and perhaps precipitating their collapse. Remember, too, that the more debt a company has, the less it is able to make independent decisions.

Cashflow/Total Liabilities

Recognizing the importance of cashflow to lenders, and the fact that debt/equity ratios do not take cashflow into account, we now turn to consider the use of cashflow/total liabilities as a measure of leverage. As is stated elsewhere (see Chapter 8), this ratio has been found by Beaver and others to be a very useful indicator of future financial problems in a firm.

Ideally, the ratio should consider all liabilities and compare them with cash from operations, rather than with net income plus noncash charges (that is, traditional gross cashflow), since it is cash from operations that will be available to repay the liabilities. In practice, gross cashflow is often used as the base instead.

A good ratio will depend both on the stability of future cashflows and on the level of interest rates. One way of looking at this is to consider an extreme case:

Example 5.5. A real estate company whose sole asset is one building has leased this to a government agency at a net $10,000 per annum for five years, after providing for all operating costs and taxes. If there are definitely no other calls on this "risk-free" cashflow (on the basis that the government agency will not default on the lease), the maximum amount that could be borrowed on this project will be the present value of these cashflows. This present value will be dependent on the interest rate used in discounting the cashflows, but at 10% with rentals payable annually in advance, the figure at the date of the signature of the lease (and the receipt of the first payment) would be $31,700 for the four remaining payments. This must by definition be true, since the present value sum represents exactly the amount that can be borrowed with annual repayments of $10,000 to cover capital and interest at 10%. Note that, if the market value of the building were to be the basis of the amount of the loan, implying that the sale of the building would be the source of the loan's repayment, a different debt maximum would be possible, based on the degree of certainty of the future sale price as well as interest rates.

Example 5.6. The Megan Company considers buying a machine for $75,000 with no resale market value because of its specialized use. This machine will produce expected net cashflows (that is, after all costs and taxes) from labor savings in production of $20,000 per annum for five years. Cashflows have been adjusted to "expected" levels based on probabilities estimated by management. After five years, the machine will be scrapped. Assuming a 10% interest rate and that the cashflows occur at the end of each period—

to make calculation easier—what is the amount which could be borrowed on these facts?

The present value of an annuity of $20,000 per annum for five years at 10% is 3.791 × $20,000 = $75,820. A lot depends on the probabilities estimated by management. In theory, it follows, that $75,820 would be the maximum debt to be supported by these cashflows alone. If this were done, however, the Megan Company would receive only $820 benefit from the machine, since the expected cashflow savings thus created would be almost entirely used up in repaying the debt required to purchase the machine. It would not, therefore, be likely to borrow $75,000 on these facts. Nor would a banker be willing to lend 100% of the purchase price of a machine! In practice, either the purchase price would be lower or the cashflows greater for such a financing.

Notice also that if the Megan Company did proceed to borrow $75,000, it would be increasing operating leverage[2] and financial leverage at the same time, which is a highly risky thing to do. Thus, it seems clear that the degree of future certainty of cashflows will influence the amount of debt which they can support.

This discussion has so far focused on debt that will be repaid by cashflows from operations. However, debt substitution may also be possible, given reasonable reliability of future cashflow. Indeed, this happens all the time with loans to finance companies and with interbank deposit placements. However, it is important at this stage to reflect on the total liabilities/cashflow ratio by itself. The question to consider is this: Is it possible to state generally what an acceptable ratio will be?

Once again, present value analysis should help us gain some perspective. Presented below is an extract from the present value of an annuity table, which can be found in many finance textbooks.

Years	6%	8%	10%	12%	14%	16%
1	.943	.926	0.909	0.893	0.877	0.862
2	1.833	1.783	1.736	1.690	1.647	1.605
3	2.673	2.577	2.487	2.402	2.322	2.246
4	3.465	3.312	3.170	3.037	2.914	2.798
5	4.212	3.993	3.791	3.605	3.433	3.274
6	4.917	4.623	4.355	4.111	3.889	3.685
7	5.582	5.206	4.868	4.564	4.288	4.039
8	6.210	5.747	5.335	4.968	4.639	4.344

[2]Operating leverage reflects the proportion of fixed costs to total costs: The more fixed costs it has, the more vulnerable a company is to a decline in revenues leading to operating losses. Operating leverage is a very important concept but unfortunately cannot be determined from financial statements.

In the first column, the figure 6.210 indicates that the present value of $1 received annually in arrears over eight years at 6% interest is today $6.21. Or put another way $6.21 of debt at 6% can be repaid at the rate of $1 per annum over a period of eight years.

Suppose we expect interest rates to be 10% and that we regard five years as the limit to the reasonably foreseeable business outlook. If cashflows remain constant, then liabilities of $3.791 can be repaid for every $1 of cashflow. This requires, of course, that these cashflows are not needed for other purposes (for example, capital investment). Perhaps a better way to estimate the ratio would be to estimate available cashflow after provision for capital expenditure.

By inspecting the table, we can see that a ratio greater than four requires either an outlook of more than five years or interest rates below 10%. That is to say if liabilities are more than four times cash flow, it will take longer than the foreseeable future (five years) to repay these, and/or it will depend on interest rates being less than 10% throughout the entire period. Whether this is realistic, is up to the banker to judge. In fact, many lenders consider that total long-term liabilities should not exceed four times gross cashflow. You should be cautious, however, about applying any number as a maximum figure for several reasons:

1. While total liabilities/cashflow is normally based on gross cashflow, some expenditure will be necessary for capital.
2. The table assumes constant cashflows. This is generally not realistic because of inflation.
3. The table is far less sensitive to interest rates than it is to the period of years being considered. Hence, the decision about what time horizon is reasonable for projections has a major effect on the outcome—that is, on what is an acceptable ratio.

Of course, you should remember that most liabilities are replaced as they are repaid in a continuing business. All that we are examining by using the present value of annuity table is the conceptual basis for choosing a maximum number, such as four times.

Debt Service Coverage Ratios

Debt service coverage ratios relate reported income to interest-bearing debt. These are popular with bond holders and with agencies that rate bonds for investors according to safety of principal and interest.

The simplest ratio is earnings before interest and taxes/interest payments. This is calculated using earnings before interest and taxes because interest is tax deductible. A ratio of less than 2, indicating that interest payments are only twice covered by available funds, would be cause for alarm. Unfortunately, the ratio uses earnings before interest and taxes rather than cash flow, so it is not adjusted for noncash charges.

A more advanced ratio would include lease payments, sinking fund payments, and all other forms of debt service required and would compare these with earnings before tax and depreciation. Adjustment would have to be made for capital repayments that are not tax deductible.

Both of these ratios are useful where debt substitution is likely to be the method of repayment for existing lenders. The ratios are also useful in that they relate current dollar interest payments to current dollar income rather than to historic cost debt; debt figures in terms of original capital amounts are distorted by inflation.

LIQUIDITY/SOLVENCY RATIOS

Many books on financial analysis frequently confuse liquidity and solvency. The ratios normally used to examine these features are the current ratio, the quick ratio, receivable turnover, inventory turnover, and net working assets/sales. While these can all be useful, it pays to know what you are measuring.

In this book, *liquidity* means "nearness to cash." *Solvency* means "ability to pay one's debts as they fall due." Frequently, a high ratio of current assets to current liabilities (a high current ratio) is described as showing a strong liquid position. Of course, that is not strictly true, since the definition of current assets includes work in progress, which may be very illiquid because of the length of the production process, and accounts receivable, where extended credit of up to three years may be granted. It all depends on the composition of those assets and liabilities and the degree to which cash demands can be met from cash resources, including undrawn short-term lines of credit. An illiquid firm can be solvent if it has the ability to borrow to pay its debts even though its assets are not near to being turned into cash. And a liquid firm could become insolvent if its combined liabilities (including its long-term debt) exceed its assets, even though the current assets are mostly cash and exceed its short-term liabilities. The trigger would be a default on a covenant in a term debt agreement that resulted in all debt becoming immediately payable.

The current ratio is, then, the simplest and most traditional method for measuring liquidity. Even though it has drawbacks, the ratio shows that any firm whose current ratio is less than unity is at first glance unable to meet its current obligations out of its current assets. Further investigation is then necessary to determine the nature of the lack of liquidity and the extent of the liabilities. Such a company would perhaps be a company that owned apartment blocks where the rental income to be received in the future would easily repay the current liabilities. Admittedly, however, such firms are rare, and manufacturing companies with current ratios of less than one are generally poor credit risks.

The quick ratio is also used to measure liquidity and consists of current assets, exclusive of the investment in inventory, compared with current liabilities. Where inventory or work in progress is substantial, this may be a more useful ratio than the current ratio.

Inventory levels are measured in terms of days of inventory on hand, and accounts receivable are measured in terms of days of sales represented by the amount of receivables outstanding. Changes in these numbers from year to year should be examined and explained. Care should be taken, however, to look for changes in the product mix of the company that can explain changes in these numbers. The formula for finding the ratio is

$$\frac{\text{Inventory}}{\text{Cost of goods sold}} \times 365$$

and this will tell you days of inventory on hand. This is discussed further in the next chapter. Similarly, days of receivables can be found thus:

$$\frac{\text{Accounts receivable}}{\text{Sales}} \times 365$$

And days of payables thus:

$$\frac{\text{Accounts payable}}{\text{Cost of goods sold}} \times 365$$

These three items can be combined to find the number of days in the cash cycle, which is discussed in Chapter 3.

The Self-financing Short-Term Growth Rate

As we have seen, net working assets as a percentage of sales can be looked on as the ratio to use to find out how much of an increase there will be next year in such items as inventory, receivables, and payables that taken together will reduce gross funds flow (that is, net income plus depreciation) to an actual figure for cash from operations. You can also use the net margin on sales to find the amount of funds generated by the profit margin on sales. Then combining these two, you can find the level to which the company can grow in the next period without having to increase short-term debt to cover an additional requirement for an increase in net working assets. In fact, it is possible to refer to the net working assets/sales ratio as the cash efficiency ratio and the profit margin as the cash-generating ratio.

In Exhibit 5.2, Paragon has a current sales level of $3,000, with a profit margin of 8% and a ratio of net working assets/sales of 20%. At a sales level in the next period that is constant at $3000, funds from operations will be $240 and no additional net working assets will be needed, thus cash from operations will also be $240. At a sales level of $4,000, funds from operations

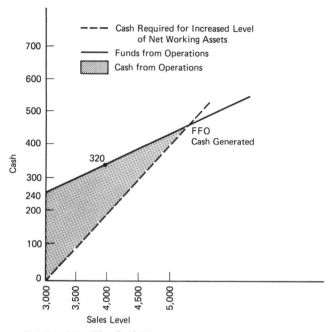

Exhibit 5.2 The Self-Financing Growth Rate, Paragon.

will be $320 (8% of $4,000) and net working assets will have to increase by 20% of the difference in sales levels (20% of $1,000), hence cash from operations will be $120. In fact, all of the shaded area will be positive cash from operations. At a sales level of $5,000, funds from operations will be $400 (8% of $5,000), but since sales are now $2,000 greater than the former level, Paragon will need $400 (20% of $2,000) more in net working assets. As can be seen, sales increases of less than this level are self-financing, whereas those above will produce negative cash from operations.

This model has several very limiting assumptions. Mostly these relate to economies of scale, operating leverage, and so on. It is probably not credible that the profit margin would remain constant with such sharp increases in sales, but the concept can be useful for seeing the extent to which increases in net working assets can be internally financed by profit margins. Note also that the profit margin excludes depreciation expense.

Generalizing, where p is the profit margin and q is the net working assets/sales ratio, the self-financing growth rate x is

$$x = \frac{p}{q - p}$$

PERFORMANCE RATIOS

Each industry has performance ratios in terms of the efficient use of assets. These ratios concentrate on the assets that are the most significant to that industry. Significance is most often determined by cost, especially where high operating leverage is present. That is to say, if an asset gives rise to a high level of fixed costs and thus to high operating leverage, it makes sense to relate sales revenues to the size of this asset.

For example, in hotels, the normal performance ratio is an occupancy ratio measured as the proportion of bedrooms filled each night, since it is these rooms that govern the amount of fixed costs. In the airlines industry, one ratio used to measure operating efficiency is the revenue passenger load factor (RPLF). Because of the high element of fixed costs, the higher the RPLF, the better the performance. RPLF is found by dividing the number of revenue passenger-miles flown by the number of available seat-miles flown. Such factors as route structure, aircraft type, and seat configuration should be taken into account and the airline compared with others of its type. Another efficiency measure is total operating expense per available seat-mile. Total operating expense generally increases with the size of the aircraft, but greater capacity usually results in lower operating expense per available seat-mile. In electric utilities, costs per unit of output are important. In retailing, sales per square foot of selling space is used. As analysts, you are advised to develop your own performance ratios to cover the industries in which you are interested, bearing in mind the data that companies disclose that can be used for comparative analysis.

SUMMARY ON USING FINANCIAL RATIOS

Single financial ratios suffer from some disadvantages in computation but are important for comparative purposes. Multiratios (that is, equations using several ratios with appropriate constants) can be very important for determining trends, especially in predicting corporate collapse, and are discussed in Chapter 8.

The following chapter on financial condition discusses how to use financial ratios and performance ratios in practice. Analysts must always remember how ratios fit together and how one set of ratios will affect another set. For example, higher leverage ratios can produce higher return on equity. Exhibit 5.3 illustrates this.

In this example, the company's balance sheet and income statement are as follows:

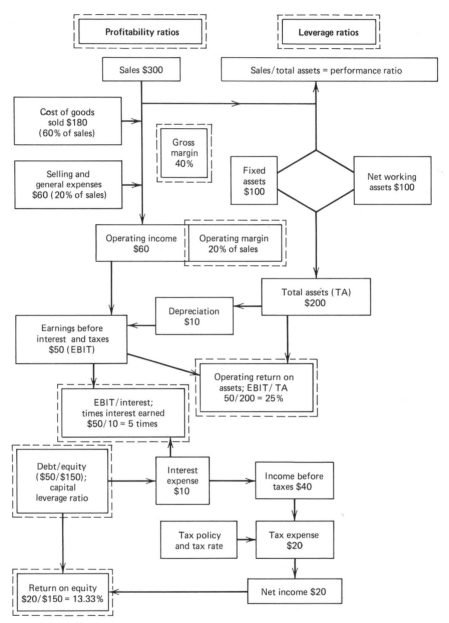

Exhibit 5.3 How Ratios Relate to Each Other

Balance Sheet

NWA	$100	Debt	$ 50
Fixed Assets	100	Equity	150
	$200		$200

Income Statement

Sales	$300
Cost of Goods Sold	180
Selling and General Expense	60
Depreciation	10
Interest Expense	10
Income before Taxes	40
Tax Expense	20
Net Income	20

Note that if Debt was not $50 but $80, Equity would be $120, Interest Expense would be $16, Net Income would be $17, and hence Return on Equity would be $17/120 = 14.16\%$.

PROBLEM

Attempt the industry identification exercise that follows:

Everyone knows that there are variations in operational and financial policies and practices and in operating results between firms in the same industry. However, the nature of each industry has an important impact on the general patterns of asset allocation as well as on the financial results of most firms in the industry. Presented in Exhibit 5.4 are balance sheets, in percentage form, and selected ratios drawn from the balance sheets and operating statements of 11 firms in 11 different U.S. industries as of December 31, 1979. Recognizing the fact of certain differences between firms in the same industry, each firm whose figures are summarized is broadly typical of those in its industry. In fact, all but the first named have debt which is rated A by Moody's Industrial Services. Here are the 11 industries:

1. Fast-food chain
2. Electric utility
3. Supermarket chain
4. Broadcasting and movie producer
5. Regional domestic airline

Exhibit 5.4 Industry Identification Exercise

	A	B	C	D	E	F	G	H	I	J	K
Cash	13.2	3.1	4.8	6.5	—	15.0	1.3	4.4	5.2	16.7	3.7
Receivables	3.5	2.0	8.0	37.1	4.9	12.9	22.6	23.3	25.6	21.3	16.3
Inventory	3.3	31.6	39.7	19.2	2.8	3.2	28.5	8.9	22.6	1.7	34.3
Other	1.2	2.2	1.1	1.1	1.0	3.6	1.2	0.5	—	16.6	1.3
Plant and equipment	78.1	60.4	28.1	33.4	87.7	47.3	42.5	58.3	28.8	23.5	24.3
Other assets	0.7	0.7	18.1	2.7	3.6	18.0	3.9	5.5	17.8	20.2	20.1
Total	100	100	100	100	100	100	100	100	100	100	100
Notes payable	—	0.6	1.5	5.5	2.1	5.0	4.1	2.6	1.7	1.0	13.9
Accounts payable	16.8	28.1	15.1	14.5	2.3	17.0	15.9	21.9	6.5	4.1	—
Other accruals	—	—	4.0	—	2.9	7.3	—	1.0	15.2	13.4	—
Current taxes	2.2	0.1	2.6	2.5	—	1.0	4.8	8.6	3.7	3.4	3.9
Long-term debt	7.6	30.8	12.5	16.0	44.9	29.4	27.2	19.8	13.1	17.7	25.9
Other long-term liabilities (including preferred stock)	1.8	1.6	5.3	4.2	18.7	8.8	7.5	15.3	10.6	1.0	2.6
Owner's equity	71.6	38.8	59.0	57.3	29.1	31.5	40.5	30.8	49.2	62.8	53.7
Total	100	100	100	100	100	100	100	100	100	100	100
Net income	10.5	1.04	6.1	1.0	11.5	4.6	1.7	5.8	6.1	7.7	5.1
Return on equity	28.5	14.2	17.5	17.9	11.3	15.4	6.7	41.8	15.8	20.9	12.9
Sales/total assets	1.91	4.42	1.62	10.9	0.28	1.36	1.53	1.74	1.26	1.61	1.40

6. Meat packer
7. Engineering equipment
8. Large electronics company
9. Rubber tire maker
10. Tobacco manufacturer
11. Oil company

Now match the industry with the firm. For instance, if column A is the supermarket chain, write A3 and give reasons.

6 Financial Condition

An important part of credit analysis is to examine the borrower's assets and liabilities, as shown by the balance sheet, and to form an opinion as to a company's financial vulnerability or its flexibility. In other words, the analyst tries to determine answers to questions beginning "What if . . . ?" For instance, "What if inventory has only half the value that is recorded on the balance sheet?" Or "What if the company has to raise new long-term capital? Could it go successfully to the equity market?"

When writing this part, you must describe major changes in the balance sheet since the previous year. You are expected to consider the quality of the assets, the magnitude and seniority of the liabilities, including any contingent liabilities, and the company's ability to react to unexpected changes in future cashflows. This is what is meant by financial flexibility.

Your purpose is to think and thus come to a judgment as to whether the borrower's financial condition is satisfactory for the bank's purpose. The question is "Will the company have cash available for our loan and to meet other requirements?" You must make use of some of the financial ratios discussed in the previous chapter. Most importantly, you must examine trends and explain year-to-year changes.

ASSET QUALITY

Asset quality means a description of what sort of assets the company has. Do they appear to generate cash on a regular basis? Do they also generate earnings? Will they be worth recorded values if sold in the normal course of events? What would the breakup value be? How much more must be spent on them to make them marketable? All of these things should be going through the mind of the trained observer. Since the most dubious asset in companies in financial difficulties is usually inventory, we will examine inventory first.

INVENTORY

Almost always the figure for inventory on the balance sheet is not a good guide to what it is worth. This is because the recorded value is based on accounting concepts, not on market value. In most accounting systems, this will be true even where the "lower of cost or market" rule is applied because, if the inventory's market value is below cost, then something is likely to be wrong with either the inventory or the firm. An exception to this might be where precious metals or other commodities are involved that were purchased at prices higher than the year-end value. If this is the case, however, then it is equally likely that today's market price is not the same as the price ruling at the company's year end. We can safely say, then, that inventory as a recorded value is an accounting concept that is needed to establish a company's cost of goods sold for historic cost accounting. It is not a guide to realizable value.

Next, it is necessary to consider whether the accounting principle being used is FIFO (first in first out) or LIFO (last in first out). This is best illustrated by a simple example, showing the substantial difference that arises between the two methods during a period of rising prices.

Example 6.1. The Broadoak Company on June 1 had 100 units in inventory at a cost of $6 each. It purchased 100 items at $7 on June 10, 100 items at $8 on June 15, and 200 items at $9 on June 25. Since 300 units were sold in June, the ending inventory was 200 units. Under LIFO, these 200 units are the 100 at $6 and the 100 at $7, giving a recorded value of $1,300. Under FIFO, the units are carried at $9 (the price of the latest purchased units), giving a recorded value of $1,800.

It can readily be seen that FIFO inventories are nearer to replacement cost than LIFO inventories.

A third complication will arise from the fact that manufacturing companies divide their inventory into raw materials, work in process, and finished goods. Asset quality relating to raw materials, which may be very marketable, will differ from the marketability of half-finished goods, which is likely to be minimal, and this will differ again from the finished article. Provided that demand for the finished goods is satisfactory, the value of these goods will reflect the added value of the manufacturing process. However, in one dis-astrous—and fortunately rare—situation, the raw materials were worth more than the finished goods because of the totally unsuccessful nature of that company's product.

The final complication in looking at the balance sheet figure for inventory is the fact that there is nearly always more than one type of product in in-ventory (even Coca-Cola is not a one-product company), and often many thousands of products, each of which will be moving at a different pace. Traditionally, banking textbooks have told the analyst to calculate inventory turnover ratios in order to determine the rate at which inventory generally is moving. This implies that a slow rate of movement indicates the probability of a large amount of unsellable inventory. To find the inventory figure in terms of days of inventory on hand, use the method shown in Chapter 5, which will give you the number of days of production which are in inventory. However, this figure depends on two highly unlikely hypotheses:

1. That ending inventory is the average inventory maintained during the year.
2. That all inventory is in the form of finished goods.

What is really needed to assess inventory turnover is seldom available. But if it were possible, you would want to know, for each major product line, the average inventory level in days, the target inventory level in days, and the average age of each product. These figures would then be compared with year-end and quarterly positions in order to see trends as they appear. Such information would also help monitor the company's ability to control its levels of inventory.

In the absence of such information, you ought to make a point of seeing the inventory. This is vital, of course, where inventory is going to be used for collateral, and certainly useful where it is not. With multiproduct firms, you should in addition ask about the inventory control system. A good inventory control system will minimize the levels of each product without the risk of being out of stock, will keep the costs of holding inventory low (a matter vitally important when interest rates are very high or when storage charges are expensive),[1] and will also help control production since it will identify items that are selling fast and therefore need replacing. Ideally, such systems are computer based.

In 1972 the W. T. Grant Company was the seventeenth largest retailing company in the United States, with over 1,200 department stores generating sales of over $1.6 billion. In 1975 the company collapsed into bankruptcy. Among many reasons, one that seems today almost incredible was that W. T. Grant's main office in New York did not know the details of each store's inventory except by a single total dollar figure. As a result, buyers did not know what to buy. There were practically no inventory controls within the stores, as the company's internal auditing procedures were no help and there were in any case not enough auditors.[2] In another case, a nut and bolt manufacturer in Latin America showed inventories equal to more than 500 days sales at the end of 1978. In fact, inventories were understated. But even so, the problems that ultimately overtook the company arose in part from a lack of inventory controls. Almost every time an order was received, a new production run was scheduled, since nobody knew—short of physically looking in the warehouse—what was in inventory. With total inventory exceeding

---

[1]There is a case for saying that the 1980 U.S. recession was less damaging to industry than earlier recessions because of the widespread improvement in inventory control systems. (**Fortune,** July 27, 1981.)

[2]*Business Week,* July 19, 1976.

$30 million worth of industrial fasteners, such a procedure was simply not feasible.

INVENTORY AND CONCEALMENT

Before leaving inventory, it is important to spend a few moments considering the fact that inventory offers the best means available of concealing information should the owners of the business wish to do so. There are several reasons for this: First, fixed assets tend to remain unchanged from year to year, with an accompanying stability of recorded value.[3] Second, the value of cash and accounts receivable is much more easily checked by auditors.[4] But most importantly, inventory values are extremely difficult to substantiate. Concealment takes two forms: either an overstatement of value, which can be disastrous to the banker, or an understatement of value, perhaps intended to frustrate the tax collector. An example of each type follows:

Example 6.2.   A wine merchant accepted delivery of a large consignment of grape alcohol that he purchased in the belief that it was 100% top-quality Greek-origin alcohol used in the making of cheap brandy. Subsequently, he discovered that it was impure and had been diluted with industrial alcohol. The market value of this was much lower than the cost of the consignment. However, he did not revalue downward the inventory he already held. As a result, his inventory was overstated, as were his profits.

Undervaluation of inventory, on the other hand, is a way of postponing profits. Writing off inventory results in an expense in the current year. If, however, the inventory is retained on the books at a low figure, it can be sold the next year with a benefit to the income statement.

Example 6.3.   An oil distributor had five tanks of heating oil, each with a cost of $10,000. Suppose purchases of oil in that year amounted to $440,000 and beginning inventory was $40,000, then the cost of goods sold would be $430,000. If, however, the owner of the business were to understate the amount of ending inventory by concealing the fact that all five tanks contained oil and declaring only four tanks worth $40,000, the cost of goods sold would be $440,000 and the next year's profits would benefit to the extent of $10,000 of oil that had effectively been written off for the purposes of cost.

---

[3]Although if fixed assets can be revalued, which they may be within the accounting principles of several countries, there is scope for concealing high values and generally less scope for hiding the lack of value in fixed assets.

[4]False sales will create false receivables, however. A known method of distorting figures is to invoice customers just before year end for goods which they have not received, and then to adjust the accounts after year end when the customer complains.

Whether or not concealment is fraudulent always depends on the facts of each case. One must make an important distinction here between concealment and conservatism. Conservative businesspeople traditionally like to carry inventory at or below cost even if replacement cost is higher. Undervaluation is not necessarily wrong or fraudulent, simply a way of being prudent in not realizing a profit until something is sold. "Never anticipate gains, always anticipate losses" is the watchword of the conservative. On the other hand, concealment generally implies factual misstatements to auditors or tax collectors and is usually fraudulent.

WORKING CAPITAL

Working capital is defined as current assets minus current liabilities, and represents the risk money which the owners of the business have at stake in relation to short-term assets. It is relevant to assessing asset quality in current assets since it is a measure of the amount by which assets could decline in value before the short-term creditors are not covered in full.

Example 6.4.   The Peter Pine Company, a wholesale florist, had figures at June 30 that looked like this:

Cash	$ 24		
Inventory	210		
Accounts receivable	430	(A)	664
Accounts payable	$160		
Short-term debt	310		
Accrued expenses	81		
Current taxation	47	(B)	598
Working capital		(A − B)	66

If current assets are worth only 90% of recorded value, the value at (A) becomes $598 and working capital is wiped out. Current liabilities are still covered on a one-to-one basis. Whether this figure for working capital would be considered adequate depends on the types of goods in inventory. Short-term lenders obviously want a higher figure for riskier or slower moving inventory items, where asset quality may be questionable. Given the nature of the flower business, with its rapid turnover, Peter Pine's figure may be acceptable.

On the other hand, if we look at the next example, a different picture is revealed.

Example 6.5.   Charles Chestnut & Company show the following figures at September 30:

Cash	$ 41		
Inventory	330		
Receivables	72	(A)	$443
Short-term debt	$120		
Accounts payable	110		
Current taxation	43	(B)	273
Working capital		(A − B)	170

Although working capital is 38% of current assets, most of the current assets are in inventory. Charles Chestnut & Company are in the business of making electronic games and toys. If the inventory does not sell well in the next quarter, which is the most important quarter for this business, then all that working capital may be needed to absorb the cut-price movement of inventory that might be necessary. Short-term lenders normally look to be repaid in situations such as this out of asset contraction, since this is a seasonal loan. In such cases, working capital is more significant than profitability, since it demonstrates the company's ability to absorb unexpected changes in cashflow. On the basis of these figures, one might say that Charles Chestnut & Company had financial flexibility thanks to a good working capital position, but such a judgment would really only be possible given knowledge of expected sales levels in the next quarter, together with knowledge of normal selling margins.

CHANGES IN WORKING CAPITAL

Analysts should perform a simple study to see how and why working capital has changed from year to year, since this obviously affects financial flexibility. Stated in brief, working capital will normally increase through retained earnings. New equity or long-term debt that is not used in fixed asset purchases will also have the same result, as will use of a lower amount of fixed assets for an equal level of sales. Conversely, working capital will decrease because of losses or because short-term debt is being used to fund capital expenditure. By itself, short term debt does not increase working capital: Depending on how it is used, short term debt could decrease working capital.

A common error among beginners is to suppose that bank lines of credit exist to provide working capital. They do not. They can only finance net

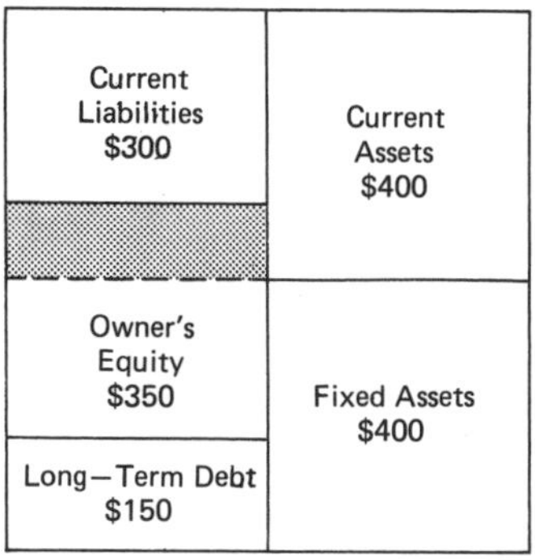

Chart A

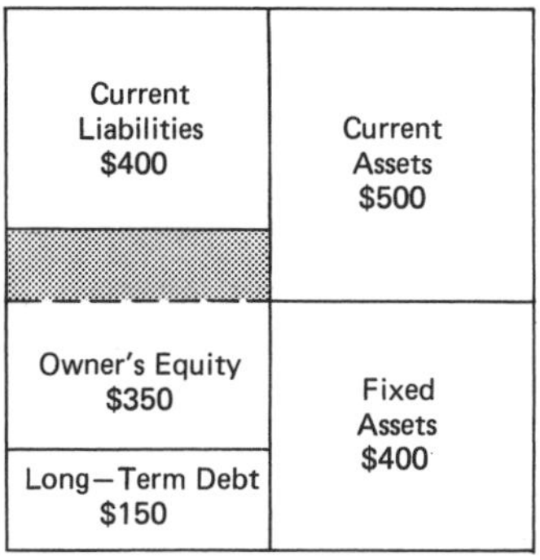

Chart B

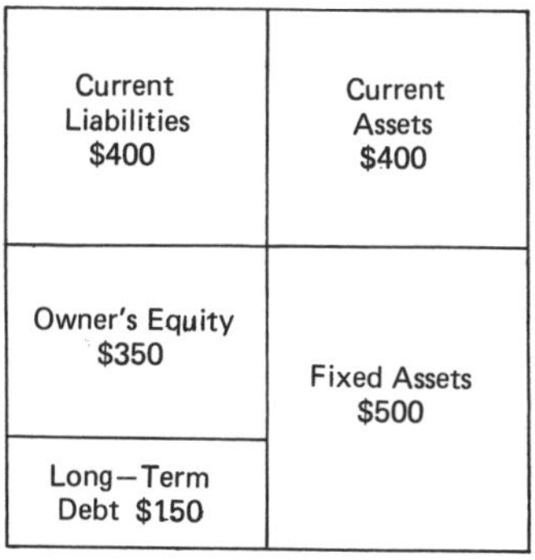

Chart C

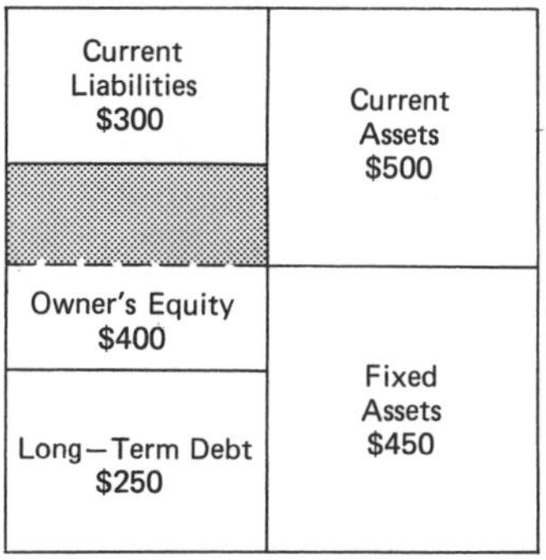

Chart D

working assets. This is best illustrated in a series of charts. (See Charts A–D.)

The dotted area is working capital provided by owner's equity. If short-term debt of $100 is added to Chart A and this is used for purchase of inventory, working capital is unchanged, as can be seen in Chart B.

On the other hand, if the same amount of short-term debt is added and used for purchasing fixed assets, working capital decreases and the firm's liquidity decreases too, as shown in Chart C. At this point, there is no working capital.

Finally, in Chart D the working capital has increased because long-term debt was increased by $100, of which $50 was spent on fixed assets. In addition, retained earnings were $50. Working capital increased by $100 to a total of $200.

ACCOUNTS RECEIVABLE

Asset quality in relation to accounts receivable depends on their collectibility. This in turn depends on who the customers are, whether there are a small number of preponderant buyers, and whether the receivables contain any overdue accounts.

It is generally much easier to determine the quality of receivables than the quality of inventory. This is because borrowers can supply lists of their principal customers, and banks then can check out the credit worthiness of these if they are not already known to the bank in other respects. As a general rule, accounts receivable are more liquid than inventory, since they represent items that have already been sold and are thus nearer to the end of a company's cash conversion cycle. There are thus usually fewer problems relating to accounts receivable, and if collateral is being offered, they provide much more acceptable collateral than does inventory.

Two tools are available to assist you in determining quality. The first of these is the receivable aging schedule:

Total receivables	0–30 days	$305,000
June 30, 19X0, $491,000	30–60 days	102,000
	90–120 days	13,000
	Over 120 days	71,000

Although this does not provide individual customer information, it can be a guide to incipient problems. In this instance, $71,000 is more than 120 days old. If normal trade terms are that payments are due within 30 days of invoice, this represents a potential bad debt, or possibly a disputed sale where the goods may be returned by the customer for any of a variety of reasons. Aging schedules are most useful when combined with monthly sales figures so that the two can be compared.

The second analytical tool is the accounts receivable turnover ratio. This can be expressed in two ways. The first method is to divide sales by the ending balance of accounts receivable. Many people, however, prefer the second method since it is easier to understand. This can be calculated by dividing the sales by 365, which gives a figure for daily sales, and then dividing the ending figure for accounts receivable by this number to obtain number of days of receivables—that is, the number of days' sales that remain uncollected.

For this figure to be meaningful, of course, certain conditions have to be met. These are basically that sales were not made for cash, that sales were at a reasonably consistent level throughout the year, and that every customer gets the same credit terms. Only the second of these needs a little explanation.

Example 6.6. Barry Beech has accounts receivable at the end of December of $600,000. Annual sales were $2.4 million. Apparently Barry Beech has 90 days of receivables. This would be incorrect, however, if Barry's business was very seasonal, with 60% of sales being made in the final quarter of the year. On that basis, sales in that quarter must have been $1.44 million, and thus there are only 37.5 days of receivables ($16,000 daily sales over 90 days).

THE CASH CONVERSION CYCLE

Inventory, accounts receivable, and accounts payable can all be measured in days, and the net result will be the number of days in the cash conversion cycle. Two examples will illustrate this:

Example 6.7. Larry Lime has a photographic equipment wholesale business distributing cameras and related products to retailers. Larry has an average of 25 days of accounts payable, 30 days of inventory and 35 days of accounts receivable. Observe that, if he acquires inventory on day 1 of trading, he will pay for this on day 25, the inventory will be sold on day 30, and he will collect the cash from receivables on day 65. Thus, we have a cash-to-cash cycle of 40 days.

On the other hand, if a business can sell for cash and take credit from suppliers, it will be able to grow quickly thanks to cash surpluses.

Example 6.8. Paulo's Pizzas, a fast-food pizza chain, makes all sales for cash, has low inventories since most ingredients must be fresh and cannot be stored easily, and takes an average of 30 days' credit from suppliers. If inventory averages 5 days and there is at most 1 day's receivables, the cash-to-cash cycle is minus 24 days. This means that 24 days' sales are represented by cash in hand. Paulo has a money machine!

QUALITY OF FIXED ASSETS

After reviewing the current assets, you should consider the fixed assets to see in what way they add to financial flexibility, if at all, and to see if the recorded values are realistic. Fixed assets may include anything from highly specialized custom-built machinery to trade investments held at a figure well below current stock market value which could easily be realized. They also include intangible assets, such as capitalized expenditures, which have no separate marketable value, although they have and continue to create some value to the owners.

Generalizations about fixed assets are dangerous, but since in many problem loans the sale of fixed assets represents the fallback position for repayment—since repayment from cashflow or new sources of outside capital is impractical—we should consider fixed asset quality to be indicated by the answers to three questions.

The first question is: *How marketable is this asset?* Some assets have a value that is tied to the success of the product which they produce. For instance, a plant of a highly specialized nature producing synthetic fibers on a continuous basis would have no value if the market for fibers collapsed. On the other hand, if there were a shortage of capacity, or if there were to be a control over the issuing of permits, to have such a plant would be quite different. Other assets, by contrast, have a value quite distinct from the business to which they belong at that moment. An obvious example is freehold land or property in a highly desirable location. If this land can be used by several different types of businesses—especially retail businesses—then its value rests with its geographic location, not with its present occupant. For instance, the well-known firm of Tiffany's occupies a corner site in the heart of Manhattan's fashionable midtown district. The value of the site does not depend on Tiffany's business so much as on its nearness to Fifth Avenue and 57th Street. Stated another way: Will the assets keep their value even if the firm's earnings decline?

Other highly marketable assets would be quoted investments, self-contained but successful subsidiaries, and exclusive or quasi-exclusive rights or contracts to perform some activity. This last category would include such things as a seat on the stock exchange, a broadcasting license from the government, or the right to receive royalties from some technical process. Be sure not to confuse marketability with the expectation of high value. You can always sell a seat on the stock exchange, but its value will depend on whether the market is doing well or not.

The second question is: *Would the sale of this asset impact severely on the remaining lines of business of the company?* Here you are considering the extent to which part of a business can be easily detached and sold off without serious effects on what remains. Consider, for instance, a finance company which is a wholly owned subsidiary of an automobile manufacturer. To what extent is the ability of the manufacturer to offer credit to his dealers and customers a key ingredient in his marketing strategy? To what extent does the manufacturer impact the interest revenues of the subsidiary by using his control to offer below-market financing to customers in order to spur his sales? Perhaps the subsidiary is independently managed and its risk portfolio diversified so that only part of its assets are related to the parent's product line. Only detailed investigation will answer this question.

The third question is: *To what extent are the fixed assets already pledged to other lenders?* This of course limits the ability of new lenders either to look to the assets for a fallback position or to expect significant undervaluation to exist in such assets. The reason for the latter statement is simply that a borrower will try to get maximum recorded value for any asset which is being used as collateral, so that there is little chance of hidden reserves existing in assets already pledged.

LIABILITIES

In considering financial condition, you must also look at the size and seniority of liabilities, and at the extent of contingent liabilities. Generally, this will require constructing a debt equity ratio. It will also necessitate considering debt priority (see Chapter 4) and the relationship between available cashflows and existing levels of debt.

In particular, you will want to know to what extent the company has reached its debt limits, such as they might be. Well-managed firms will not permit long-term assets to be funded by short-term debt. However, a short-term debt may build up from time to time, to be funded when interest rates are right by a bond issue or by raising new equity. It is tempting to discuss debt limits in terms of interest coverage ratios. In practice, you should have a good idea of the lowest acceptable coverage ratios for the kind of companies and the kind of markets in which they operate. It is dangerous, however, to offer any general magic number that should apply across the board, since the degree of leverage varies so markedly between countries and between industries. Stability and certainty of future cashflow are the most important features—the more a company can demonstrate historic stability of cashflows, the higher its leverage can be, and thus the lower its interest coverage ratios can be. Let us repeat the equation for calculating interest coverage:

$$\text{Interest coverage} = \frac{\text{Earnings before interest and taxes}}{\text{Interest expense}}$$

Traditionally, a figure of 4 has been thought to be the lowest acceptable level of interest coverage for a manufacturing company in a European or North American industry. But you should view this figure with great caution, since it has weaknesses, as discussed in Chapter 5. Basically, the problem is that the ratio is based on reported earnings rather than on cashflow. It does not take account of varying interest rate movements. Further, it does not take account of repayment of principal or of lease payments.

Two adjustments will help make the ratios more useful. First, we should add repayments of principal to the bottom line, grossed up for tax since they are not tax deductible, plus lease payments; second, we should add back depreciation to the top line so that we are comparing available funds to required payments of debt.

$$\text{Debt coverage} = \frac{\text{Earnings before interest and taxes + lease payments}}{\text{Interest + repayments}\left(\dfrac{1}{1-t}\right) + \text{lease payments}}$$

Where t is the tax rate. Even so, this ratio does not look at capital expenditure or changes in working capital.

Then, following results of research done by Beaver,[5] we might go further along those lines and look at total liabilities/cashflow, since this would be the nearest to an available cash/cash required ratio, which is what we want.

---

[5]Beaver, W. H. "Financial Ratios as Predictors of Failure." *Journal of Accounting Research 1968.* Supplement to Volume 4.

ACCESS TO CAPITAL MARKETS

The theory of capital structure is rich with discussion as to the optimal level of debt, the actual cost of capital, and the debt/equity combination that will be most advantageous to the firm. Analysts in banks writing credit analyses are faced with facts and practical realities. Many of the companies being examined do not fit the theory of capital structure for a variety of reasons, such as; they are too small to raise new equity from the stock market, or the controlling family does not wish to lose control; or the market for fixed-rate debt is not open to them. You should therefore look at a firm's capital structure from a practical point of view in terms of access to capital markets or other lending institutions and ask yourself these questions:

Is there a reasonable balance between long-term assets and long-term liabilities? Are long-term assets funded from long-term sources?

Did management exercise wise judgment in the past in the timing of its exercises to raise capital, whether debt or equity? Are there long-term liabilities that will need refinancing soon? If so, how easily will they be refinanced?

Could new equity be raised either privately or publicly? How well does management reward shareholders? Would shareholders be happy with the risks of the firm? Is return on equity satisfactory in relation to these risks and the rest of the market?

If the firm has shares quoted on a reliable stock market, does the price exceed the company's net asset value? If it is significantly below this value, what are the reasons? Could the company raise new equity in spite of this?

Access to public debt markets in the United States, whether long or short term, involves issuing debt which is then rated by rating agencies such as Standard and Poor's Corporation. Rating agencies perform a credit analysis which is very similar in form to that performed by bankers, with the emphasis for long-term debt at any rate on a longer term view. Credit analysis for short-term public debt (known as commercial paper in the United States) is performed in a fashion even more similar to bank credit analysis. Extensive use is made of financial ratios by rating agencies, although these firms are careful to state that they never overemphasize financial ratios nor do they state minimum criteria for each category of bond rating. Standard and Poor's Corporation publishes its approach to credit in *Credit Overview,* and the key ratios that they use are shown in Table 6.1. You will see that many of these are the same as those that were discussed in Chapter 5. Bonds rated AAA

Table 6.1   Three-Year (1979–1981) Median Averages of Key Ratios by Rating Category

	'AAA'	'AA'	'A'	'BBB'	'BB'	'B'
Pretax Interest Coverage	18.25X	8.57X	6.56X	3.82X	3.27X	1.76X
Pretax Interest and Full Rental Coverage	8.02	4.95	4.05	2.75	2.41	1.52
Cash Flow/Long-Term Debt	231.95%	108.19%	71.75%	43.88%	30.23%	17.89%
Cash Flow/Total Debt	136.23	80.41	57.96	36.58	26.43	13.25
Pretax Return on Average Long-Term Capital Employed	31.27	26.29	21.75	18.31	18.44	13.19
Operating Income/Sales	16.15	14.27	12.72	10.90	11.86	9.04
Long-Term Debt/ Capitalization	11.83	19.02	26.30	34.47	44.09	54.13
Total Debt/Capitalization Including Short-Term Debt	17.04	23.70	30.41	38.62	48.07	58.77
Total Debt/Capitalization Including Short-Term Debt (Including 8X Rents)	30.93	36.79	41.49	47.93	56.57	64.60
Total Liabilities/Tangible Shareholders' Equity and Minority Interest	70.24	93.16	105.76	131.97	190.37	259.76

Source.   Reproduced by permission from "Credit Overview," published by Standard & Poor's Corporation, New York, 1982.

Note.   These are not meant to be minimum standards.

are considered the best quality debt in terms of certainty of repayment and always command lower interest rates.

BREAKUP ANALYSIS

Bankers look at a business as a going concern. This is a basic precept of lending, since loans are repaid only if businesses continue to exist and to generate cashflow. Occasionally there may be a reason for looking at a business as a "gone" concern. This means trying to estimate a breakup value for the business if it had to be liquidated, and is called breakup analysis. In this process, you have to try to attach a value to each asset and then distribute this among creditors, paying special attention to the seniority of each and to any claims for collateral. Usually a breakup analysis is relevant only when cash from operations as a source of repayment appears a remote possibility.[6]

There are two steps to the process: The first is to estimate the size of the pool of assets available to creditors, and the second is to see which creditors are ahead of your bank in debt priority and which are equal. As to the first step, you must recognize that asset liquidation can be orderly, disorderly, or disastrous depending on how rapidly the business is being forced to break up. If liquidation is orderly, there is no pressure from creditors, whereas if it is disastrous, all the assets are on the auction block at distress prices. Obviously, asset values are seriously affected in the latter instance, and inventory may realize only 20% of its recorded value. When you make breakup estimates, it seems best to assume a disorderly rather than a disastrous process in the absence of any other information. The total of estimated asset values is then used as the basis for finding asset cover for liabilities.

In the second step, you must decide on debt priority. Because debt/equity ratios are a measurement of liquidation or asset coverage, the relative priorities of various debts are relevant to the calculation of the ratio. When attention is being directed at a debt capacity estimation of a going business, the priorities of the various forms of debt are of much less concern because a company cannot continue as a healthy ongoing business unless it makes all its debt payments.

The rule in the construction of a debt/equity ratio for breakup analysis is very simple: Any creditor whose claim on the assets of a company is superior, or equal, to your claim is considered debt. Any claim subordinate to yours is considered equity.

Example 6.9.

Omega Inc.

Short-term bank debt	$ 1,500
Accounts payable	1,000
Various accruals	500
Taxes payable	300
Total current liabilities	3,300

[6]Breakup analysis is not the same as calculating a firm's net asset value. The principal difference is that, as lender, the bank is interested only in the asset coverage available to it, leaving other lenders who are junior in priority out of the calculation. Net asset value is simply total assets minus total liabilities. This number divided by the number of existing units of common stock gives the net asset value per share, sometimes known as the book value per share. By comparing this with the stock market price for a quoted company, you can see if there is a discount to book value; if so, it will be hard for the firm to raise new equity. Also, it indicates that the stock market has a poor view of the firm's prospects, since it suggests that the recorded asset values in the financial statements are too high in relation to expected future cashflows.

Deferred taxes	$ 250
Term loans (banks)	1,000
Mortgages (plant)	1,500
Capitalized leases	500
Other long-term liabilities	250
Subordinated debentures	1,000
Deferred revenue	1,000
Total long-term liabilities	5,500
Preferred stock	$ 750
Common stock (all items)	15,000
Total capital	$15,750

Generally when analyzing (but particularly when calculating debt/equity ratios), the statements of the borrower should be examined first. These should not be consolidated or combined statements. In this case, Omega Inc. is the borrower and has no subsidiaries. Identifying enforceable claims on the assets of other corporations (subsidiaries) is a separate process.

If you hold the short-term debt and term loans, which of these claims is superior and which is equal to yours in the event of bankruptcy?

Superior Claims

Various accruals	$ 500 (a portion)
Taxes payable	300
Mortgages (plant)	1,500 (specific assets)
Capitalized leases	500 (sometimes and/or specific assets)
	2,800

"Various accruals" will probably contain wages payable and other items. In bankruptcy law, wage earners are given superior treatment under most jurisdictions. It is probably safer and simpler to consider these accruals superior to your claims, though some of the items will be equal, such as accrued legal fees and accrued accounting fees.

"Mortgages (plant)" represents debt carrying with it a security interest in specific assets—in this case, the plant. Such assets are often required by the operations of a business. "Mortgages" and "capitalized leases" are quite similar because they represent alternative methods of financing. Many companies, instead of buying an asset and obtaining mortgage financing, will lease the asset for an extended period. Sometimes the accountants will show the leases on the financial statements as a liability because they are required to do so under accounting principles. Often they will not, and you will have to approximate the amount. The courts and taxing authorities often treat leases as a form of debt.

Should a company find it necessary to reorganize because of financial difficulties, it will probably continue to make both mortgage and rental payments because, should the payments cease, the company might lose the use of an asset important to the continuation of its business. Unlike mortgages, leases are not always effectively superior to unsecured creditors but, if the assets being leased are critical to the operations of a company, such as a good store, or have a market value in excess of the lease amount, the leases are, for all practical purposes, superior because lease payments must be continued if the operation is to be continued. This is an important consideration when it is likely that a company will be reorganized. If rentals are unpaid on leased assets having a market value greater than the lease amount, the lessor will take possession of the asset and dispose of it elsewhere. None of the proceeds will be returned for distribution to the other creditors.

Should the proceeds from the sale of the asset be insufficient to pay the lease in full, the lessor can bring a claim against the company for damages, but the amount of the damages is often limited by law to a fixed number of years' rentals. However, if a mortgage lender similarly had to sell the asset and its proceeds were inadequate, the entire deficiency without limitation would be a valid claim on the company.

Some items must receive special treatment. For Omega Inc., these are:

Equal Claims

Short-term bank debt	$1,500
Trade accounts payable	1,000
Bank term loans	1,000
	3,500

Special Treatment

Deferred taxes	$ 250
Other long-term liabilities	250
Deferred revenue	1,000
	1,500

When a going concern perspective is being used, these "special treatment" items are best considered debt because their future cashflow implications are usually the same as a legal liability. But when a liquidation viewpoint is taken, the issue is less clear. "Deferred taxes" may not be enforceable legal claims against a company's assets. In the case of "deferred revenues" it may be that someone has paid for a service or product that the company has not yet delivered.

The best general rule is: If an item such as "deferred revenues" represents a possible claim by an identifiable group of parties, consider the item as unsecured debt. If the item is an accounting but not legal liability, do not; include it as an asset reduction. Applying this rule to "deferred taxes" is fairly simple because it is an accounting but not a legal liability. In the case of long-term liabilities," it depends on the detailed nature of the statements assume a going concern, but converting them to liquidation statements often produces results of questionable validity.

Special Item	Amount	Classification
Deferred taxes	$ 1,000	Asset reduction, neither debt nor equity
Other long-term liabilities	250	Equity
Deferred revenue	1,000	Debt

The difficulty in classifying these special items raises an important point: Accounting statements assume a going concern, but converting them to liquidation statements often produces results of questionable validity.

Below are the claims of Omega, Inc. that are subordinate to yours.

Subordinate claims	
Subordinated debentures	$ 1,000
Preferred stock	750
Common stock (all items)	15,000
	16,750

Subordinated debt, such as preferred stock, is a hybrid, possessing some of the characteristics of debt and some of equity. As mentioned, a healthy firm must make the interest and principal payments on subordinated debt. Assuming the subordination is effective, in liquidation, senior creditors will ordinarily be paid in full before subordinated creditors receive any cash. However, in one of the forms of reorganization under U.S. law (known as Chapter XI of the United States Bankruptcy Code), the approval of the subordinated creditors must be obtained if liquidation is to be avoided. This sometimes gives the subordinated creditors the bargaining power to exact settlements from the senior creditors. In calculating a debt/equity ratio, subordinated debt is normally considered the equivalent of equity, because in reorganization and liquidation, it is usually junior in its claim on assets. But subordinated debt can create problems that equity cannot, so considering subordinated debt as equity is a necessary oversimplification. No general rules are offered here since subordination depends extensively on the application of local law.

We now have total figures for liabilities senior to, equal with, and junior to your debt. Let's assume that Omega Inc. has assets of $20,000. It is then a simple matter to determine asset coverage for your debt:

Assets	$20,000
Less senior claims	(2,800)
	17,200

This shows $17,200 of assets are available to cover claims equal to yours totaling $3,500—that is, asset coverage of 4.9 times. It is not relevant that other liabilities total $20,500, since they are junior in priority to your claims.

PROBLEMS

1. Why is working capital important to short-term lenders?
2. Why do lenders prefer accounts receivable to inventory as collateral?
3. An importer sells goods on a duty-paid basis to his customers. Duties average 20% of sales value and are paid by the importer 30 days after importation. Customers on average pay the importer 10 days after importation. Suppliers are paid on shipment of goods 14 days before importation. What cash-to-cash cycle does this present? (Assume a 5% net profit margin to the importer.)
4. A highly leveraged company in a high-technology industry has good profits in the opinion of an investment banker. What considerations would affect the raising of new equity?
5. A solid industrial manufacturing company has a lot of debt and a book value for equity which is 20% above the current stock market price for the common stock. Bankers are pressing the company to raise new equity. What should be the company's reaction:
    a. If interest rates are high but expected to fall?
    b. If the stock market is high but expected to fall?
6. You have reason to believe that inventories in a certain company are of high quality but are seriously understated as to recorded value. How would you check your opinion? If correct, how would this affect your credit judgment of the company?
7. How could you use an interest coverage ratio in looking at a term loan proposal?

7 Evaluation of Industry and Management

Industries are rather like cities. They have their own characteristics and dynamic forces. In some cities, such as Hong Kong or New York, the risks are high, but the rewards for success are rapid and substantial. Some are full of bustle but achieve little; others are slow or dull but efficient. Some cities, such as Paris, hardly seem to change, yet they survive; others appear almost overnight in a burst of spectacular growth, but in a few decades, they can come to resemble the ghost mining towns of the old American West.

Management's job is to direct the firm in a constantly changing world, and it is your task as an analyst to determine two things: What are the business risks, and how good is management? In doing so, you must understand the nature of the industry in which the firm is operating and recognize the place occupied by the firm within that industry. This chapter presents a method of analyzing the performance of management and outlines a pattern for considering business risks within an industry.

EVALUATING MANAGEMENT

In 1954—only thirty years ago—Peter Drucker wrote: "Management is the least known and the least understood of our basic institutions."[1] Since that time, tremendous interest has been directed toward management, and many books and studies have been published. Drucker himself did a great deal to popularize management and make it comprehensible. When we come to consider a framework for evaluating management, we can still make good use of his concepts of objectives and key areas—areas in which, as he wrote, "performance and results directly affect the survival and prosperity of the business."[2]

The great contribution of Charles Darwin to the study of natural science was his theory of evolution based on adaptation to change and the survival

---

[1]Peter F. Drucker, *Practice of Management* (New York: Harper & Row, 1954).
[2]Ibid.

of the fittest through a process of natural selection. You should view the business world in the same way as Darwin viewed the world of Nature. There is a continual process of creation, growth, and disappearance among business enterprises. While it can hardly be graced by the name of evolution, it certainly seems that natural selection and adaptability to change are very much involved in survival. And notice too that different forms of business enterprises are successful in different countries. This is directly analogous to Darwin's observations of the natural world. Today's organizations are very different from, yet grew out of, the business enterprises of the early Industrial Revolution. At the same time, several primitive forms of enterprise, the business equivalent of the horseshoe crab, continue to exist quite happily. Examples, of this type are the general store, the country tavern, and the street market or bazaar.

Inherent in survival is the ability to make profits. As has been discussed earlier, profit is needed for three purposes: It measures the net effectiveness of a business's efforts; it is the risk premium that covers the costs of staying in business (replacement, obsolescence, and uncertainty); and it ensures the supply of future capital for growth or innovation. In the long run, profitability as measured by return on equity (see Chapter 5) is the best indicator of the health of a business and the success of management. Profitability, therefore, is one of the key areas Drucker listed. There were seven others:

Market standing
Innovation
Productivity
Physical and financial resources
Manager performance and development
Worker performance and attitude
Public responsibility

These key areas will be discussed as ways of examining how well management is doing.

Market Standing

The obvious way of measuring market standing is by calculating market share. There seems little doubt that high market share produces higher profitability than low market share,[3] since the market leader is more often able to achieve price leadership, economies of scale, and other advantages of size. But in multiproduct firms, you may find it very difficult to know what market share each product is achieving. Accordingly, another approach may

[3]Buzzell, Gale, and Sultan, "Market Share, a Key to Profitability," *Harvard Business Review* (January–February 1975).

prove more practical. This requires looking at the company's product line and placing its products as far as you can within the following matrix:[4]

	Low Market Share	High Market Share
High Growth	A	B
Low Growth	C	D

New products, known as "question marks," usually begin in Box A. They are launched because the firm believes that they have great potential for growth, but being new, they obviously do not have much market share at the start of their product life cycle. Entirely new products are very risky if developed from scratch, but without new products no firm can survive. Such products tend to use more cash than they generate. Often competition will see to it that copies of successful products or new versions appear very quickly, and for this purpose, one should not expect every firm to be original, merely responsive to change in the marketplace.

If all goes well, the products move into Box B and become stars. High growth is achieved with high market share. But, as cashflow analysis has suggested, such products tend to require substantial increases in net working assets as well as in capital expenditure. Every firm needs some products of this type, but if it has too many, it will suffer from negative cash from operations. If products fail to achieve growth, they may fall straight from Box A to Box C. These "dogs" have low growth and low market share. They are often failures, rarely contributing much to profits or cashflow. Regrettably, almost every company is bound to have some, and it is the analyst's task to try to identify these as problems that one hopes management has recognized.

Ideally, as growth of sales slows down, products move from Box B (high growth, high market share) to Box D (low growth, high market share). Popularly known as "cash cows" because they throw off good cashflows, these are the growth products that have matured. As growth has slowed, so the amount of net working assets has reduced proportionately, economies of scale are realized in production, and earlier capital expenditures come to fruition.

Company profiles will have certain distinct patterns. Some tend to have neglected new products or find that they fall straight into Box C. Some com-

---

[4]First developed by the Boston Consulting Group. See also B. Hedley, "Strategy and the Business Portfolio," *Long Range Planning* V 10 (February 1977).

panies may have some C and some D type products—both with low growth, but with the good products offsetting the losses on the failures. Here the problem is that there is little or no innovation, and therefore the future appears very risky. Others will have both A and B type products—fast growth but with cashflow shortages. Ideally, a company has enough D types to offset the A and B products and has no type C. In this case, cashflows and market strength from the old products are sufficient to support the uncertainties, risks, and expected rewards of the new products.[5]

Innovation

One can think of innovation as a response to a changing world: It is not just researching and producing new products, it also includes adapting to new ideas for customer service, distribution, marketing, packaging, advertising, and every other business activity. Furthermore, being able to copy someone else's invention is just as important as having one's own creative ideas. An assessment of management's success in this field might revolve around questions of technology, marketing, or changing customer behavior. Let's take technology first.

To what extent is technology stable in this industry? To what extent does the company control the pace at which technology is changing? Have competitors gained market share by introducing technically more advanced products? Is the technology such that once a change occurs everyone can exploit that change? Or put another way, is copying easy?

Marketing innovations are often more subtle to detect, since they may occur in distribution channels, packaging, or in the type of needs that the product satisfies. As an example of distribution changes, consider the shift in toys in Britain in the 1960s and 1970s. At one time, most toys were purchased in specialty toy shops. Meccano produced a famous range of construction toys as well as model cars and trucks that were sold principally in toy shops. However, over time, retail newspaper shops, supermarkets, and big chain stores, such as Woolworths, increased their share of toy sales, with a consequent major change in distribution patterns. Regrettably, Meccano failed to recognize this shift, and this among other factors contributed to its economic demise.

As an example of changing consumer needs, consider the needs satisfied by the private car. A few years ago, the most popular features of cars were performance, styling, and comfort, suggesting that the needs being satisfied were ego-related needs, such as status and achievement. Today, thanks to energy price changes, economy of operation and simplicity of design have become more important, suggesting that basic transportation and cost effectiveness are the relevant needs.

[5]Analysts should use this general product matrix approach with caution, since there are pitfalls especially in the absence of hard marketing data. See also S. St. P. Slatter, *London Business School Journal* V 2 (1980).

Resources

In Drucker's list, productivity meant the degree to which resources were used efficiently and the extent to which the firm contributed value by putting together labor, raw materials, and capital. By contrast, physical and financial resources as a key area meant that a firm must have reliable access both to supplies of raw material and to capital markets. In terms of management analysis, therefore, you should examine where the company obtains its resources, with what risks, what management does to minimize risks, and how efficiently it uses those resources.

Should the company depend on one supplier? While this may give it a price advantage because of volume purchasing, and it may obtain materials more closely suited to its requirements, this strategy also has the risk of vulnerability if anything happens to the supplier, and it diminishes the degree of competitive purchasing power. If the suppliers, however, have less power than the buyer because the buyer could integrate backward, or because the buyer's industry is more concentrated than the supplier's, or because there are plenty of alternative sources, this strategy could be right. This is discussed further in the section on industry dynamics. Recognizing good management means recognizing why the company has made certain choices as to its access to resources. This can be difficult to guess. By contrast, measuring the efficiency of the use of resources is relatively easy, and the reader is referred to the discussion of performance ratios in Chapter 5 and, for access to capital markets, to the discussion in Chapter 6 on financial condition.

Human Resources

The other resource besides money and materials is the people in the company. Today we refer to human resources; at the time Drucker was writing, there was a more marked distinction between managers and workers, and the company's role differed toward each group.

You must assess management in terms of its use of human resources—not just in terms of output per employee, but also in terms of the spirit of the organization, the degree to which there is corporate loyalty, the extent to which middle management is committed to the purpose of the organization, and the amount of cooperation with organized labor unions. There are not many tangible measures to use here, since in this key area, you must exercise your judgment on the basis of factors that are not reflected in financial ratios, any more than human resources are measured and recorded for the purposes of the balance sheet.

One way of looking at management's use of human resources is to consider what can go wrong, what the common mistakes are, and what risks are involved.

1. What are the aims of the organization structure? Is it decentralized enough to ensure rapid responses to change? Is it centralized enough to give control over key decisions? Is there enough depth of management?

2. Has the organization adapted to change in the socioeconomic system?
    For example, how is it reacting to the increasing numbers of women
    who work? Or, for example, how well is it adapting from the autocratic
    style of a former leader to the style of a new more democratic chief?

3. Is this an organization that gives top managers time to think and plan
    ahead? Or are they too involved in day-to-day decisions? If so, who is
    doing the planning and research?

4. Is this a business that has good union–management relations? Who takes
    the initiative for change in working conditions? What is the record for
    strikes? How high is employee turnover?

5. What is happening in communications between employees and senior
    management? Is it only top-down communications? Does management
    encourage innovation? How are employees motivated?

Public Responsibility

In this area, there are two distinct relationships: the company to the public
at large, and the company to government. The former is the more obvious,
but the latter is probably much more important. Everyone knows about the
importance of good corporate citizenship. This means both the sponsorship
of cultural events as well as a concern with protecting the environment.
However, good corporate citizenship makes little difference to credit analysis.
What is really important to the analyst is the company's relationship with
government, especially in times of increasing government involvement with
business.

Here are the issues in government relations:

To what extent are antitrust and monopoly policies likely to affect the
industry and the company?

To what extent is the company a chosen vehicle for government restructuring of that particular industry?

Are there price controls? Are prices subject to change because of special
taxes or duties that apply to this industry? What can this do to demand
for the product?

Is this an industry protected by the government because, for example, of
the high level of unemployment that would result from unrestricted imports?

Who gets government contracts? Are they a burden or a benefit to the
company?

Are exports a government priority? What is the company doing to take
advantage of this?

Is the industry an important source of tax revenue for the government?
What effect does this have?

And finally:

If there is a political upheaval in government and a radically different administration appears, what will this do to the company?

INDUSTRY DYNAMICS

We turn now to consider the framework of industry within which management must operate and to take a look at the dynamic forces which govern competition within an industry. Understanding these forces is of vital importance to bankers, especially when making decisions on medium-term loans. Just why are certain industrial sectors more profitable than others? Why too are some industries major sources of firms that go into bankruptcy? The answer to both these questions is related to competition.

The most important work in this field has been done by Michael Porter of Harvard.* "The intensity of competition in an industry," states Porter, "is neither a matter of coincidence nor bad luck. Rather, competition in an industry is rooted in its underlying economic structure and goes well beyond the behavior of current competitors. The state of competition in an industry depends on five basic competitive forces." These are shown in Exhibit 7.1.

Traditional economic theory postulates that competition in a perfect market will work to reduce profitability as new entries and existing rivalries combine to drive down returns to the level of the free market. Yet some industries, as can be seen from the following list, consistently beat the average profitability over a five-year period and others consistently fail to reach even this average level. The list is constructed from figures published annually by *Fortune* magazine for the top 500 U.S. companies. I therefore do not mean to suggest that either Group I or Group II industries in other countries will have the same results, simply that in the United States their performance appears to be this way and can be explained, in part anyway, by examination of the five forces, in particular by barriers to entry.

Group I: Above-Average Profitability	Group II: Below-Average Profitability
Broadcasting and TV	Steel (metal manufacturing)
Tobacco	Rubber
Pharmaceuticals	Toys
Cosmetics	Textiles
Oil and mining	

Exhibit 7.1   Forces Governing Competition in an Industry. Reprinted by permission of the *Harvard Business Review*. An exhibit from "How Competitive Forces Shape Strategy" by Michael E. Porter (March/April 1979). Copyright © 1979 by the President and Fellows of Harvard College; all rights reserved.

Barriers to Entry

Barriers to entry will naturally operate to the advantage of firms already in the industry. Porter identifies seven major barriers to entry.

Economies of Scale.   These can arise in nearly every function of business, including research, development, purchasing, service network, distribution, and manufacturing. Economies of scale deter entry because the new entrant must either enter at large scale and risk strong reaction from existing firms and thus a possible large loss, or enter in a small way and suffer severe cost disadvantages. Economies of scale are apparent in oil and mining (Group I), but they are also apparent in steel and rubber (Group II).

Product Differentiation.   This means that established firms have built brand loyalty and customer loyalty on the basis of several years of past advertising, customer service, and product advantages. The barrier to new entry is principally one of substantial cost as well as lack of credibility of product. Start-up costs (losses) can be very large, and thus a high degree of risk is involved, since these costs are irrecoverable.

Product differentiation is probably the reason for the profitability of tobacco and cosmetics and their inclusion in Group I. Porter also gives as examples baby care products and investment banking, as well as brewing, where economies of scale in production combine with brand loyalty to create high barriers to entry.

Capital Requirement.   The need to invest large financial resources represents a significant barrier to entry, especially if the expenditure has to be on intangible items, such as research, image building, and advertising. Capital may be needed not only for plant and machinery but also for financing customers. Porter quotes Xerox's strategy of renting office copiers as an example of a move to increase capital requirements for potential new entrants, which would also have to permit customers to rent equipment.

Switching Costs.   These are very interesting types of costs since they arise only when customers want to switch products. They create an important entry barrier since new competitors must overcome these costs to attract buyers to their products. Switching costs include the need to retain employees, the cost of new ancillary machines, and the bothersome business of testing out new equipment (especially if it is of a technical nature), with all the associated risks of loss or disruption to production. An example of a product with high switching costs would be jet engines for aircraft. Airlines require tremendous support services for their engines, a big training investment in personnel, as well as membership in a resources pool with other airlines sharing the same equipment. A product with low switching costs would be the rubber tires for the family automobile, which perhaps is one reason why rubber is in Group II in the above list.

Distribution Channels.   Often existing firms have locked up the available distribution channels. In the watch industry in the 1950s, distribution of the product was through jewelry stores and chains. Thus, when Timex tried to combat the Swiss watch industry, it was forced to create an entirely new distribution system and sell its products through a different class of outlets. Similarly, manufacturers of new products always face problems of getting shelf space in supermarkets for their new products and have to use intense selling efforts, special incentives to retailers, and costly price breaks to achieve penetration.

Cost Barriers That are Independent of Scale.   Established firms may have certain advantages that become cost barriers that are not available to potential rivals no matter what the size or scale of operations of the new entrant. The most critical ones listed by Porter are:

Proprietary Product Technology.   Firms are able to take legal protection through patents or copyrights.

Access to Raw Materials.   An example of this might be minerals; for instance, China clay is found in only one major deposit in Britain, which is controlled by one company.

Favorable Locations.   Established firms may have already obtained the best locations, or they may be able through property restrictions or ownership to prevent the establishment of rivals. Sometimes a market sector will support only one firm ("This town isn't big enough for both of us").

The Experience Curve.   In some businesses, there is a tendency for unit costs to decline as the firm gains more cumulative experience in producing a product. This is distinct from economies of scale since the time factor works to the advantage here of the oldest established firms. The argument is that costs decline because workers learn and become more efficient, also because systems for distribution and logistics are adapted and improved over time. The essential element here is, if experience can be kept proprietary, then this will lead to an entry barrier. The best way to think of this is to think of craftsmen and apprenticeships. Craftsmen can be tempted away from their employer, it is true, but since they are by nature more interested in the quality of their output than in wages, this rarely happens. And craftsmen take years to acquire their experience.

Government Policy.   Since governments regulate some industries through licensing, they can easily influence the degree of new entry. Sometimes more subtle restrictions arise from government influence over standards of product safety, pollution control, and health requirements that can create long lead times and sometimes also give existing firms ample notice of the impending entry of a new competitor. Government regulation appears to work in favor of U.S. companies with TV and radio broadcasting licenses (Group I). On the other hand, the action of foreign governments both damages U.S. industry and assists indigenous foreign firms through the establishment of new steel mills in developing countries (Group II).

Rivalry

Analysts must try to assess the degree of rivalry among existing firms, and not make simple statements, such as "This is a highly competitive industry." Why is this industry so competitive? How do firms compete? This is all relevant.

Number and Relative Size of Competitors.   It appears that, where an industry is highly concentrated or dominated by a small number of firms with a clearly defined market leader, rivalry exists but market share tends to be more stable. If, however, there is a large number of firms (fragmentation) or a small number of firms of roughly equal size, competition is stimulated by the expectation that one firm can somehow "win" in a fight with the rest.

Rate of Industry Growth. Slow industry growth tends to create conditions where rivalry increases, since in a saturated market, the only sales gains possible are those made at the expense of competitors. In rapidly growing markets, on the other hand, rivalry will be less intense, since there should be room for all to expand.

Level of Fixed Costs and Overcapacity. These two often interrelated problems can also strongly influence the degree of rivalry. High fixed costs create strong pressures to fill capacity, which frequently leads to price wars. Industries producing basic materials, such as paper and aluminum, illustrate this problem. So also does the domestic U.S. airlines industry, especially on routes where several carriers are licensed, such as the New York–California route. Here, one notes that, while fixed costs in the airlines business are very high, there is the offsetting feature that entry into this market is limited to an extent by government regulation through the Civil Aeronautics Board's control over routes.

Degree of Diversity Among Competitors. This will have an effect on the degree of competition. Where firms in the industry share common goals and strategies as well as business outlook, the degree of competition may be less, as the firms are better able to read each other's intentions. On the other hand, foreign competitors can behave very differently from domestic producers of the same product, since they may view the market as a dumping ground for their excess capacity, rather than as a primary market, or they may be unrestricted by regulations that affect domestic producers. A good example of the latter was the spectacular growth of foreign-owned banks in the U.S. domestic market during the 1970s. Foreign banks were not subject to many of the restrictions on U.S. domestic banks, such as interest rate ceilings on deposits, interstate banking, the cost of FDIC membership, certain reserve requirements, and the prohibition of investment banking activities, such as corporate underwriting. Until the passing of the Bank Regulation Act of 1980, foreign banks undoubtedly enjoyed competitive advantages over U.S. domestic banks in the United States. More recently, it is not the foreign banks in the United States that have had such advantages so much as the consumer-oriented financial service companies, such as Sears Roebuck, Beneficial Corporation, and American Express. This has created such a wide diversity in the U.S. market for financial services that rivalry has become very intense.

Substitute Products

In industrial analysis, you must also focus attention on substitute products, since these will have the effect of limiting price increases in the basic industry being studied or threatening substantial inroads if the cost structure should change for any reason or if the primary market is threatened. One example of substitution has occurred in the security guard industry. Electronic alarm systems represent a real alternative to a labor-intensive guard system. Price trends in electronics favor reducing the costs of such systems as well as improved performance as time passes. Consequently, the firms in the security industry may well seek to redefine their role as automated systems are introduced. Another example of product substitution would be the recent trend toward solid fuel or natural gas based heating systems for domestic houses in place of oil-fired systems, which have become less cost effective because of massive price increases for oil. Consider, too, the extent to which the desire for more informal and flexible vacations has, in Europe at least, made extensive inroads into the traditional tourist hotel business. Here the substitute made gains resulting from changes in life-styles and habits, combined with higher mobility because of the increased ownership of automobiles. There is also a trend among the richer classes toward the ownership of second homes, which has provided a source of supply for holiday rentals.

Buyer Power

Another factor you must consider when doing a risk analysis is the effects of buyer power on the industry. Under what conditions will the buyer be strong? Porter has identified eight situations which favor buyers.

1. Buyers are concentrated in a small group or purchase large volumes relative to the producer's sales. Large-volume buyers will be even more powerful if they are buying from an industry that suffers from high fixed costs, such as corn refining and bulk chemicals.
2. The products being purchased are standard or undifferentiated. Since buyers are able to find alternative suppliers easily, they will be in a strong position. Consumers are often in this position, especially in relation to such items as retail banking, gas stations, and ballpoint pens.
3. The products being purchased represent a substantial outlay for the consumer or, in the case of industrial companies, represent a significant portion of their input costs. The more the buyer spends, the more he or she will invest the resources and the time necessary to obtain favorable prices. Conversely, if the product sold is only a small fraction of the buyer's costs, buyers are less price sensitive.
4. There are low switching costs to the buyer. Most consumer products have low switching costs; hence, manufacturers strive to build brand loyalty through any means available.
5. Buyers with low profitability will do their best to strengthen their hand. Reportedly, suppliers to Chrysler have always faced tougher negotiations than suppliers to other members of the industry.
6. Buyers who can integrate backward will be strong. Here a buyer who can produce the goods through in-house manufacture will use this as a

bargaining tool. Further, many companies who manufacture part of their own inputs will develop a detailed knowledge of costs which will also aid them in negotiations.

7. Buyers of inputs which do not materially affect the quality of their own outputs will be strong. (For the opposite effect, see the following section on supplier power.)

8. If the buyers have full information about demand, actual market prices, and costs, this will increase their bargaining power. They will be more aware of favorable prices offered to others, of competing brands and substitutes, and of the seller's cost structure.

Supplier Power

The conditions making suppliers powerful tend to be the mirror image of those making buyers powerful. A supplier group is powerful if any of the following conditions are found:

1. Suppliers are highly concentrated and buyers are fragmented.

2. Suppliers are not obliged to contend with other substitute products.

3. Suppliers are selling to a buyer group that is not an important customer in terms of sales volume to the suppliers.

4. The supplier's product is a vital input to the buyer's business.

5. The supplier's product or service, though not expensive in itself, can save substantial amounts of money for the buyer. Buyers who are interested in top quality are at a disadvantage. Such services as investment banking and public accounting are good examples: In a bond issue, for instance, good market timing, which is the province of the investment banker, can save millions of dollars annually for the borrower through a lower interest coupon being offered. Similarly, good oil field equipment can save large potential losses arising from malfunctions of supply and subsequent blowouts.

6. The supplier group has built up switching costs.

7. The supplier group could integrate forward and absorb the buyers.

In summary, analysts should look at an industry in terms of the five competitive forces, recognize business risks in relation to opportunities, and evaluate each firm in relation to its position in the market.

PROBLEMS

1. Is there a single overriding objective for any business? If so, what is it and why? How would you measure it?

2. Why is business becoming a more frequent target for public criticism in industrialized countries? What response should business make to these criticisms?

3. Under what circumstances should governments do any business as manufacturers of goods or providers of services? Should a nationalized industry have the same objectives as private business firms?

4. "Other firms make products, but we make profits." Who said this? Is it a useful objective?

5. What evidence can you find that growth of size is important to a firm's survival? Or that innovation in products is important?

6. What characteristics would you expect to find in sectors of industry which have a higher than average profitability? Give examples.

7. What business sector would you enter today, given $50,000 capital? What objectives would you set? How would your answer differ if you had $5 million?

8. In 1977, Kennecott Corporation was forced to sell 50% of its assets (which produced 95% of its income) for cash and notes of more than $1 billion. In your opinion, what should it have done with the money?

8 Corporate Collapse

In an examination of industry and management, it becomes very important to recognize the causes and symptoms of corporate collapse. There are at least two different approaches to this subject, and in the following pages, we shall try to discuss both methods and see what lessons can be applied in credit analysis. I am convinced that too little time in a typical training program is spent in examining the causes of failure and indeed the signs, and yet the evidence is quite available and fairly convincing.

The two approaches can be summarized as the financial ratio model, which was first developed by Edward Altman of New York University and expanded in his book *Corporate Financial Distress*,[1] and the multiple management error model, which is described by John Argenti in his book *Corporate Collapse*.[2] Both approaches seem very relevant, although one is quantitative and the other is qualitative. Analysts familiar with both methods will be well equipped to gauge the extent to which a company may be headed toward bankruptcy and also to recognize causes of collapse, rather than merely the symptoms.

To return to our analogy with physical health, bodily symptoms, such as a high temperature, reflect but do not cause ill health. The doctor has to identify the symptoms in order to diagnose the causes of the illness. In the same way, analysts should distinguish symptoms, such as negative cashflows, from causes, such as a failure to respond to market changes.

THE ALTMAN APPROACH

Altman uses published financial data on publicly owned U.S. companies which have gone into bankruptcy in recent years and compares this data with a matched sample of nonbankrupt firms. His early model employed five ratios which were tested by multiple discriminant analysis and were used to compute a Z score, which was then tested as an effective predictor of bank-

[1] Edward Altman, *Corporate Financial Distress: A Complete Guide on How to Understand, Predict, and Deal with Bankruptcy* (New York: John Wiley & Sons, 1983).

[2] John Argenti, *Corporate Collapse* (Maidenhead, England: McGraw-Hill, 1976).

ruptcy.[3] His more recent approach, known as Zeta™, expands the number of ratios to seven and has improved accuracy in prediction tests.[4]

In the original form, the Z score was a linear model in which the ratios were weighted to maximize the predictive power of the model and at the same time to adhere to the necessary statistical assumptions. The model was developed in 1968 from 33 U.S. manufacturing companies that failed in the period 1946–1965 and a matched sample, matched as to industry size and date, which did not fail. All had assets in the range $1–25 million. Twenty-two possible ratios were grouped into five categories—liquidity, profitability, leverage, solvency, and performance. The five variables selected were those which combined together produced the most accurate prediction of bankruptcy. The final formula was as follows:

$$z = 0.012X_1 + 0.014X_2 + 0.33X_3 + 0.006X_4 + 0.010X_5$$

where X_1 = working capital/total assets

X_2 = retained earnings/total assets

X_3 = earnings before interest and taxes/total assets

X_4 = market value of equity/book value of total debt

X_5 = sales/total assets

Each firm was then assigned a Z score. It was found that a score of less than 1.8 indicated a company most likely to fail, whereas a score higher than this was, relatively speaking, a less risky company.

The accuracy of this model has been tested several times, and it generally shows reliable results up to two years prior to failure. The actual results were as follows: Up to one year prior to failure, 95% of firms were correctly classified as "bankrupt" or "nonbankrupt". However, with data of two years prior to bankruptcy, Altman found in 1968 that the correct classification fell to 74%. Earlier data did not provide reliable classification. Subsequent tests using the same model on firms which failed after 1968 show an accuracy level of 82–85%.[5]

In 1977 a second model was developed that made allowance for several new factors. There included the change in size and financial profile of business failures, adjustments to the model for retail companies, and adjustments to cope with changes in financial accounting data resulting from changes in GAAP.[6] The two samples in this study were 53 bankrupt firms and 58 non-

[3]E. Altman, "Financial Ratios, Discriminant Analysis and the Prediction of Corporate Bankruptcy," *Journal of Finance* (September 1968).

[4]E. Altman, R. G. Haldeman, and P. Narayanan, "Zeta Analysis: A New Model to Identify Bankruptcy Risk of Corporations," *Journal of Banking and Finance*, 1 (1977).

[5]For a complete discussion of these results as well as the data for private firms, see E. Altman, *Corporate Financial Distress*, New York: Wiley, 1983.

[6]Data was adjusted to include the capitalizing of all noncancelable operating and finance leases, and captive finance companies were consolidated with the parent company, even if treated as equity investments in published statements.

bankrupt firms. Of the sample firms, 94% failed during 1969–1975, and the average asset size of the failed group was $100 million, indicative of the increasing size of failures. The bankrupt firms represent publicly held U.S. industrial failures which had at least $20 million in assets, with no known fraud and where sufficient data was available. Of the 53 bankrupt firms, 24 were retailers, and 29 were manufacturers.

The seven-variable model was extensively tested. Its components are:

V_1, *return on assets,* measured by earnings before interest and taxes/total assets. This variable is the same as X_3 in the 1968 model and was also significant in Beaver's 1968 study.[7] It measures profitability of the underlying business in relation to the use of assets. Since it shows earnings before interest and taxes, it reflects operating results undistorted by financing policies or tax changes. In other words, it is Darwinian profitability: it is the result of management decisions made in manufacturing and selling products.

V_2, *stability of earnings,* is measured by a normalized measure of the standard error of estimate around a 10-year trend in V_1. Business risk is often expressed in terms of earnings fluctuations, and this measure was found to be very effective. It confirms our earlier comments that high leverage can be justified by stable cashflows; but in their absence, high leverage can be fatal.

V_3, *debt service,* is measured by the interest coverage ratio—that is, earnings before interest and taxes/total interest payments.

V_4, *cumulative profitability,* is determined by retained earnings/total assets. It measures cumulatively retained profits and is obviously very sensitive to two or three back-to-back loss years. It is the same as X_2 in the 1968 model. This is "unquestionably the most important variable."[8]

V_5, *liquidity,* is measured by the current ratio. Altman's results found that this ratio had greater significance than other possible measures of liquidity, such as working capital/total assets, which had been used in the 1968 study (X_1).

V_6, *capitalization,* is measured by equity/total capital. In both the numerator and denominator, equity is represented by the five-year average of the total market value rather than its book value. The denominator also includes preferred stock, long-term debt, and capitalized leases.

V_7, *size,* measured by the firm's total assets.

The most important variables in order of their contribution to total discrimination are cumulative profitability (V_4) stability of earnings (V_2) and capitalization (V_6).

---

[7]W. H. Beaver, "Financial Ratios as Predictors of Failure," Empirical Research in Accounting, Selected Studies, 1968. *Journal of Accounting Research.* Supplement to Volume 4, pp. 71–127.

[8]Altman, Haldeman, and Narayanan, "Zeta Analysis," p. 35.

Table 8.1   Percentage of Firms Correctly Classified as "Bankrupt" or "Nonbankrupt" by 1977 Altman Line Model

Years Prior to Bankruptcy	Bankrupt	Nonbankrupt	Overall
1	96.2	89.7	92.8
2	84.9	93.1	89.0
3	74.5	91.4	83.5
4	68.1	89.5	79.8
5	69.8	82.1	76.8

Source. E. I. Altman, R. G. Haldeman, and P. Narayanan, "Zeta Analysis," *Journal of Banking & Finance,* **1** (1977); reprinted with permission.

Results showing overall classification accuracy— that is, the percentage of firms which the model correctly classified as "bankrupt" or "nonbankrupt" are shown in Table 8.1. Altman tested the 1968 model on the new sample of failed firms and found that it was not as good as the 1977 model, which as can be seen obtained over 70% overall accuracy up to five years prior to bankruptcy.

Altman's research has been marketed in recent years by a financial consulting firm which applies ratio analysis to publicly owned U.S. companies. In an article published in *Business Week* in March 1980, 24 companies with scores that looked particularly worrisome were listed. Of that 24, five had filed for reorganization within two years,[9] and two others were bought out and went private. In a follow-up article,[10] 50 companies were listed, including Braniff Airlines, which filed for bankruptcy the week the article was published.

Remember, that Z scores were developed using U.S. publicly owned corporations as the source of data. Therefore, the model will not necessarily apply to other companies in other countries. However, two important lessons can be drawn. First, watch those ratios which the model uses, especially where these are confirmed as significant by other research or by lenders' experiences, and second, watch the trend in these ratios over two or three years. If return on assets, cumulative profitability, and earnings stability all show a declining trend, then you have pretty solid ground for expecting that very serious financial problems are just around the corner.

APPLYING THE ALTMAN APPROACH

A fascinating example of successfully turning around the fortunes of a business by applying the 1968 Altman "bankruptcy predictor" model occurred

[9]Itel, Seatrain Lines, White Motor, Penn-Dixie Industries, and Sambo's Restaurants.
[10]"Companies That Face Financial Strain," *Business Week,* May 17, 1982.

with GTI Corporation, a manufacturer of parts for the automotive and computer industries.[11] When James La Fleur took charge in 1975, GTI had a $4.4 million net worth (over $2 million lower than the previous year's figure) and had experienced a $5.6 million decline in working capital. The company was losing money and had a heavy burden of debt. Its Z score was below 0.5. La Fleur knew of Altman's model and consciously took management decisions to improve the Z score by working directly on the five component ratios.

Having observed as the member of the board of directors during 1973–1975 that GTI was growing rapidly by excessive use of debt and with too optimistic expectations of raising future equity, La Fleur determined to find the underlying problems. He soon discovered that inventory and work in process were out of control. Returned goods had often been set aside and not properly accounted for. These and other assets showed an excess of actual assets over what was required.

It was then decided to find a strategy that would decrease total assets without seriously reducing the numerators in the X ratios—namely, working capital, retained earnings, earnings before interest and taxes, market value of equity, and sales. The chosen strategy was to sell off excess inventory as quickly as possible. Staff cuts were also made, and capital expense programs were frozen. Employees at two plants were handed questionnaires asking why they thought their plant was unprofitable. They responded very specifically about how to improve the use of their machinery, and their suggestions were followed. A function/location matrix was devised to analyze each executive's job, how much it cost the company, and where the work was performed. This was extended to include products profitability. As a result, a major product line was identified as being only marginally profitable and absorbing a lot of capital as well. It was sold for cash and the cash was used to reduce debt. The Z score leapt from under 0.5 to 2.95. Next the company's management extended product analysis from simple profit projections to return on assets over several years, and also looked at projected working capital and capital expenditure by product line. This helped establish what costs could be expected if the company expanded within its current markets.

Then in 1978 another division was closed, with the cash from excess assets going again to pay off debt. Interestingly, this closure pushed GTI to a 29¢ per share loss for the year, but its Z score actually rose as more debt was paid off.

By 1979, from a balance sheet viewpoint, GTI's strategy had decreased the debt/equity ratio over five years from 128% to 30%, and increased owner's equity from $3.5 million to $4.7 million. Working capital improved from $1.4 million to $2.8 million, and the current ratio from 1.38 to 2.10.

---

[11]E. I. Altman and J. K. La Fleur, "Managing a Return to Financial Health," *Journal of Business Strategy* (Summer, 1981).

This case dramatically illustrates that management can use the Altman model to help make decisions that can turn around a company. The essence of GTI's strategy was to utilize a proven predictive model in an interesting way rather than in the passive way in which most forecasting models are used. In the next section, we look at the Argenti approach, which can also be applied to the analysis of failure.

THE ARGENTI APPROACH

Puzzled by the lack of any serious studies on the causes of collapse, and disappointed by the sensation-seeking "Great Business Disasters" type of book which was usually semifictional and certainly not scientific, John Argenti set out in the mid-1970s to do what no one at that time had ever seriously attempted. He undertook the task of seeing if there was a pattern to business failure and if it was possible to determine a series of causes of collapse which were repeated frequently enough to form the basis of a hypothesis. His approach, therefore, is different from Altman's in that he is seeking out business decisions that cause disaster, not merely looking at the predictive power of ratios.

In the course of gathering evidence, Argenti interviewed several leading experts. Many of these were professional receivers, but there were also investment analysts, managers, and journalists. In his book *Corporate Collapse,* Argenti presents Altman's earlier model and discusses it. He also recounts in detail two very large crashes—namely Rolls Royce and Penn Central—and tests his hypothesis on them. This is a very fascinating and readable book. His conclusion is that there are certain paths or patterns of failure. Thus, very young small companies follow one distinctive failure path; young but larger companies follow another equally distinctive failure path, which includes a period of dramatic collapse; and, mature companies follow a rather complex three-stage failure path.

In the following paragraph, Argenti states all the causes of collapse which appear with sufficient frequency to form the basis for his hypothesis:

If the management of a company is poor, then two things will be neglected: the system of accountancy information will be deficient and the company will not respond to change. Some companies, even well managed ones, may be damaged because powerful constraints prevent the managers making the responses they wish to make. Poor management will also make at least one of three other mistakes: they will overtrade; or they will launch a big project that goes wrong; or they will allow a company's leverage to rise so that even normal business hazards become constant threats. These are the chief causes, neither fraud, nor bad luck deserve more than a passing mention. The following symptoms will appear: Certain financial ratios will deteriorate, but as soon as they do the managers will start creative accounting which reduces the predictive value of these ratios and so lends greater importance to nonfinancial symptoms. Finally the company enters a characteristic period in its last few months.[12]

The remainder of this section examines what Argenti distinguished as the more significant causes of business failure and then looks at the failure paths which he observed.

Management

It is somehow self-evident that poor management causes companies to fail. It is rather like saying that abuse of the body causes ill health. What we need to know is what types of poor management we are talking about. Argenti found that six management structural defects were indicated by the experts he interviewed: One man rule, nonparticipation by the board of directors, an unbalanced top management, a lack of management depth, a weak finance function, and a combined chairman–chief executive. He claims that in 1971 Rolls Royce had five of these (it did not lack management depth) and Penn Central had three.

In my opinion, one man rule is the most important of these defects. It often manifests itself in very large companies in the form of one man combining the role of chairman and chief executive. Of course in smaller companies, this one man rule is necessarily acceptable, since some of these small companies are by the nature of things one man and his immediate employees. What Argenti means by one man rule is the kind of autocratic dominance which is exercised by unusual people who will

> allow no discussion, hear no advice, and surround themselves with colleagues who are likely to agree rather than disagree with them. And lest anyone say that many autocrats are successful and have businesses which did not fail, one must at once reply that there is no one single reliable cause of failure: It is the combination of several of the main causes which are now being discussed that is fatal.[13]

One point which follows very naturally from this is the importance of recognizing exactly when one man who has been an entrepreneur, let us say, and a successful one, should make the transition to a new management structure, with all that goes with it—delegation, division of duties, decentralizing of power, and so on. This must be a matter of judgment, but bankers very often have seen borrowers who were very successful so long as they could manage a small business directly and personally, but made serious errors when this important transition came about, either because they continued to be the sole decision maker or because they got the management structure wrong.

---

[12]Reprinted with permission from John Argenti, *Corporate Collapse* (New York: McGraw-Hill, 1976), p. 122.

[13]Argenti, *Corporate Collapse*.

The remaining five management defects will tend to reinforce the danger of one man rule. If the board does not participate in proper discussion of strategic matters, it will have contributed to failure. Of course, it will be performing its most important role if it makes a wise choice for chief executive. Then its next most important task is to watch that chief executive, considering always its duty toward the varying interests of employees, customers, the public at large, and stockholders. If the board allows itself to be dominated in its discussions by its chief executive, it is losing its grip. But how can boards know what is happening in a company when the chief executive controls the flow of information to them? And how can you detect a nonparticipating board?

An unbalanced top management team is one that is too full of engineers, or marketing people, or whatever. This suits the autocrat, who will dominate the areas which his senior management knows least well. Examples of an unbalanced top team include Rolls Royce (engineers), British Leyland in the 1970s (engineers or salesmen), and perhaps Braniff in the 1980s, although that company is a much better example of the problems of one-man rule, personified in H. L. Lawrence. Argenti's other weaknesses—namely, a weak finance function, a lack of management depth, and a combined chairman–chief executive are less significant causes, since they tend to reflect what has already been seen as one-man rule, and Argenti himself regards them as indicators of that central defect and determined by it.

Management Information

Argenti reviews what the experts told him about failed companies having very poor accounting information systems. His experts mentioned particularly the lack of budgetary control, cashflow forecasts, and poor costing systems which they had seen in failed companies. I would like to extend the lack of information principle to include not just accounting information but also management information in general. This includes knowing what is happening in the market, what is happening in the competitors' businesses, and what new developments in technology are coming that could affect the industry. Poor management information systems are a very significant cause of collapse. Just as a person will have trouble driving a car at night if the car has poor lights and the driver cannot see the road ahead, so management cannot run a company if it does not know what is happening.

A good case of poor management information, mentioned earlier, was the W. T. Grant Company, a major U.S. retailer that failed in 1975. In the retailing business, detailed knowledge of inventory is vital so that proper decisions can be made as to purchasing and internal distribution. In times of high interest rates, excessive inventory levels cost the company a great deal of money. Yet management of W. T. Grant did not know what was in the inventories of its hundreds of individual stores: It only knew a total dollar figure for inventory at each location. Similarly in the case of a Venezuelan manufacturer of steel fastenings that collapsed in the late 1970s, the lack of inventory controls proved to be a major cause of insolvency. Because the company was unable to know what was in its warehouses, nearly every new order required new production.

Poor management information systems will also make worse the next management error, failure to respond to change. If these systems are not bringing up data about patterns of market demand or about cost changes or whatever, then how can management respond?

Change

Argenti names failure to respond to change as a major cause of collapse. Earlier, I drew a parallel with natural history and suggested Charles Darwin's principle of natural selection as a useful model for the business world. Argenti's evidence supports this approach. Changes are continuous. What matters for companies is adapting to change in order to survive. Changes can be thought of as arising in five areas: competition, politics, economics, society, and technology. Some of these changes are violent and unexpected, such as the quadrupling of oil prices in 1973–1974 and the second sharp increase in the early 1980s. These changes are the most dangerous, but at least they are rare. More common are the gradual changes, such as the trend toward smaller families in industrialized countries. While the changes are outside the control of management, of course, what is definitely within management's control is how the company should respond.

Change arising in terms of competitors' actions has already been mentioned in discussing industry dynamics according to the Porter model (see Chapter 7). Remember that the presence of foreign low-cost producers, the merger of two competitors, or the entry of a new company with great financial resources into an industry will surely precipitate change. The Japanese auto industry and the Japanese motorbike industry did not spring fully formed like Athena from the head of Zeus. It took several years to achieve its tremendous export markets, and in the process, many competitors had time to react to this change. Of course, some companies went out of business even though they tried to react. Some changes are so strong that they appear to permit no opportunity for a counterstrategy.

Political changes are also important. I have already emphasized the importance of assessing the impact of government on a company. Now it is time to say that changes in political attitudes should cause companies to react. If they do not perceive such changes, disaster will follow; if they do perceive the changes but do not react to them, that too can be fatal. Think of what might happen to agribusiness in the European Economic Community (EEC) if the Common Agricultural Policy were to change so that farmers were no longer so protected against imports and against the effects of overproduction at home. One can think of what has happened to non-EEC producers of agricultural products who have found that they can no longer sell to such markets. New Zealand's lamb farmers, for example, have had to turn to new markets, such as the Middle East, in order to survive.

Changes in the economic environment frequently originate from political changes. Often, however, they are not directly politically caused. Economic changes include the devaluation of a major currency, the shift to a higher level of interest rates, the abandonment of fixed rates of exchange, and most importantly, the impact of inflation. No company can be unaware of the effects of inflation, but sometimes changes in the level of inflation may not be sufficiently recognized as a cause of financial problems. For example, a company might have adequate capital and access to reasonable bank credit lines to carry a certain level of inventory and receivables with inflation at, say, 6–7%. But if inflation shifts to 12–14%, the monetary values of inventory and receivables will be sharply increased, the need for debt will also be sharply increased, interest rates will escalate, and the company's financial resources will be overstretched, perhaps to the breaking point.

Economic changes in the level of a foreign exchange rate can also have fatal results—witness the collapse of Laker Airways in early 1982. Laker had more than $300 million of dollar-denominated debt, most of which was raised when the dollar was weak against the pound sterling. Since the airline had most of its revenues in sterling, it was already taking a foreign exchange risk with debt in one currency and cashflow in another. In the 12-month period immediately prior to its bankruptcy, the pound sterling depreciated by 27% against the U.S. dollar, with a resulting massive increase in the sterling equivalent value of Laker's debt. Here was an economic change to which the company was unable to react. Although it could have adopted the policy of hedging its foreign exchange risks by the use of forward contracts, for some reason, Laker did not take that action, which at best would only have partly lessened the flow. Such a massive increase in debt was therefore a major contributory factor to the collapse.

There remains only to mention social change and changes in technology. Since social changes are more subtle and evolve more slowly, it is hard to find examples of companies that have not reacted to such changes. Attitudes toward pollution and consumer protection, the increasing trend for women to work, rising levels of further education—all of these are gradual social changes. Employee motivation, expectations, and participation are also part of social change. Whereas once workers would obey the bosses without argument, today labor unions are more common and more widely accepted. Management which ignores such changes will be taking big risks.

Finally, changes in technology are said to be the most influential today, but according to Argenti this is a weak generalization. Very often the changes can be anticipated, and sometimes responding too soon to the change can be fatal. Sometimes the responses are just inadequate: Consider the several attempts made by AM International (formerly Addressograph-Multigraph), which failed in 1982, to adapt to the changing technology of office products, such as photocopiers. Over 10 years or so, the company tried many different products in reponse to changes in technology, but all failed for different reasons.

Overtrading, Launching a Big Project, and Leverage

Next we review the three other major causes of collapse which Argenti listed. Overtrading was the cause most frequently mentioned by his experts. It means simply trying to expand beyond the limits which a company's resources can support. Most commonly this expansion is at the expense of profitability. In other words, management is increasing sales through a conscious (or perhaps unconscious) cutting of profit margins. Growth at any price! No company can expand without debt, as we have seen, if its cash from operations is inadequate. Negative cash from operations is usually a symptom of overtrading if it is combined with rapid increases in sales and low profitability. Rapid growth for a certain period has often been associated with later collapse, especially in younger companies which go through this dramatic expansion phase. (This will be reviewed in the section on failure paths, as a Type 2 failure.)

An alternative to overtrading as a management error is launching "The Big Project." A company that is poorly managed and has disappointing results sometimes falls into the error of gambling on a big project that it hopes will restore the company's good fortune. Usually this project is financed by debt, since the company's cashflows are in a poor state already—hence the need for a big project. Usually, too, the costs are underestimated and the revenues are overestimated. A big project can include a merger, a diversification program, an expansion program, or the launching of a major new product. If the size of the project is very large in relation to a company's net worth, the risks are manifestly increased. Success will be wonderful of course, but even a small margin of error will have a huge impact on the company.

A good example of a company that launched a unsuccessful big project is Rolls Royce, which in 1967 set out to develop a new aero engine, the RB211. Initially, the development cost of the program was estimated at 60% of the company's net worth; four years later the actual cost turned out to be more than 100% of the net worth. There are plenty of other examples in the case histories, including Massey Ferguson (a major plant intended for exports from Germany that became a white elephant), Chrysler (the costs of converting to smaller more fuel-efficient cars proved huge in relation to Chrysler's capital base), Pertamina (the Indonesian oil company that massively overexpanded in the mid-1970s), and Mitchell Construction (a British engineering company which built a power station at Kariba in Africa that cost so much more than the contract that it sank the whole company).

While companies seldom commit both errors of overtrading and launching a big project, the presence of high leverage seems to be universal in failed companies. High leverage results from management decisions to press ahead with overtrading or a big project despite the fact that internally generated cash is insufficient to finance it. High leverage, as we have seen, is justifiable only if future cashflows are highly predictable. Corporate collapse comes about in a highly leveraged company usually because either interest or capital payments cannot be made, but sometimes because the company has simply run out of cash and no one will lend it any more money. This simply does not happen in companies with low leverage. Shareholder-financed companies with little or no debt are different: Dividends are not obligatory; shareholders cannot cause a company to collapse by demanding repayment; and from management's point of view, shareholders have far less influence in a low-leveraged company than bankers have in a high-leveraged company. If management's desire is for independence of action, then leverage is to be avoided. If a company has no debt, then no one can tell it what to do. High leverage therefore is a management error in that it limits what the company can do. High leverage is a hostage to fortune—when growth pays off, it is wonderful for the owners and for management, but when other strategic errors combine with it, then it is the fatal blow.

Creative Accounting

In Chapter 2, we looked at financial statements and their reliability. We saw that the nature of accounting principles is such that income and expenses involve assumptions and judgments, whereas cashflow is reliable, absolute, and not subject to manipulation. "Creative accounting" is any method of accounting that overstates revenues or understates expenses—that is, overstates or understates according to your business judgment of what is appropriate to a particular company or industry. Creative accounting is definitely a symptom of companies that are in a failure path. Usually it is employed as a smokescreen to disguise the real results in order to maintain the company's credit worthiness or to confuse the investors. But also management does not like to recognize failure; therefore, it sometimes deceives itself by employing those accounting principles that are most favorable to management.

Accounting principles in most countries permit substantial latitude in their application. Watch out then for the following "creative" signs, some of which are ingenious and some patently fraudulent.[14]

Recording as sales any inventory consigned to dealers but returnable by them.

Capitalizing expenditure which has doubtful long-term value.

Depreciating assets and later revaluing these assets upward, then taking the excess depreciation into trading profit.

Revaluing inventory upward.

Recognizing revenues on a front-end basis on the whole of rather than part of a contract where this is unjustified (for example, because the contracts are cancelable subsequently).

---

[14]Argenti presents a list of 18 techniques. This is my own list, not Argenti's, although a few are the same.

Consolidating an associate's income where this should be treated as equity accounting.

Treating revaluations of fixed assets as income where the company is a manufacturing company.

Extending the lives of fixed assets for depreciation purposes.

Using unreasonable assumptions for residual values for leased assets.

Not showing advance payments from customers as actual liabilities.

Recognizing unrealized gains on future contracts but not unrealized losses.

Making excessive allocation of overhead costs to products in finished goods inventory so as to shift overhead from the current period into future periods.

And there are many others that only await a creative mind.

Failure Paths

Argenti identifies three failure paths for three kinds of companies: the young, the fairly young but spectacular, and the established but waterlogged. This part of Argenti's book is very plausibly based on general observations of several failed companies (see Exhibit 8.1). Type 1, the young company, never gets off the ground. Some 50–60% of company failures are said to be of this type. "In some cases," Argenti writes,

> one may be entitled to predict failure right from the start, for such companies are presented with the following dubious gifts on their birthday: an unbalanced top team of one man with a weak finance function and no depth of management: rudimentary budgetary control, costing systems, and cashflow flaws; high leverage; and a project well beyond their means.[15]

That project is, of course, the business of getting started in business. Such companies live from two to eight years.

More spectacular is the Type 2 failure, but this is a rare type. Such companies are typically run by publicity-hungry enterpreneurs—undoubted leaders with a tendency toward flamboyant life-styles. A highly respected venture capitalist, Frederick R. Adler, is suspicious of a flamboyant style. Asked by the *New York Times* in January 1981 why he rejected a promising California electronics firm, he replied:

> The first thing I noticed was a giant Mercedes with initialed plates. The president said it was his, leased by the company. Then we went up to his office which was almost as big as the production area with a desk about eight feet long. After about an hour I said "Fellows I'm impressed with your desk and your

---

[15]Argenti, *Corporate Collapse*.

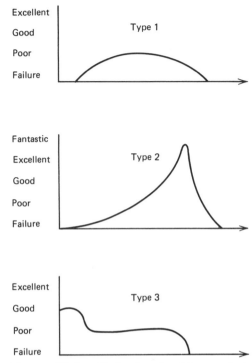

Exhibit 8.1   Three Types of Failure Paths. Reprinted by permission of John Argenti, *Corporate Collapse* (1976); Berkshire, England: McGraw-Hill, copyright © 1976 John Argenti.

car, but that's not the criteria by which I invest!" They went bankrupt 18 months later.[16]

Finally, Argenti describes the Type 3 failure path. This is the route typically taken by the large older established company, including what are often called "ailing giants." Examples of this type are AEG-Telefunken in Germany in the 1980s, British Printing Corporation in 1978–1981, or, of course, Penn Central in 1970. You might think of these companies as dinosaurs approaching extinction, but not all of them are large. Mostly they have failed to change, or have been dominated by one man who, perhaps very successfully, had guided the fortunes of the company for years but who has now departed from the scene leaving his followers still practicing his policies without thinking of their need for revision. As can be seen from Exhibit 8.1, the collapse is a two-stage affair. The first steep decline is often caused by an outside event that was not properly anticipated, while the second steep decline happens because either another shock hits the company or it attempts

[16]*New York Times,* January 6, 1981.

to gamble its way off a plateau of dismal performance. This plateau, Argenti suggests, can last for years, and changing the metaphor such a period is in his view a time when the company is "waterlogged"—that is, "leverage has become too high and at the same time the company has lost its competitive edge."[17] He is convinced that it is rare that such companies are able to get off the plateau because of their other defects (poor management information, for instance). In addition, an acute difficulty arises in that management seldom accepts the need either to contract the size of the company or to sell out to another company, and these represent the only really viable recovery plans. Nevertheless, such companies can and do survive if timely rescue work takes place.

SUMMARY

Understanding an industry is a matter of learning its dynamics, assessing where profits are made—for that is where risks are taken—and identifying changes. Good management is essential, and good management depends on Drucker's key result areas, discussed earlier. As analysts, you must develop your own measures for success in these areas, especially where financial numbers will be of no value. Some industries are inherently weak; others are strong because of barriers to entry. You must determine the nature of the industry in terms of buyer and supplier power, as well as the subject company's position within that industry. There are two separate but not incompatible approaches to predicting corporate collapse: using financial ratios and detecting multiple management errors. Both approaches are important to credit analysis. Causes of weakness are more relevant to risk analysis. You must use your own judgment, however, in decisions when isolated instances of Argenti's causes are significant, since it is normally a combination of weaknesses that proves fatal.

[17]Argenti, *Corporate Collapse*.

9 Term Loans

What we anticipate seldom comes about; what we least expect often happens.

Benjamin Disraeli

Term loans are defined as loans or revolving credits with repayment dates more than two years from the commitment date. It is important to recognize that revolving credits will tend to become solid debt once a borrower's financial condition deteriorates. This chapter discusses the purposes of term loans and why you must treat them differently from short-term loans. It includes an outline of a loan agreement, explains its key covenants, and discusses cashflow projections and how to test these.

In view of all that has been set out in earlier chapters concerning the assessment of risk in various industries and how to analyze management, it would be superfluous to repeat that here. However, it is vital to state at the outset that medium-term lenders must be even more satisfied than short-term lenders with industry and borrower characteristics. Risk increases with the passage of time, and the purposes of term loans, being different from those of short-term loans, magnify that risk. Good loan agreements do not make a poor credit risk into a good term loan simply by having strong financial covenants. Rather, the essence of what is needed for a good term loan is the ability to rely with some certainty on the future availability of cashflow.

PURPOSES OF TERM LOANS

Banks find term loans attractive partly because such loans normally have fixed repayment programs providing lenders with a degree of regular liquidity. More important, however, is the negotiation of binding promises from the borrower in return for a longer commitment from the bank. In the past, many commercial banks made loans under short-term lines of credit, then periodically renewed them because borrowers had used the short-term lines for investing in fixed assets and simply could not easily repay the loans.

During periods of recession, however, bankers often were reluctant to renew these lines. This led to further economic distress, because repayment meant fixed asset sales at low prices when times were at their hardest. By introducing the term loan concept, banks were recognizing that, although many short-term loans were in theory repayable on demand, such loans were in practice very illiquid, being tied up in capital goods or in other forms of fixed investment. At the same time as banks began to make commitments for funds to be available for longer periods and for purposes other than seasonal increases in current assets, they also strengthened their position by limiting a borrower's ability to raise other debt and by requiring a formal repayment program. Further, failure to observe certain promises which a lender had extracted from the borrower would mean that the borrower would suffer penalties, not the least of which was the risk of an immediate demand for repayment.

Not all purposes put forward by borrowers are suitable for term loans. The easiest type to accept and the most justifiable from the banker's point of view is the term loan for fixed asset expansion by a borrower who is simply expanding the size of its regular line of business. In this case, past performance will be a useful guide to future earnings and cashflow. Further, since the borrower is not venturing into an untried business but is building on successful management of his existing business, the risk of failure is far less than it would be in a new venture. The expansion of fixed assets is the most common purpose for which term loans are given.

Somewhat more difficult is the evaluation of term loans for working capital expansion. If it is proposed merely to finance an increase in inventories or the extension of longer periods of credit to customers, you must question whether this is sound business judgment. It may even be symptomatic of a fundamental weakness in either the borrower or the industry. As we have seen from cashflow analysis, the ratio of net working assets to sales should be fairly constant from year to year. Increases in the money amount of net working assets to be financed do require increased working capital, and this ought to be provided out of equity. Only when a borrower or an industry is experiencing a wave of rapid growth to be followed by a period of consolidation would it be reasonable to consider term loans for working capital. In doing so, lenders often limit the size of the term loan (or revolving credit, which is more frequently found in such cases) to a fixed percentage of inventory and receivables. This is what is meant by "borrowing base" loans. A bank will agree to lend, say, 60% of inventory and 80% of eligible[1] receivables, up to the maximum amount agreed. Such an agreement will always carry a provision that, after the period of rapid growth, the company must demonstrate a positive cash from operations that will service the debt, or that, after a certain period of time, capital markets must be more receptive

---

[1]Eligible means that the lender can exclude receivables from overseas customers or those that are 30 days past due or whatever the lender chooses.

to long-term debt or equity issues. The latter may be easier to prove than the former.

A third purpose, also fairly common but not so easy to evaluate, is the acquisition of another business, either as a going concern (most commonly) or as a breakup situation. This is obviously more risky, because when a corporation acquires another, the changeover in ownership is often accompanied by significant management turnover, especially if the acquisition was unfriendly. A second risk will arise from diversification, if that is involved in the acquisition. Some years ago (when conglomerates were fashionable) in the United States, it was believed that good management was transferable across all types of industry barriers and that diversification per se was desirable. Since then, it has been proved that synergy is often a myth and that diversified risk is something that investors can achieve for themselves by having a wide selection of different stocks in their investment portfolio. Probably the most convincing evidence that superior management performance by conglomerates was a myth was an article published in the *Harvard Business Review* in 1978 which demonstrated that almost all the large conglomerates had underperformed a representative matched sample of portfolios of independent companies in similar industries.[2] This is not to suggest that diversification is wrong, of course. What is intended is simply to show that diversification is not a magical formula for superior performance. Further, many companies who are successful in one industry frequently lose money when they invest in another industry that they know little about.

The economic justification for most acquisitions is that the combined entity can operate more profitably and efficiently than the two parts separately. Obviously this is hard to prove in advance, but in established industries, it is generally true that economies of scale, especially on the cost side, can be obtained more easily as size increases. The prudent lender will therefore tend to relate the repayment schedule to the demonstrated earnings capacity of the acquiring company (net of the losses, if any, of the company to be acquired). Furthermore, the agreement should be structured so that fairly strong covenants protect the lender from having to wait until all the acquisition problems have emerged (as this may take longer than expected) before negotiation is begun between the lender and the company.

Term loans to refinance existing obligations are often requested. The reasons usually cited are that the company cannot operate within its present maturity schedule or continued growth has caused a continuing need for funds. Sometimes the reason is that public capital markets are closed or prohibitively expensive. Closed markets are more generally acceptable to bank lenders than the first two reasons. Lenders are more able to judge the truth of such a statement, for one thing, and for another, the first two reasons simply suggest inadequate cash from operations. The irony of such a situation

[2]Malcolm S. Salter and Wolf A. Weinhold, "Diversification via Acquisition: Creating Value," *Harvard Business Review* (July–August 1978).

is that companies who least deserve debt refinancing usually have the most pressing need for it—namely, the fact that all other options are closed to them. The same thing seems also to be true for sovereign borrowers in international lending. As lenders, your response must still be to evaluate future cashflows and repayment possibilities. When this is done, it can be compared to the consequences of refusing refinancing and demanding repayment. In so doing, you should recall Disraeli's maxim, which we could rephrase as: "The unexpected tends to happen." By this I do not mean that loans should never be refinanced, or that poor loans should be rolled over to be problems later, but that you should be very sure indeed that the future survival of a borrower is impossible before refusing refinancing. After all the money has already been lent—now the skill is in obtaining repayment!

DIFFERENT EMPHASIS

Readers could regard most of this book as being about how to choose borrowers who are good term loan risks. In theory, short-term loans involve simply an advance for seasonal needs to support inventories which when sold provide repayment of the loan. The analytical approach to short-term credit is therefore based on the determination of the risk factor in current assets and consequently the amount of working capital needed to absorb potential losses in the cash-to-cash cycle. If loans were made only as short-term advances, there would be few loans made—how many truly seasonal businesses are there? Further, there would be no need for long training in credit matters. Surely anyone can see if inventory is sellable? In practice of course, bankers believe that all borrowers should be worthy of long-term relationships even if the borrowers' actual needs are only short term. The old principle still stands—"Know your customer"—and you cannot know your customer if you have only a short-term relationship in mind. Further, no one likes to be the banker to a borrower that does not have the Darwinian ingredients for survival in today's tough business climate. As a result, banks are rightly looking beyond the immediate request in making credit decisions.

It must be said, however, that term loan analysis does require different emphasis from the normal evaluation of annual lines of credit. The reason is that the borrower's cashflow, his income, rather than his balance sheet, is the key to the term loan decision. In short-term matters, balance sheets are useful. In the medium term however, analysis of several years' history, especially cashflow items, is essential. Remember too that loans can be made to loss-making companies where such loans are short-term, self-liquidating, and preferably secured. Term loans to loss-making companies, however, are another matter altogether.

To sum up, then, the different emphasis needed is for the loan officer to determine risks over longer periods and to structure a loan agreement in such a way that, if the risks become realities, the loan can be renegotiated.

LOAN AGREEMENTS

The main purpose in having a loan agreement is that it will provide for periodic review and renewal of a term credit which would not otherwise occur. The longer a borrower has a bank's money, the more likely it is that an unexpected adverse change will occur or that the plans on which the borrower based its financial plan will change. A loan agreement defines the conditions under which you as a lender have the right to review your credit decision. This should be at a point and on a level where the borrower's condition has not slipped beyond retrieval and you can still step in while the borrower has enough flexibility left to solve his problems.

The question sometimes arises as to whether the strongest companies should or indeed need to provide covenants to lenders. Market conditions have favored such borrowers for so long that banks have to accept minimal promises from such borrowers if they want top-quality term risks. Consider these points: Such companies have great depth of management; they have vast resources for asset sales, and government intervention will probably ensue if the strongest and largest companies in an industry get into trouble. This used to be doubted in the United States until Washington came to Chrysler's aid in the early 1980s. It is a reasonably sound political guideline to the banker that, in his own country at any rate, the industries employing the largest number of people will get some government help. Foreign bank lenders to a domestic industry may, however, be less well treated.

Even when the borrower is very strong, the agreement will give the lender the right to terminate if any of four events occur: nonpayment of principal, nonpayment of interest, acceleration of other indebtedness, and voluntary or involuntary bankruptcy.

Loan agreements have five main parts.

Preamble and Description

The purpose of the preamble is to describe the respective lenders and borrowers, especially when several lenders have different sized commitments. A statement of purpose may be included here, as well as commitment fees, interest rates, prepayment rights, and terms of repayment. Also, it is customary to define the terms used in the agreement.

Representations and Warranties

The representations and warranties describe, as of the date of the loan agreement, the economic, financial, and legal circumstances prevailing at the time the original credit decision was made. The purpose of the representations and warranties is not to guard against fraud, but rather to permit the lender to reassess a situation in case of unforeseen adverse changes.

Generally, the representations and warranties will recite the financial statements available to the lending institution when the basic credit decision was reached. This will include certification by a responsible officer of the borrower to the effect that there have not been any material adverse developments in the borrower's situation since the statements were submitted and that such financial statements are indeed true and correct reflections of the borrower's condition.

Less on the economic–financial side and more of a legal nature are representations that the proposed loan and its terms have been duly authorized and approved by the borrower's board of directors, that they are permitted under the borrower's charter and bylaws, and that they do not conflict with any law, governmental regulation, or other agreements to which the borrower might be subject. As a lender, you want to be assured that the proposed financing has been properly approved by the corporation, is contractually binding, and is legally enforceable in accordance with its terms. You also want to be assured that the financial plan entailed is not in conflict with existing laws, governmental regulations, or other plans or contracts to which the borrower is already committed and therefore would be subject to suit or prosecution by the government. Finally, the representations and warranties should include a paragraph dealing with any material pending litigation, to make sure that the outcome of such litigation will not materially impair the ability of the borrower to perform under the agreement.

Conditions Precedent.   Whereas the representations and warranties describe the conditions of the legal and financial environment existing when the original credit decision was made, the conditions precedent to the making of a particular loan under a legal commitment define the minimum conditions that must exist to make the commitment binding.

The basic condition precedent on the legal side is that all legal details connected with the contemplated transaction have been properly accomplished. The bank's counsel usually renders an opinion at this point and in order to do so must make an independent review of the following documents:

1. Charter of the company.
2. Bylaws of the company.
3. Resolutions adopted by the company's board of directors authorizing the contemplated transaction, together with any other required resolutions (for example, authorizing hypothecation of collateral, insurance, or guarantees).
4. Certificates of good standing from those jurisdictions where the major properties of the borrower are located or a substantial portion of the borrower's business is transacted.
5. Copies of all consents and approvals which might have had to be obtained.
6. Copies of other debt instruments to which the borrower might be subject.

A review of all the foregoing documents should enable counsel for the lender to determine that a contemplated loan and the related transactions are in a legally acceptable form. In most instances, corporate affairs of borrowers are far from simple and counsel for the lender should not be expected to become familiar with all the ramifications of the business of the borrower, guarantor, or any other party to the agreement. For that reason, opinions should be obtained from the borrower's counsel (preferably independent) stating that all necessary legal actions have been taken and that no provisions of charter, bylaws, or other applicable agreements have been violated. Such counsel should also state that the loan agreement and any notes to be issued in connection with it are valid and binding obligations of the borrower, enforceable in accordance with the terms of the loan and that all other instruments (guarantees, for example) are similarly valid and enforceable.

On the financial side of the conditions precedent, it is obvious that the lender should have obtained a signed copy of the loan agreement and of the note(s) to be issued. In those instances where collateral is to be pledged, appropriate instruments should have been executed and, if applicable, the collateral should be in the hands of the lender. A similar consideration concerns the execution and delivery of guarentees, where such are required. Certifications should also be obtained when a contemplated loan is part of a larger financing program involving the raising of additional capital funds, the discharge of other indebtedness, or the prior investment of the borrower's own funds in a venture to be financed partly by the contemplated loan.

Finally, as a condition precedent a lender will generally want to obtain two additional documents:

1. An incumbency certificate listing the names and signatures of the officers (with their respective titles) having the power to act for the borrower.
2. A certification by a responsible officer that the representations and warranties contained in the agreement and true and correct as of the closing date.

Covenants

The covenants of a loan agreement set forth, in essence, the framework of the financial plan agreed upon jointly by the borrower and the lender. The extent to which covenants are worked out in detail is a function of the financial strength of the enterprise and the depth and ability of its management, on the one side, and the length of the proposed loan, on the other.

As previously stated, the largest and best-managed companies sometimes borrow term money without restrictive covenants and with only certain basic Events of Default. (See next section). With companies that are smaller but still in the prime commercial group, lenders are often content to set broad covenants limiting debt to an overall ratio of tangible net worth, prohibiting secured debt, and providing for the maintenance of a certain minimum working capital.

Actually, the basic covenants in every term loan agreement should be constructed around these three principles: limitation of other indebtedness (or a ratio between debt and equity); prohibition of secured obligations or of obligations ranking ahead of the commercial term loan; and a provision for the maintenance of a certain minimum working capital (possibly together with a current ratio test). To these may be added the requirement to furnish financial statements.

Covenants can also be viewed as being negative or affirmative, and primary, secondary, or tertiary. Negative covenants are those that in each case will take a definite management decision to violate. For example, if a borrower agrees not to pay dividends, it cannot happen by accident that dividends are paid. On the other hand, affirmative covenants are those that are good general business practices, and management may not have control over these. Financial ratios are usually treated as negative covenants even though conscious management decisions are not always required to break these covenants. For instance, losses caused by adverse trading conditions may lead to the breach of a working capital minimum, or even a specified debt/equity ratio, even though management was not consciously trying to do this.

The three basic principles of primary covenants have been stated above, and these form the key pieces to be negotiated with borrowers. The "negative pledge" is the prohibition of secured obligations or of obligations ranking ahead of our commercial term loan. Of course, in negotiation certain exceptions will be agreed upon, including, for instance, that overseas subsidiaries may pledge their assets to support their own borrowings, that prior existing secured debt is excluded, and that a certain minimal monetary amount can be raised on a secured basis annually without having the lender's specific approval. In limiting indebtedness, lenders should include limitations on leases and contingent liabilities other than normal product warranties. Readers might also consider using as ratios the key elements in Altman's second model (see Chapter 8).

Secondary covenants may also be required even if the primary covenants are tight. This is because a lender does not want all earnings in excess of debt requirements and fixed asset maintenance expenditures to be diverted into unknown or unspecified uses. The further out in time a loan runs, the more questionable it becomes that the original credit and financial tests will adequately protect the lender.

Secondary covenants include:

1. Prohibition of the sale, discount, or other disposition of accounts receivable with or without recourse.
2. Prohibition of changes in other debt instruments.
3. Limitation of prepayment or redemption of other long-term debt.

4. Prohibitions on mergers or consolidations, asset sales, and acquisitions.
5. Prohibitions on guarantees.
6. Prohibitions on investments in other enterprises.
7. Limitations on capital expenditures.
8. Limitations on dividends, although a well-worded clause on minimum tangible net worth may make this last condition unnecessary. The trend today is to require annual increases in net worth—the so-called ratcheting net worth clause.

Tertiary covenants include the maintenance of corporate existence, the payment of taxes when due, and the maintenance of adequate insurance. Lenders to closely held corporations sometimes include limitations on management salaries as well.

Events of Default

The next section of the agreement sets forth conditions under which the long-term lender has the right to accelerate the payment of the loan. The right to accelerate affords lenders the opportunity to renegotiate terms or take other steps instead of demanding immediate repayment. The fact that the right exists does not mean that it is always used, but it does give lenders flexibility at a time when they need room to maneuver.

The most important events of default, which should be contained in every long-term debt agreement or instrument, relate to bankruptcy, reorganization, and nonpayment of indebtedness. Obviously lenders must have the right to call in their outstanding loans or be relieved of any obligation to make further loans in the case of voluntary bankruptcy or reorganization proceedings if these are not stayed or dismissed within a reasonable time. If lenders have not reserved for themselves the right to accelerate under the foregoing conditions, they might be in the awkward position of not having matured claims that they can present to the bankruptcy trustee. This, in turn, might stop them from proving their claims and from recovering in full.

Obviously lenders should have the right to review a given loan if the debtor cannot make principal and interest payments due to them on a timely basis. Whether or not such review is also warranted if other indebtedness is not paid as and when due is sometimes an open question. The argument against making such acceleration an event of default is that nonpayment could precipitate bankruptcy. This, however, might or might not be the case and the holder of other unpaid indebtedness might rewrite the obligation in such a way that it is repaid over the near term (just keeping the debtor out of bankruptcy) or the creditor might take security to protect its interests. To what extent these possibilities are serious threats depends to a large degree on the strength of the covenants. Certainly in any lending arrangement where term loans are made with only a few covenants, the acceleration of other indebtedness should cross-accelerate the subject loan.

The next group of defaults relates to such things as material falsity or representation and warranties, default under negative covenants, or default under covenants contained in other debt instruments. Certainly if a representation on which a lender has based its decision should prove to be false in a material respect, the lender should have the right to review its decision. At times this can protect the lender from serious problems, especially if the contemplated loan is in violation of other agreements or statutory regulations. As pointed out earlier, negative covenants are generally those that are under the direct control of a borrower's senior managers, and a breach of such a covenant might be considered a willful or premeditated act on their part. For this reason, if such defaults occur, lenders dealing in good faith with a borrower should be relieved of their obligation to continue to lend. The reason for insisting on the right to accelerate indebtedness if a borrower defaults under another loan agreement, even though the other lender does not accelerate its obligation, is that the default generally will be stayed by another lender only if its position is improved.

The Miscellaneous Section

The final section sets forth any matter to be specified that does not logically fall in one of the previous sections. It includes where notices to borrowers or lenders shall be sent, what law governs the agreement, the duties of the agent bank in syndicated loans, and the borrower's agreement to pay certain expenses.

CASHFLOW PROJECTIONS

Examining projections for cashflow is an essential part of the term loan analysis process. Exhibit 9.1 shows how to find what cashflow should be available to cover term loan repayments

Assumptions are necessary, of course. The key assumptions will be the annual rate of sales increase, whether net income margins will remain the same, whether net working assets will continue as a constant percentage of sales, what the level of required capital expenditure will be (as opposed to what might be called discretionary capital expenditure), and whether there will be any change in the corporate tax rate. Line 9, "margin of safety,"will represent what is left over after all the required payments have been met. If this line is negative, not only is there no margin of safety but additional debt will probably be necessary. At this point, you might wonder (correctly) how that will fit with the typical limiting covenants on debt/equity and the current ratio. It is a good policy to do the projections using several different assumptions. At least three sets of projections will be needed: best case,

Exhibit 9.1   Form for Determining Cashflow Needed to Cover Loan Repayment

	19X0	19X1	19X2	Etc.
1. Net income after tax				
2. Add back noncash charges such as depreciation.	____	____	____	____
Subtotal (funds from operations)				
3. Less increases in net working assets.	____	____	____	____
Subtotal (cash from operations)				
4. Less required capital expenditures				
5. Less required dividends (if any)				
6. Less other long-term debt payments	____	____	____	____
7. Available cashflow				
8. Less repayments of this loan	____	____	____	____
9. Margin of safety	____	____	____	____

worst case, and most likely. Then these should be compared with the ability to raise additional debt from other sources, since in this inflationary age such projections seldom show much margin of safety.

One way of testing the validity of projections is to project also the accompanying balance sheets and income statements,and then to calculate certain key ratios to see if the projections are consistent with known past performance. For instance, if projections show that earnings before interest and taxes/total assets will rise from 18% now to 30% in three years, you should be suspicious. Probably this result has occurred from underrating the required level of capital expenditure. That is, earnings before interest and taxes may be right, but total assets is far too low, producing the unexpected and probably unachievable ratio.

Balance sheet and income statement projections are most easily done by computer, but they can be done by hand if necessary. A simple method is shown in Exhibit 9.2. Base-year numbers are the current year's figures adjusted for any extraordinary income or expense.[3] Note that Net Working Assets is treated as a single entry. An explanation of how to use this model follows:

STEP 1.   *Assets*. First fill in base-year numbers. Calculate Net Working Assets as a percentage of base-year sales and use this for projections. Line 4, Capital Expenditure, should be the actual figure for the base year. Line 5, Depreciation: Use the actual figure, calculate the ratio Depreciation/Closing Net Fixed Assets, and use this for projections.

[3]A different school of thought requires the base year to be an average of the preceding three years' figures. I think this is misleading unless inflation has been negligible. However, base-year data must be adjusted for anything not likely to be repeated (for example, an unusually low figure for net working assets).

Exhibit 9.2   Form for Projecting Cashflows

Line	Base Year	Year 1	Year 2
Balance Sheet			
1. Cash			
2. Net Working Assets			
3. Net Fixed Assets (Opening)			
4. Plus Capital Expenditure			
5. Less Depreciation			
6. Net Fixed Assets (Closing)			
7. Other Assets			
8. Total Assets			
9. Short-Term Debt			
10. Other Short-Term Liabilities			
11. Long-Term Debt			
12. Preferred Stock			
13. Minorities			
14. Beginning Owner's Equity			
15. Closing Owner's Equity			
16. Residual Cash ($+/-$)			
17. Total			
Income Statement			
18. Sales			
19. Cost of Goods Sold			
20. Selling General and Administrative Expense			
21. Depreciation Expense			
22. Interest Expense			
23. Income before Tax			
24. Tax Expense			
25. Net Income			
26. Dividends			
27. Retained Earnings			

STEP 2.   Enter in line 9 the Short-Term Debt for the base year. Decide whether or not this figure can be projected unchanged (this will depend on what limitations there are in the loan agreement). In Line 11, enter the Long-Term Debt. Note for the projections what are the required repayments of Long-Term Debt. Add in the new term debt. Line 14, Beginning Owner's Equity, will be the beginning figure for the base year. Line 15 will be line 14 plus line 27. Therefore, proceed to Step 3 before returning to line 15 and line 16.

STEP 3. *Income Statement*. For the base year, use actual numbers adjusted for extraordinary gains or losses. Calculate Cost of Goods Sold as a percentage of Sales, and use this for projections. Line 21 is the same as line 5. In Line 22, Interest Expense use the actual number. For projections, decide what interest rate to apply to the total of Short-Term Debt (line 9) plus Long-Term Debt (line 11) plus the *preceding year's* Residual Cash (line 16). If line 16 is negative, it will increase interest expense; if it is positive, it will be "marketable investments" or the equivalent and therefore its interest income will reduce this expense. For the base year, enter Interest Expense on line 22 as the net of interest income and interest expense, and show any marketable investments in line 16 as a negative number. (Remember they are really an asset, so that they appear in liabilities in the negative for the purpose of calculation.) Line 24, Tax Expense, can be adjusted if deferred taxes are created, with an addition of a Deferred Tax line to the balance sheet as well. Decide if the percentage tax rate can be used for projections. If not, choose a tax rate. Line 26, Dividends: Decide if they will be constant or will increase at a fixed percentage rate. Line 27, Retained Earnings, can be added to line 14 (Beginning Owner's Equity) to take us to Step 4.

STEP 4. Line 16 is residual number. It is much the same as the margin of safety already mentioned. If in the base year there are no marketable investments and Short Term Debt is at a "normal" level, this line will be zero for the base year. For future years, this line will be either negative or positive, and this is a result of the fact that asset increases were determined as a first step in this projection process (that is, before liability and retained earnings increases). Line 16 is mainly determined by changes in Net Working Assets and Capital Expenditure levels. Line 16 is very important, since if it becomes positive and grows significantly throughout the projections, it definitely indicates the need for debt or equity increases. It also implies that the repayment program of the term loan cannot be met out of normal cash flow. It is generally superior to the margin of safety in the simple projection since it is cumulative.

Summary on Using the Projection Model

Obviously computer-based projections can be much more sophisticated than this simple model. The object here is to generate numbers and check cash flows as well as ratios to see if they are realistic given past performance. We need to have the following data and variables:

Data: for the base year, income statement and balance sheet; capital expenditure, tax rate, NWA/Sales percentage

Variables:

1. At what rate will sales increase?
2. Will Net Working Assets/sales remain constant?
3. Will the tax rate remain constant?
4. Should dividends be held constant or be increased?
5. What interest rate should be projected?
6. At what rate should depreciation be in relation to net fixed assets?
7. What is essential capital expenditure?

Tests for Projections

You can test the validity of projections by comparing these ratios to industry and company norms:

Gross margin
Net income/sales
Earnings before interest and taxes/total assets
Debt service ratio
Return on equity
Total liabilities/tangible net worth.

It is also possible using a computer to determine answers to these questions:

1. How slowly must sales grow if line 16 in Exhibit 9.2 is to stay at zero?
2. What is the maximum rate of sales growth the company can support? (Assume line 16 can increase to some percentage of net working assets, but subject to maintaining the restrictive convenant in the loan agreement on total liabilities to net worth.)
3. What happens if dividends are held constant?
4. What happens if capital expenditure is greatly increased? (Note that the reverse is almost always impracticable.)
5. What happens if the interest rate doubles?
6. Is your allowance for inflation reasonable?

PROBLEMS

1. What purposes for term loans are not likely to be acceptable to lenders?
2. If financial ratios are used as covenants, why is a current ratio as well as a minimum working capital figure needed?

3. Why would a company that produces consolidated statements only once a year resist financial covenants on a consolidated basis? How would you structure financial covenants if lending to a parent company?

4. Why would it be attractive but difficult to use cash flow to total liabilities as a restrictive covenant?

5. Some lenders offer borrowers no financial covenants but insist on having a company agree to "a material adverse change" clause which would cause an event of default if the borrower's financial condition suffered a material adverse change. Discuss the legal aspects of this as well as the negotiating points for both borrower and lender.

6. Discuss the results of a cross-default clause which permits your bank to call an event of default if there is an event of default called by or callable by another lender. Would you need any financial covenants?

7. Would you always feel obliged to decline to recommend a loan if the projections on a "most likely" basis show the borrower will be unable to generate sufficient cash flow to meet your repayments?

8. When lending to subsidiaries, what restrictions would be necessary in addition to normal financial covenants?

9. A borrower's previous history exhibits wide variations in cashflow. Would you consider attaching probabilities to projections (best case, most likely, worst case) to arrive at an expected cashflow adjusted for uncertainty? Would this be meaningful?

10. What types of borrowers do not qualify for term loans? Give reasons.

10 Analysis of Commercial Banks

Banks take risks. Banks also lose money. Since banks extend credit to other banks on a very large scale, both within their own domestic markets and in cross-border transactions, including trade finance and the Eurocurrency market for interbank placements, the analysis of commercial banks has become of special importance. Ordinary members of the public are usually unaware of the risks which banks take until something happens to make them question their confidence. Two events marked 1974 as a year when that confidence was shattered.

In May of that year, the Franklin National Bank, which at the time was the twentieth largest U.S. bank, shook the financial world by passing its second quarter dividend and announcing losses of $40 million, equal to nearly a quarter of its capital. Within days depositors began withdrawing their money, and within months the Franklin National Bank was sold to a consortium of European banks who agreed to rescue it on terms not unfavorable to them. In the intervening months, depositors withdrew more than $1.5 billion, or approaching half that bank's deposits.

In June of the same year, the West German regulatory authorities closed down the operations of Bankhaus I. D. Herstatt, a small private bank but one very active in foreign exchange. This caused New York City banks to stop making payments to each other for several hours until the chairman of one major bank telephoned several of his counterparts and settlement transactions were resumed. Without this interbank settlement system, the financial markets would have completely stopped. As it was, foreign exchange activity between banks was severely reduced for several months afterward.

Since credit is extended by commercial banks to each other in various forms,[1] it is particularly important for the analyst to be able to adapt the techniques learned in examining manufacturing and selling organizations to the analysis of commercial banks. This chapter explains how to do this, first

[1]The various forms include Interbank deposit placements, purchases of other bank's certificates of deposit or Floating Rate Notes or bonds, foreign exchange transactions involving a delivery risk, standby letters of credit, correspondent account balances, purchases of bank acceptances, and letters of credit opened by issuing banks in favor of a customer.

by examining how banks make money and later by looking at financial ratios and other methods of checking on the health of the subject in the course of writing the analysis.

HOW BANKS MAKE PROFITS

Banks are like any other business in that risk and return go hand in hand. They are unlike other businesses in that cash from operations is not a meaningful concept. In order to understand how a bank makes money, it is necessary to know not only what risks it undertakes but also how its different leverage structure is both the key to its profitability and the cause of disaster. Banks, and to a lesser extent, finance companies, are perfect examples of the old adage: "Other people's money plus a positive mental attitude leads to riches." What other business can leverage its owner's equity by 20 to 30 to 1? What other business can regularly acquire debt by performing a service for its customers in terms of money transactions? And what other business is so well placed to use its own professional expertise—namely, financial management—both externally to serve customers and internally to manage its own affairs? Yet with all these apparent advantages, banking and lending to banks is far from risk free.

There are four principal sources of revenue for banks:

Interest income
Fees and commissions
Income from associates
Trading income, especially from foreign exchange

Each of these will be examined in turn, together with their associated risks. First, however, a small digression.

Suppose you were starting a bank with a $1 million of capital. It is an ordinary commercial bank dealing with private customers and both large and small businesses. Obviously you want to maximize your return on capital. If you were not prevented from doing so, you would probably attempt to carry the largest volume of assets with the absolute minimum of capital. For instance, you would be happy with, say, $100 million of assets if you could get them using your $1 million of capital to acquire fixed assets, such as buildings and machines. If your buildings and machines were staffed with people of exceptional skills, you could perhaps acquire $100 million of liabilities in the form of depositors' money. Suppose your assets earned an average 1% over the cost of funds—not an unreasonable rate of return, in fact—your net interest income would be $1 million. Even with tax at 50%, your return on equity would be $500,000, or 50% of your original capital. What a wonderful result! Banking, however, is not as easy as this. First, there are operating expenses to be met, most of which will be the salaries of those exceptional people. Second, there is hardly a country of any size today where banks are not regulated by some form of government authority, and no regulator would allow you to leverage yourself on the scale of 100 to 1. Thus, returns of this magnitude are not possible. But it does illustrate one important fact—namely, that leverage plays a key part in banking as in every other business. And the degree of leverage that is possible rests on the confidence of the depositors. Perhaps the key reason that banks cannot be formed with such remarkable profitability is that they would never obtain the public's confidence.

Interest Income

Let's first look at interest income. For the typical commercial bank this represents the largest source of revenue. It includes income from holding bonds and other marketable securities but is mostly composed of the interest earned on loans. After deducting the cost of paying for deposits (interest expense) and other borrowed funds (for example, funds from the interbank market), a bank arrives as its *net interest income*. Identifying the reasons for changes in net interest income is vitally important for the analyst, since these reasons will be a reflection of some of the risks which the management of the bank has undertaken.

Credit risk is of the course the principal risk in acquiring assets in the form of loans. Credit risk also applies to bonds and other securities. The risk is simply that the borrower cannot pay, or can pay only part of the debt. By acquiring riskier classes of assets, banks can increase their net interest income. In the short run, this will substantially improve profits, but in the medium term, this improvement will be reduced by a higher incidence of credit losses from bad debts.

A second category of risk is *investment risk*. This is the risk involved in acquiring assets with a fixed income stream. The prime example is fixed-rate bonds, including corporate, municipal, or government bonds. The risk is that there may be a change in market interest rates that will give rise to capital losses if the bonds are sold. If they are not sold, the cost of carrying these bonds (that is, the associated interest expense) will be less than the income earned by the bonds, thus also giving rise to a drop in net interest income.

It is not only bonds that cause problems. Many banks make fixed-rate loans. In the U.S. banking system, most loans to consumers are at fixed interest rates, and so are most residential mortgages. Indeed in 1980 and 1981, the U.S. savings and loan industry, which holds most of the residential mortgages, suffered substantial losses from the sharp rise in market interest rates. What took place was a steep rise in the cost of funds paid to depositors and other sources of money, while revenue from mortgages remained at interest rates which in many cases had been fixed years earlier in preinflationary times at rates as low as 5%. The industry's troubles were made worse by the fact that many mortgages were transferable with the house on which they were secured. Therefore, unlike European practice, where mortgages last on average less than 10 years since they have to be repaid when the property is sold, these mortgages continue for their full life of up to 30 years.

Fortunately for commercial banks, most of their loans are not at fixed rates, and certainly not for periods as long as mortgages. However, there are usually some fixed-rate loans, since the temptation to maintain commercial loan volume in the face of weak loan demand that tends to be associated with low interest rates leads banks to lend at just the wrong moment from the point of view of the interest rate cycle.[2]

A third risk facing bank management is *liquidity risk*. Liquidity is needed for two reasons: first, to satisfy demand for new loans without having to recall existing loans or realize bonds, and second, to meet both daily and seasonal swings in deposits so that these withdrawals can also be met early. Bank management has to determine the ideal amount of liquidity dependent on differing local circumstances. The more liquid the asset, however, the less it will earn. The risk is either than an asset will have to be realized at an inopportune moment in order to meet a claim for a withdrawal, thus causing a loss of principal, or that liabilities will have to be switched in adverse market conditions, thus causing higher interest expense. For example, it might in the latter case become necessary to borrow from other financial institutions at top-of-the-market rates if core retail deposits, which are typically of lower cost, were to be lost for any reason and no assets could conveniently be realized. Liquid assets are generally reckoned to include only the following:

1. Cash
2. Short-term deposits with other banks and its own Central Bank
3. Marketable securities of top quality with maturities of less than one year (for example, Treasury bills and certificates of deposit).

Liquidity can also be boosted if a bank's standing in the market allows it to draw on a wide range of sources of funds without difficulty. Thus, the relationship of a bank to its Central Bank or to other financial institutions can be of key importance. It need not actually be drawing on all of these sources for funds, but the fact that it could do so will be a cause of comfort to bank management looking to its liquidity position. The best position to have would be one where one knew that more funds were available in the marketplace at or below a reasonable cost than the bank could possibly deploy in the market. Such a position would be superliquid and would seem to arise only very rarely—for example, where a bank had some uniquely high rep-

---

[2]This confirms the maxim that borrowers should borrow when money is cheap, not when they need it, since when they need it, money will be expensive.

utation or was owned by a parent organization with access to significantly greater resources than the subsidiary itself.[3]

The fourth type of risk that banks can assume is *the mismatch*. A mismatch arises where the source and the use of funds are different. There are two possible kinds of mismatch: One is a mismatch of time, the other a mismatch of currency. Mismatching of time is almost inevitable in that a retail commercial bank dealing with customer checking accounts could never be profitable if it kept as much in overnight assets as it had in checking accounts. Obviously, therefore, it is the degree of mismatch that creates risk, since almost all banks practice mismatches of time. If interest rates are very volatile, time mismatches become very dangerous, but also very profitable.

Example 10.1. Suppose one-month deposits can be taken at 6% and six-month deposits at 8%. If a six-month loan is made at 8.25% (0.25% over the cost of borrowing of funds at 8%), it could be funded for the first month to show a 2.25% profit. But what if the one-month deposit rate in the second month is 9%? What if rates stay above the 8.25%? It would have been better not to mismatch. On the other hand, one could find out the deposit rates for two, three, four, and five months at the end of the first month to see if the original mismatch could be undone without an overall loss.

Example 10.2. A bank has a large deposit for 12 months on which it is paying 10%. One-, two-, and three-month rates are higher than the 12-month rate. Provided they stay that way for long enough, mismatching by keeping the funds in the short-term market will be profitable. But this is a risky practice.

Example 10.3. Currency mismatches involve foreign exchange risk unless forward cover is obtained. If a foreign bank makes U.S. dollar loans without matching dollar deposits, it could always buy dollars in the foreign exchange market in exchange for its local currency. The risk, of course, is that the dollar to foreign currency rate might have changed against it by the end of the mismatch period. If a contract for forward cover is obtained, the bank is engaging in covered interest arbitrage, not currency mismatching. (Covered interest arbitrage is a specialized market technique.)

Now that we have examined the risks involved in net interest income, it is worth repeating that a key task of the analyst is to understand why net interest income changes from year to year. Below is a list of some possible causes. Notice that only some of these are external. Some are internal and therefore subject to management control. Some are both external—for example, in the sense that interest rates rise—and also internal in that management may have planned its asset portfolio in such a way as to avoid the risk of a large portion of fixed-rate assets whose income is not interest rate sensitive.

[3]Saudi International Bank, in London, which is 50% owned by the Saudi Arabian Monetary Authority, would be a case in point.

	Internal/External
Possible reasons for net interest income going up (as a percentage of assets)	
Proportion of risk assets increases (more loans)	I
Rate of return on risk assets increases (more risky loans)	I/E
Rate of return on liquid assets increases (higher interest rates)	E
More checking account balances	I
Higher interest rates affect interest-sensitive assets	E
Decline in nonperforming loans	I
Decline in cost of funds due to change in deposit mix	I/E
Removal of interest rate ceilings	E
Successful funding policies (mismatching as to time)	I
Increase in loan demand	E
Increase in spreads arising from less competition	E
Decrease in competition for deposits	E
Reduced reserve requirements for deposits	E
Possible reasons for net interest income going down as percentage of assets	
Proportion of risk assets decreases (fewer assets)	I
Increase in nonperforming loans	I/E
Interest rates rise, but interest-sensitive assets are large	E
Increase in loan quality arising from switch to more wholesale loans	I
Decline in spreads arising from more competition	E
Change in deposit mix; more bought funds	I/E
Run-off of checking deposits replaced by borrowed funds	E
Unsuccessful mismatching as to time	I
Long funding when rates fall	
Short funding when rates rise	
Large proportion of non-interest-sensitive assets	I
Fixed-rate bond portfolio	
Fixed-rate loan portfolio	
Excess of nontaxable income in relation to taxable income, (for example, too much tax-free municipal bond income for U.S. banks)	I
Increased competition for deposits	E

Fees and Commissions

It is sometimes said that commercial banks live on their deposits, whereas merchant or investment banks live by their wits. While this may once have been true, in modern times in many countries the divisions between the two types of banks are becoming blurred. One obvious fact can be observed: A bank that has a significant portion of its revenues arising from fees and commissions gets a better return on capital since no owner's equity is needed to support its professional staff. Increasingly today, banks of all types use highly skilled people to generate fee income, since this type of revenue is also not sensitive to interest rates. Such revenues arise from diverse sources. Among many, the following could be listed:

Letters of Credit issued or confirmed
Underwriting commissions
Selling commissions on securities sold to investors
Custody of valuables
Investment management
Pension fund management
Corporate advisory work
Mergers and acquisitions
Loan syndication fees
Real estate management
Trusteeship for bonds and debentures
Wills, trusts, and executorships
Guarantees issued
Standby letters of credit
Acceptance commissions
Performance bonds issued[4]

In reviewing a bank's sources of income, the analyst needs to see how the net interest income was augmented by these other sources. Since some of them have substantial costs attached, it would be valuable to know their net contribution, though this is seldom disclosed. For example, while underwriting bonds produces fee income, it also carries a substantial cost when the underwritten issue is poorly received (that is, fails to sell well) and the bonds have to be taken up and held by the underwriter until such time as they can be dumped onto the market.

Special emphasis must be given to examining revenue generated by contingent liabilities. This area, normally not reflected in bank balance sheets, can have particular significance but is often overlooked. The size of contin-

---

[4]The last three sources are often limited by the size of a bank's capital, although they are not reflected in the balance sheet the way other sources of revenue are.

gent liabilities can sometimes be found in notes to the balance sheet. An example will best illustrate the point: Penn Square Bank of Oklahoma, which failed in 1982, had capital of $31 milion and total assets of $485 million. However, it also disclosed in footnotes to the balance sheet contingent liabilities of $116 million. As it happens, some of these were standby letters of credit issued by Penn Square in favor of other financial institutions who had participated in Penn Square's loans. The standby letters of credit were contingent liabilities because they would be drawn on only if the loan sold was in default or nonperforming. Penn Square's income was increased by taking a slice out of the income arising from assets which had been on-sold to others even though it had none of that asset on its books. When Penn Square's capital/assets ratio was computed *without* these assets that had been sold (but sold with recourse to Penn Square), it was not unreasonable. However, when the assets are adjusted for those "with recourse" participations, the picture looks very different.

The fact is that contingent liabilities tend to become actual liabilities when the bank gets into difficulties. Contingent liabilities also include guarantees and letters of indemnity. Ideally, they are matched by counter indemnities from customers. But there should be some limit to these, and analysis must examine them in relation to the bank's actual capital resources. In the United States, banks cannot give guarantees, but federal limitations on such items as standby letters of credit have only recently come into effect. In many other countries, there are no restrictions.

Income from Associates

Income from associates is fairly common among European and Asian banks but less so among U.S. banks because of U.S. banking restrictions on crossing state boundaries and on investing in nonbanking subsidiaries. However, where such restrictions do not apply, it will be important to consider the following questions:

1. Is the income computed on the basis of a share of the reported net income of the associate? Or is it computed only on dividends received from the associate? Or is some other method used?
2. What is the obligation to the associate in terms of the requirement to put in further capital?
3. Is the associate under a different or under the same regulatory system? For instance, if it is incorporated in another country from its parent, what are the regulations there and what accounting principles apply?
4. How much cash could the associate pay its parent in dividends? How else does (would) the associate support its parent?
5. If the associate is also a bank or financial institution, can an analysis of its position be prepared?

Trading Income

The major part of trading income is foreign exchange trading, but also included are revenues from trading in bonds, certificates of deposit, Treasury bills, and other marketable securities. In some countries, profits on trading the bond portfolio might also be included in reported income under this category. Banks make considerable sums from foreign exchange, although the accounting principles applied can vary. Consider, for instance, the following situation:

Example 10.4. Hickory Bank has a forward foreign exchange position at year end that includes profit from forward sales that have been locked in by matching contracts for forward purchases, producing a certain gain of $2 million. Should the $2 million be included in this year's income, since the contracts were made in this year, or in next year's income, since the contracts do not mature until next year? What could take place that would cause the profit to be lost?

In principle these are unrealized gains, and conservative opinion requires that they not be recognized until the maturity date. The best argument for this is that, until delivery of the foreign exchange takes place on the due date, there is always the risk that the counterparty might default on the contract, and then the bank would have to close out the position with uncertainty as to profit or loss.

Accounting for foreign exchange is extremely complex. However, it is clear that a bank makes money in two main ways—namely, acting as agent and acting as principal. When it acts as an agent, it executes an order for a customer to buy say, 3 million deutsche marks (DM) in exchange for dollars. The customer is quoted and accepts a rate of, say, DM 2.1020, but the actual rate at which the bank acquired the marks in the market was DM 2.0970. Accounting problems arise because, where several transactions are done, it is often difficult to know which purchase to match to which sale of currency, and during any single day a bank can move from a short to a long position and back again more than once. When banks act as principals, they are deliberately "taking a position," which means either that they are not matching customer's orders with contracts as soon as orders are received, or that they are using depositors' funds (some might say "the bank's money") and buying or selling either spot or forward one or more currencies so that they are either long or short in that currency. To this extent, they are like bulls or bears in stock markets.

Risks arise in two ways—either the exchange rate does not move in the way the dealer expected (market risk) or the counterparty fails to deliver because it is bankrupt (credit risk).[5] Fortunately the latter is rare, but when

---

[5]Very rarely, the counterparty might fail to deliver because of a force majeure, such as war, government intervention, the imposition of exchange controls, or the closure of markets.

it happens, as in the case of Bankhaus I. D. Herstatt, it is extremely disruptive. In order to appreciate the credit risk, it is vital to realize that, in a foreign exchange transaction involving, say, dollars and marks, the dollars must be delivered in New York and the marks must be delivered in Frankfurt. Since there is a time difference of six hours between these two cities, delivery of marks must take place in Frankfurt many hours before the counterparty can deliver in New York. Thus, typically one side has handed over his money before the other side has even got to work. In August 1974, Bankhaus I. D. Herstatt was closed down by the German regulatory authorities in the middle of a business day in Germany, causing substantial uncertainties. By the time New York banks opened for business, news of its closure had already been received there, and Chase Manhattan, Herstatt's principal clearing agent, held up all payment instructions that Herstatt had sent to Chase, many of which were dollar payments for marks purchased by Herstatt that it had already received earlier that day in Frankfurt. When this news reached the market, business stopped almost completely, and the major New York banks withheld all payments for over an hour until there were several phone calls at Chairman level, the panic died down somewhat, and payments were resumed (apart from the Herstatt account at Chase).[6] A point that should also be remembered is that, even if transactions take place in the same city on the same business day, the simultaneous exchange of settlements cannot take place because of the volume of payments. There is another reason, too—namely, that any bank will have "receives" (funds coming into its account) from which payments will be made that day, and if funds were held up for want of "receives," the whole system would come to a halt since working balances are always kept to a minimum.

In theory, foreign exchange is a zero-sum game with a myriad of players, some of whom are banks, some are Central Banks, and some are corporations. The alarming thought is that, since there are many large banks who derive substantial income from this source, there must be several losers among the smaller banks, but these things are seldom discussed. The next alarming thought is that in today's foreign exchange market the number of deals which are related to an underlying trade transaction is estimated to be fewer than 1 in 10. That means that 9 out of 10 trades are carried out between professional dealers for their own account. Without making a judgment as to whether this is speculation, one must at least say that foreign exchange trading income should never be treated by the analyst as repeatable (core income) from year to year. It is safest to expect breakeven when making a projection.

---

[6]It should be mentioned that the two major bank creditors ultimately recovered more than 90¢ on the dollar in relation to their claims against Herstatt.

WRITING THE ANALYSIS AND USING RATIOS

Ideally, two things should always take place: Banks should be analyzed in relation to a peer group, not individually, and the analyst or the credit officer should meet the management of the subject bank on a regular basis. If the ideal cannot be achieved, then at least one of these rules should be applied. In my judgment, the latter is the more important since ratios can be misleading, especially if the bank is in trouble and in a country where financial disclosure is at a low level. For instance, in 1981 a major commercial bank in Argentina, Banco Intercambio, was closed by the authorities: However, its most recent financial statements gave no clue as to the fundamental problems in the asset portfolio. Management remains the most important factor that a lender has to judge, and that can only be done by personal visits and by asking the right questions of both the subject bank and its peer group.

Below is a *recommended outline for bank analysis:*

Summary of analysis
Management
Asset structure
Liabilities
Equity
Earnings
Questions
Spread sheets

Management

An analysis must begin with an assessment of the quality of the bank's management. What is known about this bank's strategy? Is it expansionary or static? Is it defending market share? Does it innovate? What are its key business sectors? Is it a retail or a wholesale bank? What is its relationship with the Central Bank and the regulatory authorities? What is its overseas strategy? What is the degree of competition? What has been the continuity of management? Are there signs of one man rule? (See Chapter 8). Is this bank noted for contributing many talented people to other banks? Is there rapid management turnover?

Another important area for concern will be the decision-making and control process. Who makes credit decisions? How are they made? Can single individuals approve large sums? What is the internal control system like? How strong are the regulatory authorities? How often do they conduct in-depth audits? Is there a limit to loans to single borrowers, such as the U.S. legal lending limit?[7] How well is the foreign exchange function controlled?

---

[7]It is often a surprise to U.S. bankers to find that this does not exist in many countries.

Management can also be assessed by its choice of accounting policies. Are earnings on an accrual or a cash basis? What is the policy for recognizing loan losses? What influence does the external auditing firm have? Are secret reserves permissible? What is the estimate of their size? Are capital projects expensed, or are they capitalized and depreciated over several years?[8]

Finally, management's attitude to risk must be known. Often this is part of the bank's reputation in the marketplace. Innovative banks are risk takers, but in commercial lending, risks should be assessed. Not all innovative banks are risk takers in this sense in that their innovations may be in noncredit areas such as telecommunications or the marketing of personal financial services. Dangerous signs of management's attitude to risk would be a large concentration of assets in one business sector, unduly large foreign exchange positions or activity in relation to certain currencies, or overreliance on purchased money, as opposed to core deposits, as a basis for expansion. Anyone can lend money in order to expand a bank's asset base, but ensuring an equal growth of retail credit balances through the confidence of depositors is extremely difficult. Generally, overrapid growth is a cause for concern, especially when it is "lending-led" expansion.

For the best financial indicator of management quality, look to the stock market's evaluation of the bank's share price.

Asset Structure

Information is usually inadequate for a wholly satisfactory analysis based on published figures, but an attempt should be made along the following lines:

1. Liquid assets using the liquid assets/deposits ratio.
2. Loan portfolio by regional or industrial sectors. Changes in loan portfolio on a year-to-year basis—for example, an expansion into real estate loans, international loans, or whatever. Is this strategic or just fashionable?
3. Loan loss experience. What was the loan loss coverage ratio (if available). That is, how many times did pretax income cover the year's loan loss provision?
4. The Bond portfolio. How much is above or below book value? How much of it is government bonds that a bank may be obliged to hold (that is, effectively illiquid?)
5. Maturity structure of the assets. Are there any signs of serious mismatching by borrowing short and lending long?

Ratios to use here include:

---

[8]Bearing in mind the cost of large computer projects, this can be very significant.

Exhibit 10.1   Bank Income Statement Spread Sheet

Interest Income	$100,000
Less Interest Expense	(70,000)
Equals Net Interest Income	30,000
Other Revenues (Fees and Commissions)	3,000
Provision for Loan Losses	(2,000)
Overhead	(19,000)
Pretax Operating Income	12,000
Other Income/Expense	1,000
Income Taxes	(6,500)
Net Income	6,500

Notes: Other Income/Expense should include transfer to general reserves, income from associates, depreciation, and other subjectively determined items. Overhead includes any operating expense but will mostly consist of personnel expenses. Since personnel expenses typically account for more than 80% of all expenses, a useful measure of efficiency to calculate will be profit per employee (that is, Pretax Operating Income divided by number of employees).

Income Taxes may be struck after deductions for various inner reserves, depending on local tax authorities.

Net Interest Income/Average Earnings Assets.   Average earnings assets means loans plus Treasury assets—that is, loans, bonds, marketable securities, but not cash or reserve requirements. This ratio is the spread on the portfolio, and changes can be explained in relation to the causes listed earlier, in the section on interest income.

Loans/Core Deposits.   All deposits that are placed by consumers and commercial customers, including demand, time, and savings deposits, are compared with loans. This ratio will usually increase as a bank becomes more involved internationlly and/or pushed for increased profit from asset growth. A decrease will need explanation, since it may indicate a cutback because of loan problems or a strategic shift to nonlending income, such as trading income or underwriting.

Liabilities

Experience has shown that liability management in banks is as important as asset management. One reason is that a run on the bank is always a technical possibility, and another is that successful funding techniques contribute substantially to profitability.

The following questions are suggested for assessing liability management:

What is happening to core deposits? Is there a trend towards a declining proportion of interest-free balances?

Exhibit 10.2   Bank Balance Sheet Spread Sheet

Assets

Cash and Equivalents	$ 8	Includes balances at Central Bank, and nostro accounts.
Treasury Assets	22	Interbank deposits, bonds, marketable securities.
Loans	65	Split between short- and long-term if possible.
Other Assets	5	Fixed assets, associates, and all nonbanking assets.
Total Assets	100	

Liabilities

Core Deposits	70	Customer deposits.
Money Market Borrowings	19	Noncustomer deposits, including certificate of deposit and foreign currency deposits.
Other Liabilities	2	Accruals, and so on.
Loan Loss Reserves	1	Reserves against loans other than those included in other reserves.
Other Reserves	2	All reserves that were created by tax-deductible expense.
Equity Capital	6	
Total Capital and Liabilities	100	
Contingent Liabilities	9	

What is the net position in the interbank market? Do placements with other banks exceed funds received from them?

What use is made of Central Bank lines?

What is the matching or mismatching as to foreign exchange?

What, if any, long-term debt exists? On what terms? If subordinated, who holds it?

Is the bank vulnerable to any sudden change of circumstances—for example, a change in government regulation of competition through interest rate ceilings on deposits?

Equity

The subject of equity always involves a discussion of capital adequacy. One can do no better than to begin this discussion with a quotation about the purpose of equity from a Bank of England paper:

> The following have been identified as the two most important objectives of capital ratios:
> (i) to ensure that the capital position of an institution is regarded as acceptable by its depositors and other creditors; and

Exhibit 10.3   Calculation of Capital Base and Free Resources

Share capital

Plus

Loan capital which is fully subordinated to other creditors (including depositors) which has a minimum initial term of five years and up to a maximum of one-third of the total capital base net of outstanding goodwill and to straight-line amortization in the last five years of life.

Plus

Minority interests

Plus

Reserves

Plus

Provisions (general bad debt provisions)

Equals

Capital base

Less

Goodwill

Less

Investments in subsidiaries, associated companies and trade investments

Less

Premises and other fixed assets

Equals

Free resources

Notes: Not included are specific bad debt provisions for current or deferred tax.

(ii)   to test the adequacy of capital in relation to the risk of losses which may be sustained.

The first objective makes it desirable that one of the measures of capital to be employed by the Bank should be constructed of elements as far as possible available to the public. Depositors and other creditors have to form judgments about the capital adequacy of an institution using published information, and their reaction to these judgments will have an important bearing on the stability of each institution. The second objective requires information, an important part of which is likely to be available only to the supervisory authority and the institution itself. And the more sophisticated the testing mechanism, the less likely it is that the information will be available to the public in the necessary detail.[9]

[9]*The Measurement of Capital.* Published by the Bank of England, September 1980, with quotations reprinted and table reproduced with the permission of the Bank of England.

Exhibit 10.4   Classification of Assets and Risk Weights Held by U.K. Offices of Reporting Banks

(i)	Nil weight	Bank of England notes and UK coin Other sterling notes Balances with Bank of England Special deposits with Bank of England Debits in course of collection on banks in the United Kingdom Balances with overseas offices of the reporting bank Lending under special schemes for exports and shipbuilding Certificates of tax deposit Items in suspense Refinanced lending at fixed rates Gold physically held in own vaults Gold held elsewhere on an allocated basis
(ii)	0.1 weight	Foreign currency notes and coin UK and Northern Ireland Treasury bills
(iii)	0.2 weight	Debit items in course of collection on overseas banks Market loans with listed banks, discount market, etc. Market loans to UK local authorities and public corporations Balances with banks overseas with a maximum term of up to one year (including claims in gold) Bills other than UK and Northern Ireland Treasury bills Other loans and advances to Northern Ireland Government, UK local authorities, public corporations and other public sector British government stocks with up to eighteen months to final maturity Acceptances drawn by UK and overseas banks and UK public sector Claims in gold on UK banks and members of the London Gold Market
(iv)	0.5 weight	British government stocks with over eighteen months to final maturity Northern Ireland government stocks UK local authority and other public sector stocks and bonds Acceptances drawn by other UK and overseas residents Guarantees and other contingent liabilities
(v)	1.0 weight	Market loans placed with other UK residents Other loans and advances, net of specific provisions for bad debts, but excluding connected lending

(v)	1.0 weight	Assets leased to customers
		Working capital provided for overseas offices of the reporting bank, both in the form of deposits and in other forms
		Balances with banks overseas with a term of one year or over (including claims in gold)
		Claims in gold on non-banks
		Aggregate foreign currency position (to be defined in the Bank's paper on 'Foreign Currency Exposure')
		Other assets 'other', e.g. silver, commodities and other goods beneficially owned by the reporting bank
		Other quoted investments, not connected
(vi)	1.5 weight	Connected lending (to be looked at case by case and to exclude market-type lending where this can be separately identified)
		Unquoted investments (subject to case-by-case treatment)
(vii)	2.0 weight	Property (includes all land and premises beneficially owned by the reporting bank)
Items to be deducted from capital		Plant and equipment
		Intangible assets
		Investments in subsidiary and associated companies and trade investments

Source: The Measurement of Capital. Published by the Bank of England, September 1980, with table reproduced with the permission of the Bank of England. This table is in fact relevant in practice only to assets held by the U.K. offices of banks reporting to the Bank of England.

The paper goes on to propose two methods of assessing the adequacy of capital—a free resources ratio and a "gearing" ratio, based on risk assets. The first broadly relates current liabilities to capital resources, adjusted to exclude that part of the capital thought to be locked into infrastructure and other nonbanking assets. The second attempts to relate the risk of losses which are inherent in the assets of the business to the capital which is available to finance such losses. The free resources ratio is defined as Capital Base, minus certain deductions for fixed assets, divided by all other noncapital liabilities, including acceptances (see Exhibit 10.3).

As implied in its name, the free resources ratio shows the bank's own capital funds that are not tied up in fixed assets and are available in semiliquid form as a cushion against losses, or taking another point of view, as assurances to depositors that the bank's owners are more than covering all the long-term requirements of doing business. This liquidity aspect is conceptually the same as working capital in a manufacturing company and can be compared to the risk assets to see by how much these could contract in value before public noncapital liabilities are not fully covered.[10]

The risk measure developed in the same paper is also interesting in that it became apparent to the Bank of England that a highly detailed differentiation between degrees of risk attaching to various categories of assets was appropriate, since the limitation to the three broad classes of risk (credit risk, investment risk, and forced sale risk) was not refined enough. More risky assets, it is argued, require more capital—a fundamentally sound approach. The Capital Base—as defined earlier but modified in that premises are not deducted, because they have perceived salability—is then compared to an adjusted total of risk assets, as shown in summarized form in Exhibit 10.4. This calculation represents only the first step in the assessment of Capital adequacy by this method. Final assessment will take into account the particular circumstances of each institution."[11]

Analysts working with the published figures of commercial banks may not always have this degree of detail, but the two capital ratios certainly represent useful guidelines in assessing the adequacy of capital. So what is the right number for capital adequacy? What are the ratios which are acceptable to the Bank of England? Since this Central Bank not only supervises the U.K. banks but also keeps a watchful eye on another 250 banks from overseas who have offices in London, it would be nice to know what their experience is. Naturally, however, there is no magic number, and even if there were, publishing it would be foolish. "The Bank remains of the view that to publish such numbers would allow insufficient flexibility to take account of the different circumstances of particular banks."[12] The final word on the subject belongs to Citicorp Chairman Walter B. Wriston: "You have capital adequacy when you give the marketplace of your area or your country or the world confidence that their needs will be met with enough margin for error to take care of the mistakes that we're all going to make."[13]

Earnings

Although we have already said a lot about how banks make profits, three more risks need to be mentioned briefly. The first is losses from inefficiencies, interest penalties, and compensation for error. The second is the risk of fraud—namely, losses arising from malfeasance or dishonesty of staff or

[10]Some analysts are required to reduce owner's equity by any known figure by which the market value of the bond portfolio is below the book value.

[11]*The Measurement of Capital.* Published by the Bank of England, September 1980, with quotations reprinted with the permission of the Bank of England.

[12]*The Measurement of Capital.* Published by the Bank of England, September 1980, with quotations reprinted with the permission of the Bank of England.

[13]A.B.A. Correspondent Banking Conference, November 1976.

customers. The third is the fudiciary risk—namely, losses arising from the improper discharge of fudiciary responsibilities.[14]

Earnings need to be analyzed to see how they have been achieved. Here ratios are indeed important. The chief measures of profitability are return on assets (net income/average total assets), which combined with the degree of leverage produces return on equity (net income/capital funds), which as has already been discussed is the most important long-term ratio for any business enterprise.

As analysts, you should be concerned with how stable, how reliable, and how good income is relative to other comparable banks. You should also seek to explain changes in net interest income, operating expense, tax expense and non-asset-based revenues, so as to obtain an overall picture of why these changes happened. In particular, what happened to loan loss experience? What was the economy of that region or country doing? The strongest banks are not always those who make the most money in good times; they are those who are most able to weather the storms and survive. Steady growth in earnings is much more useful than rapid expansion achieved at the expense of profits.

COMPARATIVE ANALYSIS

As was said earlier, banks must be compared to others of the same type in the same country. There will be structural differences, of course, between government-owned banks, regional banks, and investment banks. Table 10.1 gives examples of what is meant. Good analysis should spot where a bank is significantly different from its peer group and seek an explanation of this. A good case for examination is the different French banks.

PROBLEMS

1. Read the case "What Really Went Wrong at Franklin National" in the case study appendix at the end of the book. What types of risk did management undertake? What evidence is there for supporting the Argenti theory of corporate collapse? On what terms would another bank be willing to buy the bank as of October 1974?
2. The managers of the international division of a major bank are trying to determine the lowest average spread on the loan portfolio which is acceptable to them. They know that the target return on equity for the

---

[14]The best example in recent years was the experience of the Credit Suisse at Chiasso where losses (which were easily absorbed by such a strong parent) are believed to have exceeded $250 million.

Table 10.1 A Comparative Table of Bank Ratios for 1980

Bank	Loans/ Deposits	Quick Assets/ Deposits	Loans Divided by Equity	Equity/ Assets	Return on Equity	Return on Assets
French Banks						
Banque Nationale de Paris	77.5%	29.05%	21.28	3.38%	20.42%	0.75%
Credit Lyonnais	47.21	56.17	33.38	1.23	12.25	0.16
Societe Generale	47.36	51.35	20.32	2.0	10.52	0.22
Credit Commercial de France	54.92	47.81	18.88	2.51	12.16	0.32
Credit Agricole	139.09	26.49	11.98	6.13	NA	NA
Credit Industrial et Commercial	59.48	38.63	18.97	2.65	15.92	0.39
Banque de L'Indochine et de Suez	49.14	53.47	22.09	1.89	6.73	0.13
Banque de Paris et des Pays-Bas	59.61	40.99	27.65	1.95	11.18	0.24
Average	66.78	43.0	21.82	2.71	12.74	0.31

British Banks					
Barclays	62.76	41.49	9.58	5.64	18.87	1.10
Lloyds	75.81	27.72	18.99	3.73	10.78	0.39
Midland	74.39	29.61	12.33	5.45	12.97	0.75
National Westminster	76.28	27.50	13.24	5.31	18.65	1.0
Average	72.31	31.65	13.53	5.03	15.31	0.81
Italian Banks						
Banco di Roma	44.0	44.21	24.25	1.63	18.14	0.31
Banco Commerciale Italiana	38.0	51.98	20.81	1.61	26.81	0.46
Credito Italiano	32.0	52.15	14.73	1.95	32.57	0.62
Banco Nazionale	30.0	61.58	17.22	1.53	27.6	0.45
Average	36.0	52.48	19.25	1.68	26.28	0.46
U.S. Average	71.0	37.0	21.05	3.8	14.0	0.50

bank is 16% before tax and equity is 5% of total assets. Loans average
70% of total assets, while the remaining 30% of assets normally earn
0.25% above the cost of funds. Remember that loan losses decline with
the equity of the loan, and it is argued that one must accordingly accept
lower spreads. In the past, loan losses have averaged 0.65% of loans,
and the division has had to provide for this out of its own operating
income.

   a.   Ignoring this operating expense, what is the required average spread
        on loans?
   b.   If the average spread can be determined, can there be a minimum
        spread consistent with this average? If so, how would it be deter-
        mined?

3.   A bank's annual statement indicates that it is moving from the historic
     method of treating loan loss expense as being the actual amount written
     off annually, to charging off as an expense an amount equal to the five-
     year moving average of the loan losses actually experienced. The ar-
     gument put forward is that, since loan losses fluctuate with economic
     activity, but the loans that give rise to them have a life of more than
     one year, a five-year average will give a more appropriate picture in that
     it will eliminate sharp fluctuations.
     You know that the bank has expanded rapidly in recent years. Loan
     loss expense is not disclosed separately. What could be another expla-
     nation for the change in accounting policy? What would be its effect on
     an expanding bank?
4.   Interest rates have fallen sharply in the past 12 months, yet Bank of
     Surrey's return on assets ratio has increased. What could be the expla-
     nation? Bank of Surrey is a middle-sized domestic retail bank.
5.   A European bank is reviewing its foreign exchange limits and its interbank
     deposit limits with a series of very large U.S. commercial banks who
     are many times the capital size of this bank. This bank is an extensive
     placer of dollar funds in the interbank market because of a shortage of
     suitable domestic loan opportunities, a reluctance to participate in me-
     dium-term syndicated international loans, and an abundance of dollar
     deposits. What sort of limits are appropriate? How would you reconcile
     these limits with the size of this bank's capital?
6.   The senior credit committee of a major domestic European bank with
     little international involvement asks you to prepare an explanation of
     the risks attached to lending to less developed countries (LDCs) through
     sovereign risk credits (that is, loans directly to governments or govern-
     ment agencies). The committee is particularly concerned with reports
     that major U.S. banks have very large sums at risk in these types of
     loans. What is your explanation?

7. A commercial bank in a developing country in Asia is known to have excellent relations with the government of that country and accordingly derives a lot of business from this relationship. You will shortly be visiting this bank at its head office. What anxieties will you want to dispel?

8. You believe that the published financial statement of a certain group of foreign banks are quite unreliable owing to the accounting conventions of that country. There are only four principal commercial banks there, and they all need your bank's assistance with credit lines to expand the financing of trade with your country. You have the occasion to meet at lunch the Director of Bank Supervision at the Central Bank. What questions would you ask him?

APPENDIX A: FINANCE COMPANY ANALYSIS

Finance companies are usually much easier to assess than banks in that the risks which they undertake are fewer and their revenue sources are much less diversified. For instance, they do not have much fee income, other than loan origination fees, and they seldom have income from trading securities or foreign exchange. On the other hand, they have more fixed-rate assets and higher operating leverage than banks. Like banks, however, finance companies lose money sometimes, and before you can understand them, you should appreciate the nature of their risk taking. Several different factors may lead to the failure of a finance company. These include overly aggressive expansion; use of too liberal a method of revenue recognition with insufficient reserves for losses; disguised asset deterioration; borrowing short and lending long; relaxed credit and security standards; and the replacement of sound credit investigation with undue confidence in guarantees and repurchase agreements. Lenders can protect themselves against such dangers by acquiring detailed continuous knowledge of the borrower's management, operations, and portfolio. This appendix addresses mainly the analysis of a finance company's financial statements, an approach which may be classified into three sections: the asset portfolio, the capital structure, and the income statement. Comparative analysis should highlight ratios where the company being analyzed differs from its competitors, and such differences should be explained.

ASSET PORTFOLIO

A finance company, by its nature, has a heavy debt position, usually comprised of several types of liabilities which differ in maturity, source, and seniority. Bank loans to a finance company are generally repaid from the proceeds either of an advance from another lender or from a new investment. Ultimately, however, the lender must look to the finance company's receivable portfolio as the source of loan repayment. The quality of this portfolio will, to a great extent, govern the willingness of another lender to enter the credit. In other cases, the lenders are looking directly to the liquidation or sale of the portfolio for their repayment. In the light of this, finance company analysts generally adopt a liquidation approach by which the protection afforded to the senior creditors can be assessed.

Factors to consider in evaluating the quality of receivables are discussed below.

Type of Finance Company

While differences exist between individual companies, each operation will normally fall into one of four distinct groupings—consumer finance, sales finance, commercial finance or "captive" finance.

Consumer finance companies are engaged primarily in the making of cash loans to individuals for a variety of purposes, such as the payment of medical bills, education expenditures, or travel costs.

Sales finance companies finance the installment sales of cars and household appliances.

Commercial finance companies supply additional working funds to all types of businesses in amounts that would not normally be available on an unsecured basis from other sources because of the borrower's existing high gearing levels. Advances are usually fully secured by varying types of collateral, often in the form of an assignment of accounts receivable or a mortgage on owned machinery.

Captive finance companies are so called because of their 100% ownership by a company identified with something other than the finance business. Captives are ostensibly organized for the purpose of providing supplementary financing facilities as a selling aid to distributors, dealers, and end-users of the parent company's products. Because company philosophies differ, even those captive companies operating in similar product fields are often quite dissimilar in their operations. For this reason, each company must be considered individually in the light of its particular area of operation, the product being financed, the terms being extended in relation to those prevailing in the finance industry on similar products, the position of the parent company (both financially and in its industry), and the basic operating philosophy of the company involved.

Management

Since the portfolio of a finance company is inherently composed of paper of varying but relatively short maturities, it is volatile and can shift character rapidly. For this reason, it is necessary to ensure first of all that management is honest and capable. This can be done only through personal contact between lending officer and customer, supplemented by confidence in the independent auditor's opinion regarding internal controls, standards, and accounting policies.

Internal Controls

The analyst should identify the customer to whom the finance company lends, the relative proportions of loan types (for example, whether the company is diversifying into new lending areas), the terms on which the loans are made, the amount of the advance in relation to the assets being financed, and the security arrangements, if any. The finance company's internal credit checks on its debtors, both prior to and during the transactions, should be discussed in detail.

Aging of Receivables

When does a receivable become past due or delinquent? What action is taken? When is a loan written off against reserves? What are the recoveries of loans written off? A chart should be produced for at least two years to show how much (both as a figure and a percentage) of total gross finance receivables are current, one month in arrears, two months in arrears, and so forth.

Are any receivables rewritten for any reason? (It is possible to disguise asset deterioration by rewriting so as to make overdue receivables current.) It is sometimes possible to detect this if the company is prepared to tell the analyst the average life to maturity of its receivables. This given figure can be checked against the following formula:

1. Add business written during year to net finance receivables beginning balance; subtract net finance receivables ending balance. This gives the amount of net collections received during year.
2. Divide net collections into average net finance receivables (from beginning to ending balance sheets) and multiply by 12. This gives you the average liquidation period in months.

   If this average liquidation period is significantly lower than the given figure, it is a fair assumption that some receivables are being rewritten. This may be for marketing rather than credit reasons, but it should be noted either way.

Adequacy of Bad Debt Reserve The method of providing for bad debts should be explained, and a reconciliation of the debt reserve should be prepared, showing beginning balance, provision for the year, write-offs during the year, and ending balance. The reserve as a percentage of gross finance receivables should be compared with historical loss experience and with receivables past due.

CAPITAL STRUCTURE

A finance company, like a bank, is a permanent user of debt to support its assets. The composition of the individual company's portfolio, its size, maturity, and quality will determine the mix of debt as well as the amount of capital necessary to protect the lenders against loss. Assuming an adequate equity base, the structuring of debt between long term (senior and subordinated) and short term is a function of liquidity and financial flexibility. As a permanent borrower, a finance company should have a certain portion of its debt of a long-term nature. This ensures a steady source of funds to support the portfolio. For a new long-term lender, confidence can be gained if there are short-term lenders who also extend committed facilities to the finance company; they will be less inclined to withdraw their lines if the company strikes difficulty.

The maturities of debt and receivables should be compared to ensure that cash from receivables, plus unused available lines, is sufficient to cover debt maturity. Long-range financial strength and liquidity depends on an adequate capital base, capable of absorbing losses with enough margin to enable the company to attract additional debt, if necessary. Even if a finance company has a portfolio of high quality, lack of liquidity and capital adequacy can result in failure.

INCOME STATEMENT

Revenue Recognition

Many finance company loans are made on a discount or "add-on" basis, which gives rise to a large amount of deferred income. How this is taken into the profit and loss accounts during a given period will materially affect stated profitability. There are a number of methods of allocating deferred or unearned income. For instance, all of it can be taken in the first year. Or each year, an equal amount or an amount equal to an "interest equivalent" charge based on the size of the loan still remaining can be taken. The method used should be identified, and its effects on profitability discussed.

Interest Rate Sensitivity

For a finance company, interest expense is effectively its cost of goods sold. Unless the company is able to alter the interest rate it charges to customers at will or it is borrowing money at a fixed rate, it faces the risk of paying more interest on its debt than it receives on its existing loans. The risk of this situation leading to losses should be analyzed, and the company's protection should be discussed. The buffer to prevent a finance company from sustaining a loss as a result of a sudden rise in its borrowing costs can be identified from its earnings before interest and taxes/average capital employed percentage. This will reveal the maximum interest rate which can be applied to the company's borrowings before a loss is sustained. The finance company's ability to raise its interest charges on future transactions to reflect an increase in its own borrowing costs should be discussed.

Operating Performance

Trends in the finance company's operating performance should be analyzed in the light of previous years and of the results of similar companies (where available). Explanations of year-to-year changes are needed.

APPENDIX B

SUGGESTED OUTLINE FOR ANALYSIS TEXT

Exhibit 10.5 Format for Finance Company Analysis

A. Company Background
1. Location, size, type of company
2. Bank facility (amount, source, repayment)
3. Comment on management

B. Volume Analysis
1. Shifts and trends
   a. Average loan size
   b. Average term
   c. Type (by collateral)

C. Portfolio Analysis
1. Delinquency
   a. How measured
   b. Trends and industry comparison
2. Loss experience
   a. Charge-off policy
   b. Trends and industry comparison
3. Comment on overall portfolio risk

D. Reserves
1. Loss reserve—adequacy versus portfolio risk
2. Deferred finance charge—comment on method of taking in income
3. Comment on adequacy

E. Leverage and Debt Structure
1. Leverage related to portfolio risk and reserve adequacy—trends and industry comparison
2. Short-term borrowings
   a. Comment on bank line usage
   b. Comment on commercial paper coverage
   c. Trends, adequacy of short-term facilities
   d. Results of bank checkings
3. Long-term debt (senior and subordinated)
   a. Comment on ability to service current maturities
   b. Comment on new debt plans
   c. Comment on adequacy and trends

F. Operating Statement
  1. Comment on significant results
  2. Comment on trends

G. Summary
  1. Conclusions
  2. Recommendation
  3. Loan risk classification

SUGGESTED PORTFOLIO RATIOS

Use this list as a guide, but do not limit yourself to the ratios suggested here. If you think further study is warranted in a given area, this attention should be given.

Direct Cash Loans

Volume
Liquidations
Cash liquidations
Gross outstandings
Percent loans to present borrowings, total
Percent old balances renewed/total
Percent number loans renewed less than 10% new cash
Percent delinquent (recency) total 60 days to 179
Percent delinquent (recency) 180 and over
Percent interest, charges, and partial payment
Percent net losses/average of outstandings
Percent recoveries/charge-offs
Percent deferred income/related receivables

Retail Installment Notes

Volume
Liquidations
Cash liquidations
Gross outstanding
Percent advances over 100% dealer cost
Percent account 61 days past due (contractual)

Percent net losses/average outstandings
Percent recoveries/charge-offs
Percent deferred income/related receivables

Wholesale Notes

Percent Volume
Gross outstanding
Percent wholesale volume/related retail volume
Percent net losses to average outstanding
Percent receivables outstanding over six months

Accounts Receivable, Inventory, and Plant and Equipment

Dollar volume
Net outstanding
Name of accounts exceeding 3% capital funds
Dollar amount of net losses
Percent net losses to average outstandings
Percent recoveries to charge-offs

Industrial Time Sales Receivables

Dollar volume
Gross outstanding
Average size of contract outstanding
Weighted average maturity of receivables in months
Percent 60 days past due

Lease Contract

Dollar volume
Gross outstanding
Average size of contract outstanding
Weighted average maturity of contracts in months
Percent accounts 60 days past due
Dollar net losses
Percent net losses to liquidations
Percent recoveries to charge-offs

Factored Receivables

Dollar volume
Gross outstanding
Due factored clients
Amount due from five largest debtors
Overadvances to factored clients
Percent invoices 60 days past due
Dollar net losses
Percent net losses to average outstanding
Percent recoveries to charge-offs

Rediscount Receivables

Dollar volume
Gross outstanding
Percent cash advance to gross collateral
Dollar net losses
Percent net losses to average outstanding
Percent recoveries to charge-offs

Charge Account Receivables

Dollar volume
Gross outstanding
Percent accounts past due (60 and 90 days)
Dollar net losses
Percent net losses to average outstanding
Percent recoveries to charge-offs

Commercial Finance—Total

Dollar volume
Gross outstanding
Number of accounts exceeding 3% capital funds
Percent 60 days past due (contractual), excluding Accounts Receivable & Rediscount
Dollar amount of net losses
Percent net loss to average outstanding
Percent recoveries/charge-offs

FINANCIAL HIGHLIGHTS

Loan Portfolio (000's Omitted)

	31 Dec X0	%	31 Dec X1	%
Total Direct Cash Loans[1]	$		$	
Total Retail Installment Loans				
Total Commercial Loans				
Other Finance Receivables				
Gross Receivables Less:	$	100%	$	100%
Reserve for Deferred Income				
Reserve for Losses				
Net Receivables				

Operating Ratios

Gross finance income/average net receivables
Provision for loss/average net receivables
Interest and debt expense/average total debt
Consolidated net income/average net worth

REMEMBER THIS!

The heart of a finance company analysis is the study of its receivable portfolio. This is the company's largest asset category by far and the ultimate source of repayment of your loan, together with those of all other senior and subordinated creditors.

[1]Use only appropriate captions for the company being studied.

11 How to Write a Credit Analysis

Vigorous writing is concise. A sentence should contain no unnec-essary words, a paragraph no unnecessary sentences, for the same reason that a drawing should have no unnecessary lines and a ma-chine no unnecessary parts. This requires not that the writer make all his sentences short, or that he avoid all detail and treat his subject only in outline, but that every word tell.

WILLIAM STRUNK, JR., AND E. B. WHITE
The Elements of Style

English is a difficult language, full of curious grammar, inconsistent usage, and strange pronunciation. Yet most people who speak English find that in everyday conversation they can make themselves easily understood. Of course, in speaking, there is more being communicated than just the words. There is gesture, tone of voice, body language, and so on. Speakers can also see the effect of their words on their audience and can recognize, if they so desire, a lack of comprehension or of belief. How much harder it is to *write* English well! Writers cannot see their audience, cannot respond to ques-tioners who interrupt, and have to rely entirely on the printed page to convey their messages.

In this chapter, we first set out some principles of good writing, especially as they apply to analyses, and second we provide a standard outline which should generally be followed when writing analyses. For those who want to know how to adopt an excellent style of writing in English, I strongly rec-ommend the little book from which the quotation at the head of this chapter is taken. It is a goldmine of information on rules of usage, principles of com-position, and, in a phrase, good style.

SIX RULES FOR GOOD ANALYSES

An analysis is a form of report. Some of the rules which follow apply to any kind of written report. In business writing, it is customary to use words and

199

phrases which are not flowery but factual. That does not mean that business writing has to be dull and unimaginative. In fact, the more dull it is, the less easily it will be understood, and the more quickly it will be forgotten. Although good communication is more of an art than a science, in its written form one can still demonstrate certain truths.[1]

Rule 1: Be an Analyst, Not a Copywriter

This is the most important rule in writing credit analyses. Analysts think about facts, are selective of those facts, then commit their thoughts to paper. These thoughts are opinions and facts that are relevant to the study of risk. Credit analysis is, after all, just that. Put another way, what the reader wants to know about a company is not what a commercial copywriter would write about it in describing its physical facilities or the social life of its top management. They want to know the company's strengths and weaknesses and how these affect the risk of repayment.

By contrast, copywriter's material that will be used for advertising or selling purposes, commonly called "blurbs," will be more detailed in describing company products, may be biased though not necessarily inaccurate, and will emphasize the product's value to the consumer in terms of need satisfaction. Also, if writers become too involved with the human interest aspects of a story, they are likely to stress matters which are not relevant to risk analysis.

Let's look at some examples. The corporate advertisement for NL Industries shown in Exhibit 11.1 may sound fine, but it is full of analytical weaknesses. The long-term outlook for the petroleum service industry is stated as being excellent *because* of a continuing need. But this is not necessarily true. We know from our study of industry and management that a continuing need is not a key factor in determining levels of profitability. There is, for instance, a continuing need for people to fly on airlines, yet look at that industry's problems. Second, the text says "vigorous cost reduction programs have saved millions a year"—an unquantified statement that would not be difficult to achieve in a company whose total costs run into billions a year. On this scale, $1 million is only one-thousandth of total costs of $1 billion. Not very impressive! Finally, we have no evidence as to whether net income in 1972 or in 1981 was at some level in line with the supposed trend. That is, if 1972 was a very poor year, and 1981 was very good, the claimed "average gain of 27% a year" may be statistically correct, but analytically misleading. One small clue to the company's performance is that in 1977 (was this year representative of the trend?) return on equity was 11.4%, not much of an improvement over 8.9% five years earlier. None of this criticism is intended to suggest that NL Industries is not a good com-

[1]Some of the examples used here are from Strunk and White's *The Elements of Style*. Others have been collected by the author.

HOW NL INDUSTRIES HAS CHANGED IN THE PAST SAYS A LOT ABOUT WHERE IT'S GOING IN THE FUTURE.

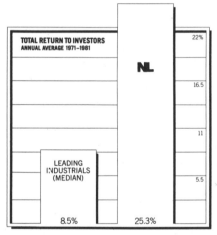

TOTAL RETURN TO INVESTORS
ANNUAL AVERAGE 1971-1981

NL

22%

16.5

11

LEADING
INDUSTRIALS
(MEDIAN)

5.5

8.5%   25.3%

There's a continuing need to find and develop new reserves of natural gas and oil. Which means the long term outlook for the petroleum service industry is excellent. And the outlook for NL Industries is even better.

Because back in the early 1970's our company began a major transformation. We invested $1.3 billion to become a leader in the petroleum service industry. At the same time, we successfully divested over 50 unrelated, low growth operations.

Today, NL Industries provides premium products and services for deep wells and hostile drilling environments. The number of these wells already is growing faster than industry averages. And as easy-to-reach reserves of oil and gas are depleted, the demand for our products and services can be expected to continue to outpace industry averages.

In the last 10 years, NL Industries' sales have grown from $1 billion to $2.5 billion. Vigorous cost reduction programs have saved millions a year and have contributed to our 740% increase in net income, an average gain of 27% a year. And return on shareholders' equity grew to 30.6% in 1981, over three times the rate just 10 years before. Total return to investors over the last 10 years

averaged 25.3% annually, making NL one of the decade's most rewarding equity investments.

At NL Industries, we've spent the last 10 years taking the long term view. And while the near term benefits have been outstanding, perhaps the greatest benefit is how we've positioned ourselves for the future.

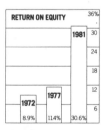

RETURN ON EQUITY

36%

1981   30

24

18

1977   12

1972

6

8.9%   11.4%   30.6%

NL

Petroleum Services
and Equipment Worldwide

NL Industries, Inc., 1230 Avenue of the Americas, New York, NY 10020

Exhibit 11.1   NL Industries Corporate Advertising

pany; what is demonstrated is that the statements in the text of the advertisement are analytically unsatisfactory.

The following two quotations are taken from the financial statements for 1980 of Teleflex, a U.S. corporation.

Statement A

The company's business is divided into two business segments: Technical Products and Commercial Products. The Technical Products and Services Segment includes the manufacture of precision mechanical and electro mechanical control equipment, anticorrosion coatings, fluid transfer systems, electrical/electronic interconnect systems, and the manufacture of a line of extended fluoroplastic products used in the aerospace chemical processing and medical industries. The company's Commercial Products segment involves the design and manufacture of Commercial controls, control system, hydraulics, instruments and other products having application in the automotive, marine, and other industries.

Statement B

Teleflex was founded to manufacture mechanical controls for aircraft. From this single market single product line the company has expanded over the years into an engineering company whose primary forte is problem solving through new technology. Market groupings are classified into two segments—Technical and Commercial. In the early '70s the mix of the business was slanted toward Commercial with attendant cyclical swings. The first energy crisis in 1973–75 intensified this cyclicality and the company's vulnerability. A new corporate plan was developed which would not only lessen our vulnerabilities but also allow us to significantly progress in a dramatically changing world economy.

Briefly stated the plan had its objectives:

Structuring a better balanced less cyclical company

Reducing our sensitivity to oil prices

Concentrating our investments in higher technology, higher return markets

Improving our profitability with a target of returning a minimum of 20% on average shareholders' equity.

To accomplish these objectives, sizeable investments were made in the last half of the decade in our operations which serve technical markets. As the '80s began, we included the automotive market in the investment program directed at the development of new applications on small fuel efficient cars.

Any credit analyst should know that Statement A tells the reader nothing about risk. In contrast, Statement B says a lot which is relevant. It says something about how and why the company is positioning itself in relation to its markets. It refers to capital expenditure, technology, and profitability, making clear the reasons why the company has done what it has done. It represents good material for risk analysis. Further reading of the full text of the Teleflex statements also discloses the company's marketing strategies, especially in relation to the difficult market which it was at that time experiencing in supplying controls to the aerospace industry.

Rule 2: Make the Figures Speak for Themselves

Analysis requires a lot of number crunching and ratios. The temptation is to present figures in quantity and leave the reader to judge which ones are relevant. That is a wrong approach. Make the figures speak for themselves, and be especially careful how they are presented. P. G. Moore in his excellent book *Reason by Numbers*[2] gives a good example, quoted here in full:

> The following information is extracted from the front page of the 1977 Annual Report of ITT. The data is clearly designed to give an overview of the company's activities and is not part of the legal accounts given later in the report. For this purpose the plethora of figures is rather overwhelming. Can they really measure sales to the nearest $500? Do you get much feel for the differences over the previous years?

Highlights	1977	1976
Sales and Revenues	$13,145,664,000	$11,795,244,000
Insurance & Finance Revenues	3,542,030,000	3,082,030,000
Income Before Extraordinary Items	562,294,000	492,380,000
Per common Equivalent Share	$4.14	$3.85
Etc.	etc.	etc.

> Would not an alternative presentation such as that shown below, be more revealing to the reader? (The abbreviation bn stands for billion or a thousand million.)

Highlights	1977	% Change Over 1976
Sales and Revenues	$13.1 bn	+11.4
Insurance & Finance Revenues	3.5 bn	+14.9
Total Revenues	16.7 bn	+12.2
Income Before Extraordinary Items	0.56 bn	+14.2
Per Commmon Equivalent Share	$ 4.14	+ 7.5

This shows first of all that the income/revenue percentage is about 3.5. Is this reasonable for such an industry? Secondly, the earnings per share have gone up between the two years by only about one half of the rate that revenue or net income has gone up. No doubt many shareholders will then want to examine the report to see if they can ascertain why; but I doubt, from the original table by itself, that the question would ever be asked.

Just how detailed should the numbers be in an analysis? This is easily answered: Keep to three figures! It is surprising how well this rule works. Consider the following pair of statements, which will also illustrate another rule:

[2]P. G. Moore, *Reason by Numbers* (London: Penguin Books, 1980).

Statement C   Income before taxes of $8,659 M (19X0 = $7,172 M) was after interest expense of $1,640 M ($1,220 M) and corporate expenses net of other income of $2,003 M ($1,435 M).

Statement D   Increases in interest expense (up 34.4% to $1.64 million) and corporate expenses net of other income (up 39.7% to $2 million) resulted in income before taxes rising only 20.9% to $8.66 million.

In Statement C we have greater detail but less interpretation. In Statement D we have less detail, but there is no doubt that it is more meaningful. Consider also the other difference which is apparent: In Statement C we have M as an abbreviation of thousand, and this goes with MM as an abbreviation for million. This can be very confusing, since in many instances M is also used for million. The other rule to which I referred earlier is that abbreviations should not be used unless their meaning is clear. The conclusion which follows from this is "Don't write M for thousand or for million—write in full which one you mean!"

While we are on the subject of presenting numerical information, let's consider also that aspect we have described as comparative analysis. Are the numbers for this company above or below what you would expect? Are they above or below an average for the industry? If sales grow at 25%, is that good or bad, taking account of inflation? Don't hesitate to use graphs where these will help convey the point dramatically. Graphs are especially useful when presenting time series data (see, for example, Exhibit 11.2).

Rule 3: Use Plain Words When You Can

A common error in business writing is using fancy language. Avoid the use of abstract words, verbs made up from nouns[3], long technical words based on Latin and Greek roots, and other jargon. Official announcements are often good examples of these errors. At a busy subway station in a big city, I recently heard the following come over the loud speaker system: "Would passengers about to board the train kindly allow arriving passengers to exit the train before attempting to board. Your cooperation is appreciated." Wouldn't it be easier to say, "Let them off first, please"?

H. W. Fowler in an early twentieth century text book, *The King's English*[4] laid down some simple rules for choosing words for good effect:

> Prefer the short word to the long
> Prefer the Saxon to the Romance [i.e., Latin or Greek]
> Prefer the familiar word to the farfetched
> Prefer the single word to the circumlocution
> Prefer the concrete word to the abstract.

---

[3]For instance, *moisturize* instead of *moisten*, or *prioritize* when what is meant is *set in order*.
[4]H. W. Fowler: *The King's English* (Oxford: Oxford University Press: 1906), p. 11.

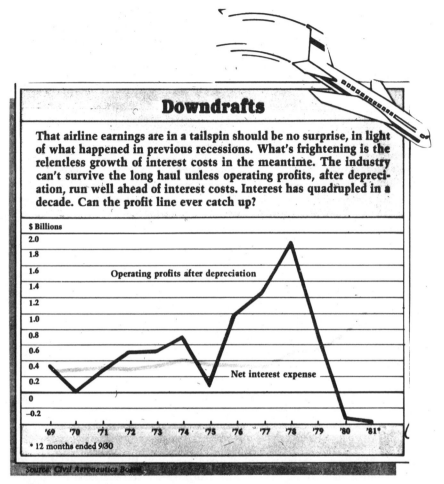

Downdrafts

That airline earnings are in a tailspin should be no surprise, in light of what happened in previous recessions. What's frightening is the relentless growth of interest costs in the meantime. The industry can't survive the long haul unless operating profits, after depreciation, run well ahead of interest costs. Interest has quadrupled in a decade. Can the profit line ever catch up?

$ Billions

Operating profits after depreciation

Net interest expense

* 12 months ended 9/30

Source: Civil Aeronautics Board

Exhibit 11.2 Example of a Time Series Graph. Reprinted by permission of *Forbes Magazine*, March 29, 1982 issue. Copyright Forbes, Inc., 1982.

He was unwittingly laying the foundation for what later has been described as "The Fog Factor." This is really the province of the next rule.

Rule 4: Omit Needless Words

Rule 4 is what Strunk and White were describing in the passage at the beginning of this chapter. Inexperienced analysts are convinced that they must write long and serious-sounding analyses. Some organizations are known to consider the importance of a report to be in direct relation to its weight—that is, the more pages it has, the better it must be. Do not be misled by such ideas! It is the quality of thinking which matters, not the quantity of words which are written. A good analysis must be selective, but it is much harder to write a short analysis than a long one, since being selective requires judgment. Wordiness has been measured by something called "The Fog Factor." To find your own Fog Factor, take a sample of your business writing. First, find the average number of words per sentence. Now count the number of words with three syllables or more (not including verbs ending in -ing or -ed). Add these two numbers and multiply by 0.4. The product is your Fog Factor. Readable prose has a Fog Factor of less than 12.

Next, consider the following pair of statements:

Statement E

The authors also show that in a multiple regression model consisting of ratios with common denominators no serious adverse effects on estimation are usually to be expected. Under a wide range of circumstances, the regression coefficients of the deflated variables will not be greatly biased when application is made to cross-sectional data.

Statement F

When an investigation is carried out in the presence of many disturbing factors, we find that there is no simple relation between the factors on which the experiment was based. We plot graphs on one thing against another and find that instead of the nice functional relationships so dear to the heart of the mathematician and the student at college, instead of nice straight lines and elegant looking curves, we get plum puddings, the points in our graph being scattered very much at random.[5]

On investigation we find that Statement E has a Fog Factor of 13.2 based on an average of 26 words per sentence with an average of 7 long words per sentence. Statement F, with a Fog Factor of 18.4, has longer sentences (average 42 words) but many fewer long words (only 4 per sentence). Both statements are from textbooks on statistics. If you find F is easier to understand than E, it may be because the author of F avoids jargon.

Rule 5: Present the Summary and Conclusion First

Don't forget, the reader wants to know what your decision is: Do you recommend the proposal or don't you? If you leave that question to the end of the analysis, you may have a more logical order, but your reader will skip to the end anyway before reading the main text. It makes sense, therefore, to state your summary and conclusion at the start of the analysis. Of course, that does not mean that you actually write this part first! You should have an open mind as you work, making your conclusion only after careful thought. As Napoleon is reported to have said in a somewhat different context, "It is not genius which reveals to me suddenly and secretly what I should do in circumstances unexpected by others; it is thought and meditation."

[5]M. J. Moroney: Facts from figures: London: Penguin Books, p. 276.

Rule 6: Following a Plan for the Structure

Make notes as you examine the evidence, whether working with financial statements or examining industry dynamics. Follow a plan for the main part of the analysis. Revise and rewrite something until you are happy with it. A basic structural design underlies every kind of writing, whether it is a letter or a sonnet. Skill lies in executing the design without spoiling the general pattern.

In the next section, I set out the basic plan for a standard form of credit analysis.

OUTLINE FOR A CREDIT ANALYSIS

Section I: Description, Purpose, and Source of Repayment of Proposed Facility

Each analysis should begin with a clear description of the proposed credit facility under consideration, with sufficient detail to identify (1) the borrower; (2) the type of credit facility (for example, a three-year revolving credit expiring December 31, 19X1, convertible into a four-year term loan amortizing in quarterly installments, with a 50% balloon payment on December 31, 19X5); and (3) the contemplated usage of the credit facility (for example, fund capital expenditures, support working capital, back up commercial paper, acquire XYZ Company). The anticipated source of repayment should be stated. This is good discipline in that analysts often forget that the purpose of the analysis is to identify risks affecting repayment. Further, you should sometimes indicate a fallback or second way out of the loan if the expected source of repayment does not come about.

Section II: Risk Analysis Summary and Recommendation, Risk Ratings

Here you should state the pros and cons of extending credit and evaluate the credit risks sufficiently to justify the credit decision. Some banks employ a borrower rating system to classify borrowers by expected risk category. For example, very strong companies are rated 1 and very weak companies 9, with others on a spectrum between these two points. If this method is used, then you should also state the rating in this section, with your reasons. It should be noted that the borrower rating reflects the credit worthiness of the borrower. Where applicable, a risk rating may be added to refer to the loan repayment risk when special circumstances, such as a guarantee, collateral, or loan structure, may warrant a rating (either better or worse) other than the rating assigned to the borrower. For instance, a weak subsidiary of a strong parent, where the parent guarantee is relied on for the subsidiary's debt, will have a low borrower rating but a better risk rating. Reasons for either a recommended upgrading or downgrading of ratings must be explained. The risk summary will simply be a short description of the principal risks which the company faces. Each risk should be matched with whatever action has been taken to reduce the risk.

Section III: Sources of Information

This section should detail and give background information on your sources of information:

Indicate the type of financial statements which are being analyzed (consolidated, consolidating, consolidated excluding a finance subsidiary, parent company alone, or whatever) and the relationship, if appropriate, to other financial statements published by the company.

State whether the financial statements are audited or unaudited. If financial statements are not audited but prepared by an accountant or company official, a statement must be made as to your confidence in the accuracy of such financials.

If the accounting firm auditing the company's financial statements is not generally recognized to be a leading public accounting firm, a statement should be made as to the reputation and reliability of the auditors as determined from checks with local banks and others capable of assessing the objectivity and professionalism of the firm.

Any change in accountants should be noted with an explanation of the reasons for the change.

If the analysis relies on company and/or industry projections, the source of such projections should be identified, and a statement concerning their reliability should be included.

Section IV: Business and Industry

This section should provide a concise yet meaningful description of the company's business and the industry in which it operates, focusing on industry dynamics, competition, current movements and changes, and so on. Avoid purely descriptive remarks without conclusions attached. For example, do not say "This company has the largest bacon factory in Europe" unless you state whether this is a strength or a weakness and why. Discuss all significant risks related to the company's type of business and method of operation. How does this company compare with its competitors in market share, productivity, and other performance ratios? Why is it different?

Explain the key management skills in this industry. To what extent does the company have those skills? What are their vulnerable points? Think about worst-case situations: What would happen then to your loan? What is the company's strategy in relation to its industry? Does the strategy make sense? What is the nature of the industry? Is it expanding? Is it high risk? What are the barriers to entry? Is it buyer dominated? How do firms differentiate themselves?

If a company has a complex corporate structure, you should explain how this fits together and where the borrower belongs in the structure. If dealing with a subsidiary, explain whether this subsidiary is or is not a key element in its parent's strategy or chain of operations.

Discuss the impact which government action can have on the company. If this is a regulated industry, describe past, present, and projected regulations and their impact. If there are import or export restrictions, what effects are these causing? How long will they last?

Section V: Management

An in-depth discussion of management, including all key officers, should focus on their strengths and weaknesses (where known) and any particular areas of expertise, such as finance, production, marketing, sales, or research. Any appraisal of management should include an evaluation of past strategies as measured by such factors as historical financing and operating results, accuracy of projections, and performance within the industry. Consider the extent to which continuity of management is a strength or weaknesss. Is the organization structure appropriate? Consider the extent to which one-man rule may be apparent. Is it justified given the nature of the firm? Consider also the degree to which management owns the firm's equity. Is this a strength?

Section VI: Source and Application of Cash

A summary of the sources and uses of cash for the last three years should be presented in the following format:

	19X1	19X2	19X3	Three-year Total
Sources				
1. Funds from operations (Less net working assets required)	——	——	——	———
Cash from operations				
2. New long-term debt				
3. New short-term debt				
4. New equity or preferred stock	——	——	——	———
5. Sales of assets	——	——	——	———
Total	——	——	——	———

	19X1	19X2	19X3	Three-year Total
Uses				
1. Capital expenditure				
2. Long-term debt repaid				
3. Short-term debt repaid				
4. Dividends paid				
5. Other	____	____	____	_____
Total	____	____	____	_____
Increase (decrease) in cash	====	====	====	======

Notice that only the major items need be set forth, others may be consolidated and called "Other." On the other hand, too large a figure in "Other" suggests poor cash flow analysis.

Section VII: Interpretation and Analysis of Financial Information

This section represents the heart of the analysis, as the major financial factors are interpreted in the light of the credit risk. The written interpretation and analysis of financial information should reflect the understanding and resourcefulness of the writer. Trends are more important than single observations. Dynamic analysis is more important then static analysis. Financial information on spread sheets should not be repeated in this section except as a reference to an analytical statement. Although no specific format is prescribed, the following categories are offered as samples of relevant areas of analysis:

Operations.   The past and projected operating performance should be analyzed as to significant trends and the major factors causing these trends. Special emphasis should be placed on the quality of earnings; that is, does the company's earnings reflect true performance and a source of cashflow or merely unique accounting, extraordinary items, or other factors. Where a company has several lines of business, the contribution of each to the whole should be shown. The company's performance vis-à-vis other similar firms should be compared and explained.

Cashflow.   Past and projected cashflows should be analyzed in connection with expectations of future financial performance and ability to meet the cash requirements of the business. The company's capital expenditure program should be considered in the light of internal cashflow as well as the availability of external financing. The debt repayment schedule should be analyzed in view of existing and new debt and in relation to past and projected cashflow.

Financial Condition. This section should analyze changes in financial condition, working capital, and debt/equity ratios, and the reasons for such changes. The liquidity of the company should be noted. Special emphasis should be placed on the quality of current and fixed assets, with appropriate explanation of how the accounting principles affect recorded values. For instance, if LIFO is being used, is there a significant "inventory cushion"? Consider corporate structure, and contingent and other off-balance-sheet liabilities. The composition of liabilities and the relationship of the structure of liabilities to the company's assets and operations should be examined. Sometimes it will be appropriate to include in debt ratio calculations liabilities which are in fact off the balance sheet. A debt priority schedule may be included showing secured versus unsecured debt (see Exhibits 4.2 and 4.3) separated between parent and subsidiaries, indicating debt that ranks prior to your facility. The key question to answer is, "Is this borrower financially healthy?"

General. If you are lending to a holding company, company-alone analysis is essential in addition to the analysis of the consolidated entity. The analysis of significant financial factors should specifically focus on those factors that are unique to the company being analyzed. When examining a subsidiary, you must consider its relationship with the rest of the group.

Capital Markets. When the company is a quoted company, market capitalization should be compared with tangible net worth and appropriate comments made. The date of the last capital raising exercise should be noted. You should also comment on future access to the capital markets for equity and debt finance, as well as on whether any significantly large shareholding in the borrower is a strength or a weakness.

Section VIII: Related Analytical Areas

In addition to the standard analytical information presented in the preceding sections, the following categories of analysis should be included, as appropriate, along with other areas which may contribute to a meaningful analysis of the credit.

Indenture Reviews. This should include a statement of the margin of coverage on ratio covenants, interim loans, and any particular features that may have an impact on your decision to extend credit. Where subordinated debt is involved, the type of subordination should be described together with acceleration and other provisions.

Legal Commitments. A complete outline of proposed terms and covenants should be included as a separate attachment. The credit analysis should contain a review of the salient controlling financial covenants and an evaluation of the effectiveness of the covenants in relation to past performance and projected future performance.

SUMMARY

The best credit analyses are not the longest, but the most thoughtfully written. They follow a clear pattern. They focus on risk rather than general description. They place a company in the context of its industry. They identify both trends in markets and trends in the financial condition of the borrower. If done really well, they form a sound basis on which credit decisions can be made.

12 Eighteen Credit Principles

The preceding chapters have outlined the kind of information needed for credit analysis. Now it is time to make a decision. Just how are you going to make that decision? You can never know everything about a borrower, but even if you could, there would still be unknowns since repayment of a loan depends on what will happen in the future not what has happened in the past. All businesses exist to earn a return for taking risks. Banks are no different in this respect from other businesses, and like other businesses, banks are successful only as long as the risks they assume are reasonable and controlled within defined limits. Credit decisions are a matter of personal judgment, taken within the context of a lending organization's overall policy toward the balance between profitability and liquidity. Liquidity will decrease as loans become longer term or more risky in character, but at the same time, profitability should increase as liquidity decreases.

This is not the right place for discussing bank asset portfolio strategies, but all lending officers must be aware of what is or is not an acceptable degree of risk for their institutions. One goal of portfolio management is diversification of risk. Another goal must be adequate profitability. It is easy to see that the capital base which supports the asset portfolio must be earning a rate of return which is related to the riskiness of that portfolio. If the shareholders expect to earn 13% net of taxes and each dollar of capital supports $26 of assets, then the net-of-tax return on assets must be one-half of 1%. That is, to provide a net income after all expenses of 13¢ per share implies a net return of 0.5% on assets of $26. On the other hand, if because of the riskiness of the portfolio the expected return is increased to 18% net of taxes, and the asset portfolio is held at a constant level, the net return on assets will have to rise to 0.69%.

It is equally possible to see that, if loans earn an average 1.5% over the cost of funds and if 1.5% of the portfolio is uncollectible, then the net return from lending is zero. It follows, therefore, that there ought to be a relationship between the net margin on loans and their riskiness. Loans which are twice as risky as the average ought to produce twice the average margin. Competitive pressures, however, work against this, as does the difficulty of determining just how risky a loan is.

Let's return to making the credit decision, and look at some rules that have been found to be helpful in making these decisions. Remember that no loan is free of risk, and no bank would be able to continue in business if it never made risky loans. Of course at the time of the decision, if you decide not to approve a loan, be sure that the reasons are clear in your mind. The principles fall into two groups: The first 7 relate to the lenders; the second 11 relate to the borrower.

1. *Quality of credit is more important than exploiting new opportunities.* Put simply by a wise old banker, "Any fool can lend money, but it takes a lot of skill to get it back." Banks are not in the business of providing risk capital, because to do so they would have to pay depositors much higher rates to compensate for potential loss of their deposits. Remember that the bulk of the bank's resources are short-term deposits from people who trust the bank to keep their money safe. This kind of money is not the bank's for risky lending or even for equity type investments.

You cannot charge a high enough interest rate to compensate for loans that are likely never to be repaid. But in times of loan expansion, it is easy to seek to override this rule about credit quality. Such an attitude is just as dangerous as that of the businessman who is sales not profit oriented.

In analyzing the degree of risk which a bank will assume in a credit, careful consideration should be given to the borrower's management experience, capabilities, policies, profitability, cashflow, and net worth. As a lending officer, you must decide for yourself how much money the borrower should borrow, how long it will take before repayment is complete, and the true purpose of the loan.

2. *Every loan should have two ways out that are not related and exist from the beginning.* Obviously, the first way out will be successful completion of the transaction—for example, the sale of goods whose purchase has been financed by the bank, perhaps under an import–export arrangement. In a term loan, it will be the successful achievement of cashflows sufficient to repay the bank from the company's operations. The second way, in the event of failure of the project, will be action by the borrower either in realizing assets or in drawing on his resources, which would include raising debt by other means in other markets.

Lenders sometimes require borrowers to accept unrealistic constraints so that the loan does not break any of the lender's normal rules. If you need to do this in order to feel comfortable, you should question whether to make the loan at all.

3. *The character of the borrower—or in the case of corporations, the principal management and shareholders—must be free of any doubt as to their integrity.* If you have any questions as to the integrity, or honesty, or good intentions of the borrower, you should not approve the loan. You must, therefore, check on the moral standing and style of business before beginning negotiations. Remember that banks who associate with people of

less than acceptable character damage their own reputation far beyond the profit obtained on the transaction.

4. *If you do not understand the business, do not lend to it.*   Successful banks specify precisely their terms of lending for appropriately differentiated risk assets, and they take pains to understand the market sectors in which they engage. The head of a lending group will decide what types of borrowers are acceptable and what form of borrowing, amounts, periods, security, documentation, and so on. But more important, the group head will understand the risk and return features of each class of risk asset and, if necessary, employ specialists or adequately experienced personnel before undertaking the business. After all, if you do not understand the industry or the sector, how can you evaluate the risks? Furthermore, customers will have respect only for the banks which take the trouble to understand their position.

5. *It is your decision, and you must feel comfortable with it according to your own judgment.*   Credit decisions are personal. They cannot be made solely on the basis of guidelines or analytic techniques. Each lending officer must exercise common sense and good judgment. You must also be sure that it is your own independent judgment on each transaction and that you are not unduly influenced by your associates. Remember that your bank, as a respected member of society, must act responsibly in evaluating risks, in negotiating terms, in competitive positions, and in credit administration.

In a decentralized credit procedure, group heads and other lending officers continue to bear responsibility for credit within their areas. It is easy to forget in times of economic growth that the business cycle also has a downswing. During the 1980–1982 recession, the dangers of poor credit judgments shook many banks to their roots. These lessons must be borne in mind whatever the phase of the cycle. The cost of loan losses is not just the write-off of the bad debt, it is also the cost of using talented human resources to manage recovery situations. Our first principle could, in fact, be restated as follows: It takes a lot of good bankers' time to clear up the mess of one bad decision.

It is clear, then, that as a lending officer you must anticipate, not react to, situations. You must be comfortable with this decision because you will have to live with it.

6. *The purpose of a loan should contain the basis of its repayment.*   For a fuller understanding of this principle, you must look at a bank's distribution of assets in terms of liquidity. Some loans are short term; others extend to 7 or 10 years. Of course, the shorter the term is, the greater the liquidity. Short-term finance is typically of a seasonal nature to cover seasonal asset expansion where repayment arises from subsequent asset contraction. Loans to fund other assets of a noncurrent nature carry greater risk.

As liquidity diminishes, certainty of repayment is reduced because of the longer time horizon. For both lender and borrower, it is desirable to have a realistically defined program of repayment agreed on in writing at the time the loan is made.

In the case of commercial and industrial loans when lines of credit are extended for short-term working capital purposes, there must be evidence of seasonal or cyclical needs for this purpose, and of the regular conversion of receivables and inventories into cash. It is not generally appropriate for a bank to provide continuous short-term working capital through constantly used lines of credit, except for companies in a healthy condition. Of course, it is recognized that strong borrowers with clearly open access to the term debt and equity markets frequently use their banks as a bridge until the financing of their permanent capital requirements is achieved, but the lending officer must have regular evidence that access to such markets remains open. The same holds true of lines to support commercial paper where continued access to the market is a vital requirement.

7. *If you have all the facts, you do not need to be a genius to make the right decision.* Unlike the cat in the proverb, curiosity never killed a lending officer. It pays to know. The more questions you ask, the more you understand the case. Also, the more respect you will gain in the end from borrowers who prefer to deal with a lender who understands their industry. Facts are helpful and, properly organized, will often make the decision easy.

Now we come to the second group of credit principles, which are related more directly to the borrower, rather than to the lender.

8. *The business cycle is inevitable.* Simply stated like that, this does not seem to have much to do with credit. But as lenders, you must always be conscious of the current point in the business cycle so that you can evaluate the risks likely to arise when economic conditions change in the future. Things are always either getting better or getting worse, but sometimes the change is imperceptible. At certain points in the business cycle, lending appears less risky. It has been well said that bad loans are made in good times. Similarly, lending becomes more apparently dangerous in very bad economic conditions. In fact, banks that lend in bad times will, provided they have made a wise credit decision, gain permanent friends.

All the same, one must bear in mind that capital markets do open and close. In some economies, companies have to substitute bank term loans for public market debt simply because fixed rates are exorbitantly expensive. In these situations, banks will recognize a shift in the demand for funds and together will decide, as they have in recent years in the United Kingdom, that neither fixed-rate debt nor equity should be raised regardless of cost.

9. *Although it is harder than evaluating financial statements, assessing a company's management quality is vital.* Quality of management is displayed in many ways: the choice of an appropriate style for the industry (autocratic or democratic), the ease or difficulty with which senior positions can be filled from outside the company, the style of the company's offices, the way in which innovation is treated, the reputation among competition. There are, of course, many other ways in which it shows: Do senior executives have a flamboyant life-style? Are employees encouraged to own part

of the company? What are the feelings of frontline management? Asking questions of others in the industry will also help you assess a company's management quality.

If managers own the company or a major part, this may be in itself no comfort. They can bankrupt themselves just as easily as a professional management can bankrupt a company owned by holders.

10. *Collateral security is not a substitute for repayment.*

11. *Where security is taken, a professional and impartial view of its value and marketability must be obtained.* Repayment, as said before, comes from cashflow; security is taken partly to prevent these assets from being available to other lenders and partly to place the lender in a stronger negotiating position because the assets are usually necessary to operate the business. When security is valued, there must be no conflict of interest by the valuer. You must also be conscious of differences in market value, liquidation value, and forced sale value. Such differences can sometimes be recognized by insisting on margins: That is, loans must be covered by, say, 150% in collateral security, valued at current market prices.

12. *Lending to smaller borrowers is riskier than lending to larger ones.* Although the same principles apply to small firms as to large ones, in a small firm managerial resources are fewer. In large firms, there can be many decision makers, all running their own divisions or subsidiaries. In this way, there can be more jobs for good managers—and thus greater depth of management—than in a small firm, where there is greater dependence on the chief executive and his or her immediate subordinates.

On the other hand, smaller firms are better able to get commitment to company goals from their employees because there is a feeling of greater personal involvement by the work force in the success or failure of the firm.

In small firms, too, financial resources are more limited. In a private firm, access to new equity from shareholders is restricted. Similarly, both domestic and international capital markets require a minimum size of firm before access is possible either for debt or equity. Thus, size favors the large firm here.

13. *Do not let poor attention to detail and credit administration spoil an otherwise sound loan.* A high proportion of write-offs are associated with sloppy administration or documentation. Never assume that loan agreements will not be relied upon. As fate has it, it is just those that are prepared in a hurry that are most likely to be tested in court! In a recent case, only 3 lending banks out of 30 had structured their loans to a group of companies by careful choice of borrowing subsidiary and guarantors. As a result, these 3 are in a superior position to the other 27. When in doubt, ask for help from those more experienced.

14. *Local banks should be participants in lending to local borrowers.* It is often a danger sign if local banks are not lenders to local firms. They may already know too much about the risks of such a credit. In the same way, be cautious with those who seek to change to a new bank because they are dissatisfied with their present bank. New accounts, it has been said, go bad more often than old ones.

15. *If a borrower wants a quick answer, it is "No."* Anyone who rushes you into a lending decision should be told this principle. On the other hand, it pays to be prepared for requests from borrowers. Indeed, the best approach is to be sure that officers seeking new business check out their target companies with their superior officers before visiting the companies.

16. *If the loan is to be guaranteed, be sure that the guarantor's interest is served as well as the borrower's.* When a guarantor signs a guarantee and you are likely to have to depend on the guarantor for repayment, you should be very careful. You must also see to it that the guarantor knows his or her obligation. Guarantors should not sign if they are not in principle willing to lend the money to the borrower themselves, since they may one day in effect have to do just that.

17. *See where the bank's money is going to be spent.* If you do not visit the company, you will not get a feel for the atmosphere, corporate style, and other intangible effects. It often pays, especially with smaller companies, to check out what the management tells you.

18. *Think first for the bank. Risk increases when credit principles are violated.* Good judgment, experience, and common sense are the marks of the good banker. The principles set out here are not perfect but are broken at your peril. If in doubt, ask yourself: "Would I lend my own money?"

Appendix 1 Case Studies

CASE STUDY 1: KWAI LAM ELECTRONICS

In the spring of 1979, Harry Jackson, assistant vice president of Commercial Bank of California's (CBC) Taipei Branch, was considering a request from one of Taiwan's emerging growth companies for a credit line of $3 million. This company, Kwai Lam Electronics (KLE), had been a prospect for CBC Taipei for the past two years, but this opportunity represented the first real chance of doing business with them. KLE was the eighth largest member of the industry and was principally engaged in making color TVs and transistor radios.

ELECTRONICS INDUSTRY IN TAIWAN

The development of the electronics industry over the past decade has shown a rapid rise, as indicated both by increase in production as well as growth of exports. In 1977, the total annual production value of the electronic and electric appliance industry reached US$2.01 billion, increasing nearly 10 times over 1968. Exports jumped by almost 17 times during a similar period, rising from US$79 million to US$1.48 billion to account for 15.81% of Taiwan's total exports for 1977, next only to the textile industry. As the electronic and electric appliance industry continues to exhibit strong growth for the first half of 1978, it is expected that before 1981, when the current six-year economic plan is completed, the industry will replace the textile industry as the largest exporting industry. This is because the future of Taiwan's textile industry is gloomy because of problems of overcapacity, weak demand both at home and abroad, and growing competition from Southeast Asian countries, South Korea, and possibly the People's Republic of China. On the other hand, local industrialists maintain that the prospect of Taiwan's electronic and electric appliance industry is bright in spite of the import quota restriction on color TV exports imposed by the United States effective February 1, 1979. CBC Taipei's outstandings to 11 electronic and electric appliance manufacturers increased 59.7% from US$10.6 million as of January 1978 to US$16.9 million as of January 1979, representing 14.8% of the total loan portfolio as of January 1979, versus 7.4% as of January 1978.

It is anticipated that the loan demand will continue to increase from this industry mainly because total sales of CBC customers accounted for 22% (on an average) of total electronic and electric appliance sales on this island for the past three years, while their total exports accounted for only 9% (on an average) of Taiwan's exports over the same period. Consequently, it was thought that a study of the structure, the growth potential, and the future trends of this industry could enable CBC to formulate a marketing as well as risk strategy.

History

Since 1947 Taiwan has had the ability to produce electric fans and radios, although the quality of these products was not good. However, the first major progressive step was the establishment of the Taiwan Television Corp. in 1962, which started local assembly of TV. The establishment of Taiwan General Instrument Corp. in 1964 by the General Instrument Corp. of the United States has led an impressive and continuous inflow of foreign capital investment into Taiwan's electronic and electric appliance industry. With the abundant cheap and skilled labor force, and the favorable investment environment supported by the infrastructure—namely, transportation systems, communication channels, electric power, industrial complexes, and export processing zones—the electronic and electric appliance industry in Taiwan has made tremendous progress and become the fastest growing industry in Taiwan during the past decade. The Japanese yen's appreciation of 32% over the past 12 months and a high rate of domestic price inflation in South Korea has prompted the foreign buyers to switch their purchase from Japan and South Korea to Taiwan. As a result, the pace of growth of the Taiwan electronic and electric appliance industry has accelerated.

In the late 1970's, there were 1,160 firms engaged in the manufacture of electronic and electric appliance products, of which 858 were owned by local investors, 50 exclusively by foreign investors (mainly U.S. companies), with the remaining 252 being joint ventures. Although the number of foreign firms and joint ventures is far less than that of local firms, the role of these firms in the development of Taiwan's electronic and electric appliance industry is significant—mainly in terms of production scale and the quality of their products. Over 60% of total industry sales is contributed by only 25 companies (see Exhibit A1.1).

Electronic Appliances

The electronic products made in Taiwan include video and audio products, and are mainly televisions (both black and white and color), digital watches, electronic calculators, telephones and switchboards, transistor radios, and sound systems. A brief review of past supply and demand as well as the prospects for television production is given below, followed by a brief discussion of the other major sectors of the industry.

Exhibit A1.1 Industry Figures

In terms of 1977 sales, the leading companies in Taiwan in electronic
and electric appliances were (figures in US $ Millions):

1.	Tatung*	200.2
2.	Matsushita Electric (Taiwan)	108.3
3.	Sampo*	106.6
4.	RCA Taiwan*	101.1
5.	Sanyo Electric Taiwan	88.8
6.	Texas Instrument Taiwan	65.3
7.	Admiral Overseas Corp.	55.0
8.	Kwai Lam Electronics	50.3
9.	TECO Electric*	50.0
10.	Capetronic (Taiwan)	45.2

*CBC Taipei has relationships with those marked with an asterisk.

Note. The top 25 companies account for 64% of the total industry sales.

Exhibit A1.2 Summarized Financial Statements, Kwai Lam Electronics, 1978 (in NT $ million)

	1976	1977	1978
Cash	12	2	10
Receivables	462	504	880
Inventory	796	890	1,247
Advances to Suppliers	60	60	170
Other Current Assets	42	50	55
Total Current Assets	1,372	1,506	2,362
Net Fixed Assets	446	506	642
Investments			
Other Assets	34	46	50
Total Assets	1,852	2,058	3,054
Bank Debt	720	790	1,268
Other Current Liabilities	564	662	980
Long-Term Liabilities	158	130	150
Total Liabilities	1,442	1,582	2,398
Capital	336	348	398
Retained Earnings	74	128	258
Total Liabilities and Net Worth	1,852	2,058	3,054
Sales	1,870	2,105	3,450
Cost of Goods Sold	1,567	1,703	2,656.5
Gross Profit	303 (16.2%)	402 (19.1%)	793.5 (23%)
Depreciation	70	82	110
Other Expenses	183	141	373
Taxation	22	80	138
Net Income	28	99 (4.7%)	172.5 (5.0%)

Exhibit A1.3 Summarized Financial Statements of the Principal TV and Radio Companies in Taiwan (in NT $1 million)

| | Tatung | | Sampo | | Teco | |
	1976	1977	1976	1977	1976	1977
Cash	44	68	111	267	105	111
Receivables	1,462	1,947	691	922	277	390
Inventory	1,814	2,062	814	947	441	511
Advances to Suppliers	520	654	51	70	64	60
Other Current Assets	239	252	9	19	3	1
Total Current Assets	4,079	4,983	1,676	2,225	890	1,073
Net Fixed Assets	1,698	1,954	433	545	359	430
Investments	366	455	71	97	75	91
Other Assets	200	422	85	82	44	44
TOTAL ASSETS	6,343	7,814	2,265	2,949	1,368	1,637

Bank Debt	2,100	3,005	900	1,210	490	583
Other Current Liabilities	2,007	2,000	572	503	284	350
Total Current Liabilities	4,107	5,005	1,472	1,713	774	933
Long-Term Liabilities	427	487	143	379	13	27
Total Liabilities	4,534	5,492	1,615	2,092	787	960
Capital	1,124	1,657	395	550	330	400
Retained Earnings	685	665	255	307	251	277
TOTAL	6,343	7,814	2,265	2,949	1,368	1,637
Sales	5,366	7,600	3,055	4,050	1,587	1,900
Cost of Goods Sold	3,864	5,472	2,108	2,754	1,174	1,311
Gross Profit	1,502	2,128	947	1,296	413	589
Other Expenses	1,002.4	1,459.4	687.2	832.4	73.8	207.3
Depreciation	220	245	50	70	40	50
Taxes	124	188	92.9	174.9	131	147.4
NET INCOME	155.6	235.6	116.9	218.7	168.2	184.3

Television.   As of 1979, Taiwan was the biggest producer and exporter of black and white TVs in the world. Total production reached 4,515,102 units in 1977, a jump of 35.7% over the previous year, and represented 22.6% of 1977's world black and white TV production. Of the total sales, 96.6% was for export, with only 3.4% for local consumption. This is because the saturation rate for black and white TVs in Taiwan had reached 90%, leaving very limited room for growth. In fact, of late, the sales of black and white TVs in Taiwan have shown a declining trend. Major exports have been to the United States (80%), Western Europe (7%), Central America (5.2%), and Southeast Asia (4.5%). Although the world demand for black and white TVs has declined continuously, Taiwan's exports in the first half of 1978 continued to show a big jump, up 41.5% over the same period in 1977. This is mainly because Taiwan's black and white TV manufacturers have a competitive edge in the international market in both price and quality. The growth is also attributed to the successful market promotion in Western Europe and Southeast Asia (Indonesia and Thailand), which uses the CCIR system instead of the U.S. system, as well as the introduction of such new products as the mini TV/recorder/radio, which has been widely accepted by the consumers.

The annual production growth rate for color TVs during 1974–1976 showed a 19.7% increase on average. Color TV exports as a percentage of total TV sales over this period, however, showed a declining trend, from 67.3% in 1974 to 45.6% in 1975 and 47.7% in 1976, mainly due to the fierce competition among color TV producers, especially from Japanese firms. Fortunately, the increase in domestic sales during this period, which can be attributed to the improved living standard and the preference for color TV, has partly cushioned the reduction in the growth rate of exports. However, the pace of color TV exports rapidly accelerated in the second half of 1977, with the U.S. quota against Japanese color TV exports in July[1] and the Japanese yen's appreciation. Local color TV manufacturers seized the opportunity presented by the U.S.–Japanese color TV orderly marketing agreement to expand exports to the United States. As a result, color TV exports increased from 238,784 units in 1976 to 563,302 units in 1977, representing a 135.9% increase versus a 50.7% increase in 1976. Color TV exports as a percentage of total sales thus increased sharply from 47.7% in 1976 to 63% in 1977. Local sales of color TVs in 1977 also increased sharply, from 261,838 units in 1976 to 330,776 units in 1977, or by 26.3%. This was mainly due to the continuing rise in per capita income. Color TV sales both at home and abroad continued and showed a big jump for the first half of 1978 to 207,279 and 507,137 units, respectively, representing a 37.5% and 156.7% increase, respectively, over the same period of the previous year. Listed on page 225 are the production and sales of TVs for 1974–1978.[2]

---

[1]This quota contract regulated that Japanese color TV exports, including chassis (that is, partially assembled color TVs, excluding picture tubes, speakers, and cabinets), to the United States, could not exceed 1.75 million units per year.

[2]From Taiwan Industrial Production Statistics Monthly, MOEA.

Black and White TV Sets

	Production	Percentage Change	Sales in Volume	Percentage Change	Local	Percentage Change	Export	Percentage Change
1974	3,617,746	-13.9	3,769,126	-8.9	277,977	-13.9	3,491,149	-8.5
1975	2,599,311	-28.2	2,641,246	-29.9	207,314	-25.4	2,433,932	-30.3
1976	3,326,432	27.9	3,556,352	34.7	152,922	-26.2	3,403,430	39.8
1977	4,515,102	35.7	4,027,923	13.3	135,229	-11.6	3,892,694	14.4
1978 (6 mos)	2,668,193	20.2*	2,406,267	39.1*	54,150	-18.4*	2,352,117	41.5*

Color TV Sets

	Production	Percentage Change	Sales in Volume	Percentage Change	Local	Percentage Change	Export	Percentage Change
1974	418,453	23.2	506,141	14.6	132,667	109.0	273,474	-6.0
1975	335,661	-19.8	347,741	14.4	189,301	42.7	158,440	-42.1
1976	523,614	56.0	500,622	43.9	261,838	38.3	238,784	50.7
1977	910,589	73.9	894,078	78.6	330,776	26.3	563,302	135.9
1978 (6 mos)	802,646	125.5*	714,416	105.1*	207,279	37.5*	507,137	156.7*

*This represents a comparison with the same period of 1977.

Major manufacturers of black and white TVs and color TVs are as follows:

1. U.S.-controlled companies
   RCA Taiwan
   Zenith Taiwan
2. Japanese-controlled companies
   Matsushita Electric (Taiwan)
   Sanyo Electric (Taiwan)
   Hitachi Electric (Taiwan)
3. Local companies
   Tatung Co.
   Sampo Corp.
   Kwai Lam
   Taiwan Kolin
   United Electronics
   TECO Electric
4. Overseas Chinese-controlled company
   Admiral Overseas

Harry Jackson knew that the U.S. government had begun an import quota system against Taiwanese color TV exports in February 1979. According to the orderly marketing agreement signed in December 1978 by Taiwan and the United States, Taiwan was to be permitted to export 127,000 fully assembled color TVs between February and June 30, 1979, and 373,000 sets between July 1 and June 30, 1980. As regards chassis (partially assembled color TVs), Taiwan was to be permitted to export 270,000 between February 1 and June 30, 1979. Jackson thought that the above measure would undoubtedly adversely affect the development of the Taiwan color TV industry, as it was just in the pre-take-off stage. Although the export of color TVs to the United States in 1977 registered a high of 460,000 units (including chassis), only 81,000 units were made by three Taiwanese-owned firms (Tatung, Sampo, and Kwai Lam). U.S. and Japanese manufacturers, such as Admiral Overseas, RCA Taiwan, Zenith Taiwan, and Hitachi Electric Taiwan, set up as subsidiaries of their parent companies to escape skyrocketing labor costs at home, contributed the remaining color TV exports. Moreover, although the export of Taiwan-made color TVs to the United States started in early 1971, the history of the three Taiwanese-owned TV manufacturers started in the late 1970s. As a consequence, the quota system was most likely to affect adversely the development of the local color TV industry, as the allotment of quota in general was made on the basis of producers' past export records, and the three local manufacturers held only a 20% share of total color TV exports.

As a result of the development of this unfavorable condition for the local color TV industry, the Ministry of Economic Affairs announced (effective October 1, 1978) a ban on entry of Japanese firms to manufacture color TVs in Taiwan. Additionally, the Ministry had informed the local Japanese color TV producers to restrict their exports to the United States to the level of 1977. Market diversification to Western Europe, which used PAL system instead of NTSC system, appeared to be the best solution. However, even though the local manufacturers do not have the technology to produce color TVs with PAL system, the situation could change within a year or two because Grundig Taiwan plans to introduce PAL system, as the existing license for such a system, which is held by Telefunken Corporation, the patent holder, expires at the end of 1978.

Product diversification was also a possibility for this industry. Sampo and Kwai Lam were planning to produce more combination models of small-screen monochrome TV, radios, and cassette recorders, and other new products that are not subject to quotas. Also, the availability of a local supply of picture tubes made by Philips Taiwan since September 1978 should make local color TVs more competitive in international markets.

The prospect of local sales of color TVs was promising, as the saturation rate of this sector for home use was only 40% in 1979. As for black and white TVs, although the demand for this sector both at home and abroad was declining as a whole, it was expected that black and white TV sales in the near future will continue to be steady, provided that Taiwan producers could continue to maintain a competitive edge in international markets and produce a new style of black and white TV, such as a battery-powered portable TV, which is anticipated to replace the most popular 12-inch model to meet the consumers' demand.

Other Sectors. Other major sectors of the electronic and electric appliance industry, in which CBC has some important relationships are as follows:

Digital watches. Although only begun in 1975, the development of this sector has been spectacular. Production has increased from 284,000 units in May 1975 to 7.5 million units in 1978, and the number of participating firms from 8 to 30. Over 90% of output is exported. The industry uses imported components from Japan, and assembles and reexports principally to the United States. Growth is slowing as competition increases from Korea, Hong Kong, Japan, and Switzerland.

Electronic Calculators. From 1972–1977, production of calculators increased 81 times from 55,000 to 4.4 million sets, of which 92% was exported. Major producers are Tatung, Santron, Calcomp, and Logitech. Production in 1978 was 46% ahead of 1977. Taiwan has a labor cost advantage here over Hong Kong, Korea, and Japan, its principal competitors. Mostly operations are assembly of imported parts for subsequent reexport. Profits are low because of intense competition.

Telecom Equipment. In 1979, production was running 24.8% ahead of 1977, and much of this was sold locally. Owing to improvements in the domestic standard of living, Taiwan was now second in Asia only to Japan in telephone density, at 9.2 telephones per 100 persons. Locally made telephones account for 97% of domestic sales, and prospects are bright because this sector is not dependent on exports.

Audio Equipment. The transistor radio has been the flagship of Taiwan audio products. In the 1960s, components and parts were totally imported from abroad, mainly from Japan, and the radios were only assembled. By now in early 1979, the transistor radio industry manufactures 90% of components locally and exports 95% of its output, mostly to the United States, West Germany, Canada, and Japan. Growth had slowed recently because of intense competition from other industrializing Asian countries, such as Korea and Hong Kong. Production in 1978 exceeded 8 million units compared with 7 million in 1975. Prospects are good, as the industry produces new models, such as clock radios. Kwai Lam is the number three manufacturer of transistor radios, behind Tatung and Sampo.

"1978 turned out to be a boom year for our industry," said Mr. Wong, president of Kwai Lam, when Harry Jackson called on him in April 1979. "The main reason appears to be that we were able to grab a large share of the U.S. color TV import market, which previously was held by Japanese manufacturers. Our color TV exports were more than 100% ahead of 1977's figures and account for most of our overall sales gain of 63%." When questioned by Jackson about future prospects, Wong replied, "Of course competition is intensifying, but we expect further sales growth in 1979 in the United States, and our penetration of European markets, which is low at present, is expected to increase as soon as we are able to produce PAL sets. Sales of transistor radios will probably grow at about 10%, in line with industry forecasts."

Jackson pressed him about financing opportunities: "Of course, with all this growth, you'll be needing to add to your bank lines for financing inventory and other short-term assets." Wong confirmed that was true: "We are looking to add another bank to our inner group of four banks. I think you know we already use two local banks, as well as Chase and Bank of America. We use all these four banks for letter of credit and preexport financing."

Jackson knew that this meant the banks were willing to lend an amount of money equal to a fixed percentage of the recorded value of inventory and receivables to the subject company, provided that letters of credit existed to support export sales. Currently, CBC lent to another member of the electronics industry in Taiwan on the basis of 85% of receivables and 45% of inventory. He was wondering whether those figures would be acceptable to Kwai Lam.

In reply to his questions, Wong told him that their inventory figures typically consisted of 30% raw materials, 50% work in progress, and 20% finished goods. Most of the materials were locally produced, apart from TV tubes, which were imported from Japan. This was considered to be cheaper than making them in-house because of economies of scale in production. Sales were made principally to the large retailing groups, such as K-Mart, Sears Roebuck, and Macy's department stores, although 30% of U.S. sales were also made to an independent distributor, who sold to smaller specialized TV and radio shops.

HISTORY OF THE COMPANY

Kwai Lam Electronics (KLE) was founded in 1965 by Wong and his father-in-law K. L. Chen (after whom the company is named) with a small amount of capital. Over the next 10 years, they established themselves as a dominant feature in the transistor radio export market through a strategy of combining reliable quality with low profit margins but substantial volume. Thus, they penetrated well into the North American market and became suppliers to many large "own label" retailers. In 1974, the decision was taken to move into manufacture of color TVs, although KLE had previously avoided the black and white TV market completely. This proved to be a very successful move because of the marketing expertise already acquired and the fact that TV tubes, a major expense component, could be imported from Japan. Thus, assembly operations continued in Taiwan, with the goods destined for eventual reexport. KLE is privately owned by the Chen and Wong families, who controlled 88% of the shares. Wong, president, is 43 and was educated in Taiwan, although he attended the University of British Columbia Business School in the late 1960s, where he obtained an MBA.

TRADE FINANCING

Substantial volumes of trade all over the world are financed by means of letters of credit. In essence, a letter of credit is an instruction from a buyer's bank to a seller's bank to pay out money to the seller provided the seller can produce documents evidencing that the goods being sold meet the buyer's requirements, have been shipped, and are insured. Obviously, this is of vital importance to manufacturers dealing with buyers in foreign countries whose credit standing is unknown. In place of the unknown buyer, the seller is able to deal with a local bank, which the seller knows, and the bank in turn relies on the strength of the foreign bank (the buyer's bank), which will refund the local bank in exchange for the documents any money paid to the seller. In addition, documents include bills of lading, which represent title to the goods in question, giving both banks collateral over the goods in transit should the buyer fail to pay in the end. Thus, the credit risk of an opening bank (the buyer's bank) is that the buyer is not good for the money. The advising bank (the seller's bank) has the credit risk only of the foreign bank, and the seller is able to get his money when the goods are shipped.

    KLE used letters of credit to pay for imports of TV tubes from Japan and

	1976		1977		1978	
	Units	Percentage of Total Sales	Units	Percentage of Total Sales	Units	Percentage of Total Sales
Color TVs	121,000	57.2	139,000	56.7	280,000	70.1
Radios	775,000	42.8	810,000	43.3	900,000	29.9

was paid through letters of credit opened by its foreign buyers through banks in Taipei for goods which it exported. However, with some of its customers of long standing, open account sales were made by KLE. These customers usually paid within 30 days of invoicing.

The sales split (home market and export sales together) between transistors and color TVs has been (see page 230):

As can be seen, the expansion of color TVs and their higher sales volume per unit has dramatically changed the sales mix of the company. "Seventy percent of our sales now [1978] are color TVs, and 92% of these are exported," said Wong. "In fact the United States accounted for 220,000 units of our production of TVs in 1978, and we hope to maintain this market share in 1979. As you can see, we are not in black and white television manufacture and really only began in color TVs in 1975. Our strategy has been to aim for high added value in this sector to compensate for the increased competition in transistor radios."

As Jackson reviewed the whole file, he wondered if this was really such a good prospect for CBC. The longer range expectations, however, of KLE's growth and the chance to obtain additional noncredit business appeared to offset some of the immediate difficulties in lending to the company.

CASE STUDY 2:   SILMARAX S.A.

In March 1982, Silmarax S.A., a French company based in Chalons Sur Marne, was seeking bank financing for a $5 million five-year term loan to be used for capital expenditure in the older of its two plants in France. Jim Arlington, treasurer of Silmarax, who was on assignment from Silmarax's parent company, Melvin Corporation of Cleveland, Ohio, had originally decided to invite several banks to bid for the loan. He had narrowed the choice to Melvin's lead U.S. bank and also Banque Nationale de Paris, a nationalized French bank with whom Melvin did a lot of its French business, especially because the U.S bank's Paris office had limited ability to obtain French francs owing to government restrictions. BNP provided them with a FF 30 million line of credit.[1]

Silmarax was an old established firm engaged in making axles, transmissions, and other parts for trucks. The original owners had sold out for $20 million to Melvin Corporation in 1979, when Melvin was seeking to expand within the EEC and needed a larger base for manufacturing. Silmarax had two plants in northern France, one of which had extensive land available for building. Melvin had no other French subsidiaries, but its European companies included a plant for tractor engines in Italy, which supplied Fiat.

[1]FF 6.00 = U.S.$1.00 as at March 1, 1982.

Melvin was a U.S.-based multinational corporation, whose principal business was the manufacture of truck axles, transmissions, and parts. It also made industrial handling equipment, safety locks, keys, and security devices. Until 1968, it sold only in the United States, but in that year, it began expanding in Europe, first of all in Scotland. Its most recent financial results for the year to September 1981 showed net income of $64 million on sales of $1.52 billion. Its summarized balance sheet and income statements are shown in Exhibit A2.1. Its publicly held funded senior debt was rated BAA by Moodies and BB by Standard and Poor's. Of the net income for the fiscal

Exhibit A2.1   Melvin Corporation Balance Sheet and Income Statements (in millions of dollars)

	1981	1980
Cash	$ 121	$ 58
Accounts Receivable	1,391	1,255
Inventory	349	376
Other Current	85	31
Total Current	1,946	1,720
Investments in Affiliates	132	137
Other Assets	201	146
Net Plant	369	387
Goodwill	46	46
Total Assets	2,694	2,436
Short-Term Debt	550	516
Accounts Payable	144	147
Taxes Payable	3	21
Other Current	380	316
Total Current	1,077	975
Long-Term Debt	890	735
Deferred Taxes	42	62
Preferred Stock	95	30
Revenue Reserves	576	620
Capital Funds	14	14
Total Liabilities and Owner's Equity	2,694	2,436

Income Statements

	1981	1980
Sales Revenue	$1,520	$1,714
Cost of Good Sold	814	1,032
Selling and General	316	286
Depreciation	47	35
Interest	208	175
Write-off of Investments	25	—
Taxes	46	59
Net Income (Loss)	64	127

year ending 1981, 92% was contributed by the industrial handling and safety lock divisions, although these two division's sales totaled $412 million.

Management of Silmarax consisted of two Americans and a Scot: Jim Arlington, was the senior financial officer for Europe in addition to his role as treasurer of Silmarax, and Harry Roberts, managing director, was also from Cleveland. Bruce Maclaren had joined Melvin Corporation in 1967 when they opened in Scotland and had recently transferred to France as marketing director following the dismissal of Robert Dugard, the previous holder of the job, who had been the senior French national in the company.

Truck parts were manufactured in the newer factory, and transmissions and axles in the older factory. About 34% of materials were imported from the United States in a semicomplete form and finished locally. Total employees in France were 1,300 men, most of whom were engaged in manufacturing. Management intended to cut labor costs drastically by the new capital expenditure, which would consist of automated machinery and some robot devices which had already been successfully used in Cleveland.

Customers for Silmarax's products included Renault Vehicles (the French nationalized truck plant), other Melvin subsidiaries, plus Ford, Volvo, and International Harvester; also, there were two large export contracts for truck bodies to Iraq and Nigeria. Sales by sector were as follows:

French domestic	52%
EEC exports	18%
Non-EEC exports (mostly to Africa and the Middle East)	30%

Exhibit A2.2   Melvin Corporation Comfort Letter

To: _____ Bank.

Gentlemen,

We understand that you have agreed to provide a $5 million term loan to our subsidiary in France, Silmarax S.A. We appreciate very much your willingness to lend and assure you that it is our company's intention to maintain its 100% ownership of Silmarax S.A. unless the company notifies you to the contrary.

It is the policy of Melvin Corporation to manage its subsidiaries in such a way that they are able to meet their obligations and to comply with local exchange control regulations.

Please let us know should you have any questions in connection with this matter.

Very truly yours,

Melvin Corporation Inc.
Arthur E. George
Treasurer

Exhibit A2.3 Silmarax, S.A. Balance Sheets and Income Statements (in thousands of dollars)

	December 31, 1981	December 31, 1980	December 31, 1979
Cash	$ 1,432	$ 1,724	$ 3,535
Accounts Receivable	15,123	24,330	19,600
Inventory	19,645	17,088	14,147
Current Assets	36,200	43,142	37,282
Fixed Assets	7,400	8,205	7,965
Long-Term Receivables	4,230	2,110	2,200
Intangible Assets	470	550	630
Total	48,300	54,007	48,077
Short-Term Debt	10,970	378	290
Accounts Payable	13,030	13,506	9,499
Due to Parent Company	9,950	17,143	13,608
Accrued Expenses	1,150	1,080	1,575
Current Liabilities	35,100	32,107	24,972
Long-Term Debt	1,150	1,300	1,400
Revenue Reserves	2,050	10,600	11,705
Capital	10,000	10,000	10,000
	48,300	54,007	48,077

Sales Revenues	56,132	59,832	53,200
Cost of Goods Sold	52,397	51,661	42,559
Gross Margin	3,735	8,171	10,641
General Administrative Expense	12,281	8,546	5,064
Depreciation	1,280	1,200	1,120
Interest Expense	1,343	402	351
Profit (Loss) before Tax	(11,169)	(1,977)	4,106
Tax Expense (Refund)	(4,186)	(872)	1,829
Profit (Loss) after Tax	(6,983)	(1,105)	3,277

Notes: 1. Long-term receivables arise from exports made under government-sponsored financing programs and have terms of repayment of two to five years.

2. Inventories are recorded on a FIFO basis.

3. Capital expenditure was $400 in 1981 and $1,400 in 1980. No assets were revalued, but some were sold at book value.

4. Sales include exports classified as long-term receivables in the following amounts: 1981 $2,500; 1980 $750; 1979 $1,150.

5. Accounts are prepared in French francs but shown here in US$. The exchange rate per US$1 at the end of December was 1981 FF5.90; 1980 FF5.26; 1979 FF5.19.

Sales units were expected to grow between 3%—taking the most pessimistic view—and 15% per annum over the next five years. Jim Arlington's profit plan was based on 8% per annum volume growth and 7% per annum inflationary increases in costs and selling prices. Non-EEC exports were priced in U.S. dollars, but the rest of sales were priced in French francs. France is a member of the European Monetary System, which Arlington believed would be a steadying force in terms of possible fluctuations of EEC currencies. The term loan was to be in U.S. dollars because the machinery was to be purchased in the United States. Melvin Corporation would be willing to provide a comfort letter in the form shown in Exhibit A2.2. Arlington expected to be asked to agree to some financial covenants but had decided to wait until proposals were made to him from the two banks before making up his mind as to what was acceptable. As he waited for the two offers, he reflected that the BNP appeared very eager to do more business with Melvin, since so far it had dealt directly only with the French subsidiary. He had noticed some hesitation, however, on the part of the U.S. bank's Paris account officer, which he put down to inexperience, as the officer had apparently only just graduated from the bank's training program. Knowing that Martin B. Melvin, Jr., chairman of the board of Melvin Corporation and grandson of the founder, was visiting Paris next month, Arlington was keen to get the proposals as soon as possible. (Silmarax's consolidated balance sheets and income statements are shown in Exhibit A2.3.)

CASE STUDY 3:   CLAVO

This case study presents some problems for you to identify. The date is December 1978. You are head of the Venezuelan territory of a New York bank. You have just received a visit from the president of a substantial Venezuelan manufacturer of fasteners (nuts, bolts, and so on) called CLAVO, seeking your bank's $5 million participation in a $15 million term loan to his company (the other lenders are American Express, which will lead the syndicate, and another unnamed U.S. bank). The term loan is to refinance short-term debt. At present you have $2 million outstanding on an offering basis to CLAVO, and CLAVO has been a regular borrower under a $2 million line of credit that expired recently.

CLAVO was created in 1958 by a small group of Venezuelan businessmen with an initial capital of Bs 500,000,[1] in order to provide an import saving local production. The company grew rapidly, and in 1978 its total revenues amounted to Bs 113 million (around $25 million). During its first 10 years of existence,the regional shareholding group was expanded to include a number of foreign partners from Argentina, Japan, and the United States that could

[1]Bs 4.4 = U.S.$1.00 as of Dec. 1978.

provide technical expertise and, in the case of Japan, guarantee a supply of raw materials. The company also built up a network of exclusive distributors to cover its home market, where it has a market share of 75%. The import of fasteners into Venezuela has been subject to very high tariffs and license controls since 1966 in order to protect local industry.

In the past five years, CLAVO has expanded rapidly. Sales in 1973 were Bs 32 million and are now nearly four times that figure. To meet its financing needs, CLAVO raised equity capital of Bs 22 million in 1977 on the local stock market and planned a bond issue of Bs 70 million in 1978, but this was deferred, as conditions in the bond market went against them.

Carlos Rodriguez, the president of the company, a strong manager who has been with CLAVO since it was founded, tells you that they will definitely raise Bs 50 million in a bond issue within the next two years to repay part of the term loan. Projections for the period of the term loan have been provided which show inter alia:

1. Costs of goods sold will improve from 58.9% to 56.9% of sales over seven years by the installation of cost controls and a computerized inventory control system.
2. Inventories will decline from the current level of 574 days to 491 days by 1982.
3. The company will modify its product mix to include a greater proportion of high-priced items whose market is growing rapidly and concentration on autos and the petroleum supply industry, since CLAVO is the only manufacturer in Venezuela which has met the quality standards set by the government for high-resistance fasteners.
4. Sales will grow as follows:

| 1979 | 19.6% | 1980 | 13.5% | 1981 | 11.1% | 1982 | 10.4% |
| 1983 | 10.2% | 1984 | 9.4% | 1985 | 9.3% | | |

In the past, you have felt CLAVO to be an important but difficult customer: important because of its strategic position in the Venezuelan economy, its rapid growth rate, and the influence of Rodriguez with the government (his sister is the wife of the minister of finance), but difficult because Rodriguez has led CLAVO into a big project involving participation in a steel mill to provide high-quality steel, which at present has to be imported, and this diverts funds from CLAVO. Further, although you have met with Rodriguez on many occasions, attempts to talk to financial officers in the company have proved disappointing. In the past, the company has also had difficulty "cleaning up" its line of credit.

The company is said to be profitable at present, with a big backlog of orders (six months). Although Venezuelan accounts are not totally reliable, its significant financial figures for the past five years are shown in Exhibit A3.1.

Exhibit A3.1   CLAVO Balance Sheet and Income Statements (year to October 31, millions of bolivars)

	1974	1975	1976	1977	1978
Cash	3	5	4	12	19
Receivables[1]	5	3	5	12	14
Inventories	40	66	76	86	120
Total Current Assets	48	74	85	110	153
Investments	1	1	2	2	6
Plant	25	33	40	53	62
Other Assets	7	9	13	43	49
TOTAL	81	117	140	208	270
Bank Debt	7	25	41	65	113
Long-Term Debt	—	2	6	4	4
Suppliers	17	19	16	34	37
Accrued Interest	1	1	1	1	2
Employee Profitsharing	2	4	5	5	6
Estimated Income Tax	3	5	5	5	4
Other Accruals	1	1	2	2	4
Dividends	1	1	1	1	1
Total Current Liabilities	32	58	77	117	171
Long-Term Debt	12	17	16	19	8
Due to Associates	3	3	2	11	7
Other Provisions	4	4	4	5	5
Minority Interests	1	1	2	2	3
Owner's Equity	29	34	39	54	76
	81	117	140	208	270
Sales	48	65	80	98	113
Net Income after Tax	6	8	8	10	5

[1]Net of discounted Receivables

238

Pricing on the proposed deal is attractive at 2% over LIBOR, and your territory is below budget on loan volume.

NOTES ON VENEZUELA

A recent study of Venezuela was generally very favorable and concluded as follows:

Oil will remain of paramount importance to Venezuela in the next decade (export revenues from oil exceed $13 billion annually).

The major policy concern is inflation. This is currently 12% in 1978, but it has been as low as 7.5% on average in 1975–1977.

While external debt is generally considered large, "net debt" (allowing for international reserves) is relatively modest.

Per capita gross national product is $3,500 per annum. Venezuela is a member of OPEC, and oil contributes 18% of gross national product.

QUESTIONS

1. Would you approve the term loan? If so, on what conditions? Suggest useful covenants.
2. If you do not approve the term loan, does that imply that you will try to get complete repayment—that is, cease offering basis loans? If so, what does that mean for your territory?

CASE STUDY 4:   NORTHERN ENGINEERING INDUSTRIES LIMITED: A PROBLEM IN CASHFLOW ANALYSIS

This case study presents an exercise to be worked out by the reader: Northern Engineering Industries Limited is a substantial British company engaged in mechanical and combustion engineering. During 1978, it acquired some subsidiaries, principally Baldwin and Francis. The information reprinted here (Exhibit A4.1) is taken from the annual report published in April 1979. Find cash from operations using the transaction analysis form shown in Chapter 3 and sources and uses of cash.

The solution to this exercise is presented in Appendix 2.

Northern Engineering Industries Limited

Contents

Notice of Meeting	2
Directors and Officers	3
Results in Brief	4
Statement of the Chairman	5
Report of the Directors	8
1978 Accounts	10
Consolidated Profit and Loss Account	10
Balance Sheets	11
Consolidated Source and Application of Funds	12
Notes to the Accounts	13
Report of the Auditors	22
Financial Calendar	22
Principal Subsidiary & Associated Companies	23

Exhibit A4.1 Northern Engineering Industries (Northern Engineering Industries Ltd. Annual Report 1978, pp. 1–23). Reprinted with permission.

Notice of Meeting

NOTICE is hereby given that the second Annual General Meeting of the Company will be held at the Gosforth Park Hotel, Newcastle upon Tyne on Thursday, 14th June 1979 at 12 noon.

Business

To receive and consider the reports of the Directors and Auditors, and the accounts for the year ended 31st December 1978.

To declare a final dividend on the ordinary shares.

To re-appoint Directors.

To re-appoint the Auditors and to authorise the Directors to fix their remuneration.

Special Business

To consider and, if thought fit, pass the following resolution which will be proposed as an Ordinary Resolution:

That the authorised capital of the Company be increased from £26,181,999 to £56,181,999 by the creation of 120 million ordinary shares of 25p each and that the sum of £18,854,965 (being as to £7,188,183 thereof the amount standing to the credit of the share premium account and as to the balance of £11,666,782 part of the amount standing to the credit of the Company's reserves) be capitalised and accordingly the Directors be authorised and directed to appropriate such sum to the holders of the ordinary shares of the Company on the register of members at the close of business on 21st May 1979 in the proportion of one new share for every one ordinary share held by them respectively on that date and to apply such sum in paying in full 75,419,861 ordinary shares of 25p each in the capital of the Company to be allotted and distributed credited as fully paid up amongst such holders as aforesaid: the said new shares ranking *pari passu* in all respects with the existing ordinary shares of the Company including all future dividends, except that they will not rank for the final dividend for the year ended 31st December 1978.

By order of the Board
R. S. Lock
Secretary

Newcastle upon Tyne

11th May 1979

Only the holders of the ordinary shares are entitled to attend and vote at the meeting. A member so entitled to attend and vote may appoint a proxy to attend and vote in his place, and such proxy need not be a member of the Company. A proxy form is enclosed herewith.

There will be available for inspection by members at the Registered Office of the Company during normal business hours from the date of this notice until the conclusion of the annual general meeting,

a) Particulars of transactions of Directors and their family interests in shares and loan stock of the Company and its subsidiaries and

b) Copies of particulars of contracts of service (unless expiring or determinable without payment of compensation within one year) of Directors with the Company or with any of its subsidiaries.

Directors and Officers

Directors	Sir James Woodeson CBE TD	*Chairman*
	D. McDonald CBE BSC FH-WC CEng FIEE FBIM SMIEEE FRSE	*Group Managing Director*
	R. Baker FCIS	*Financial Director*
	W. H. Bell ACCA FCIS	*Managing Director, NEI Electrical Engineering Ltd.*
	M. H. Bower MA LLB	*Director Corporate Affairs*
	G. T. Coughtrie CEng MIEE FBIM	*Chairman, NEI Overseas Ltd.*
	T. Harrison BSC CEng MIMechE MIMarE	*Managing Director, NEI Mechanical Engineering Ltd.*
	C. R. Thompson	*Chairman, NEI International Ltd.*
	*T. A. Ennis BA JD (USA)	
	*J. V. Sheffield	
	*L. V. D. Tindale CBE CA FBIM	
	*Sir John Wrightson Bt TD DL	
	Non-Executive Directors	
Secretary	R. S. Lock FCIS	
Registered Office	NEI House, Regent Centre, Newcastle upon Tyne NE3 3SB England	
Auditors	Peat, Marwick, Mitchell & Co. 1 Puddle Dock, London EC4V 3PD	
Registrars	Flambard Registrars Limited Milburn House, Newcastle upon Tyne NE1 1NH	
Principal Bankers	Barclays Bank Limited Lloyds Bank Limited The Royal Bank of Scotland Limited	

Results in Brief

	1978 £'000	1977 £'000
Turnover	451,000	387,000
Trading profit	31,824	26,611
Profit before taxation	30,464	25,157
Profit after taxation and minority interests	22,763	18,896
Assets employed	160,930	143,922
Earnings per ordinary share	29.63p	28.87p
Dividends per ordinary share	7.5p	6.0p
Equity interest per ordinary share	176p	160p

Note: The comparative figures in respect of 1977 have been restated to reflect the change in accounting policy for deferred taxation.

Statement of the Chairman

**Statement by
Sir James Woodeson CBE TD**

I am pleased to introduce the Annual Report of Northern Engineering Industries Ltd. for 1978 which covers the first full year of operation of NEI as an integrated Group following the merger in September 1977 of Clarke Chapman and Reyrolle Parsons.

The 1978 Results

The improved profit and performance in 1978 reflect the confidence expressed at the time of the merger in the capabilities and potential of the enlarged enterprise. Profit before taxation, at £30.5m, is some 21% higher than the corresponding figure (£25.2m) for 1977; and the increased trading and development activities continue to be supported by a strong balance sheet. The Board declared an increased interim dividend at the half year and are now proposing a further increase for the final dividend.

Trading Activities

NEI is now firmly established as a comprehensive mechanical, electrical and combustion engineering group serving industry worldwide with a turnover in 1978 of £451m and employing some 32,000 people in the UK and 4,000 people overseas. The range of activities, (described from page 25 onwards of this report) cover a diversity of products and markets, which helps to counteract some of the adverse effects of cyclical trading patterns in particular sectors of industry. More positively this breadth of activity provides NEI with a strong foundation for current and future progress.

The general level of activity in most of the NEI trading companies in the UK has remained high, despite the depressed state of certain sectors of industry, particularly shipbuilding, steelmaking and construction, which are traditionally significant customers for heavy engineering equipment. This satisfactory pattern within NEI is being sustained by a progressive orientation towards exports and overseas markets, accompanied by a continuing programme of product diversification and development.

Exports and Overseas

Direct exports from the UK in 1978 amounted to £115m. In addition the overseas companies increased their turnover to some £70m, making a total of £185m in overseas trade.

Our principal overseas companies in Australia and South Africa continue to make a substantial contribution to the Group; and we are looking to the Australian companies in particular to take a leading role in developing NEI business in the Pacific area. However the time is long past when exports 'followed the flag', and when this country was able to rely on more or less captive markets in areas of British supremacy or influence. The NEI trading companies in the UK have not been slow to react to the continuous process of change which has followed the erosion of traditional export markets and have continued to develop their overseas businesses successfully both through direct sales and through licensees. Our policy is to supplement their export effort by the formation of joint ventures, the development of well-chosen overseas manufacturing and assembly bases, and by a growing involvement with local partners. The overseas operations will themselves generate new business for the UK factories, particularly for higher technology components and without this type of arrangement we could lose out altogether in certain overseas territories.

The acquisition of Ferranti Packard, which has manufacturing operations in Canada and the United States, will represent a significant expansion in the Group's overall presence in the North American market and provide increasing export openings for a wide range of NEI products and services. Other areas which we are exploring for the development of local facilities and joint venture operations include Latin America and South East Asia.

The export drive is being supported by NEI Projects which is taking the lead in tendering for major comprehensive projects in many parts of the world and by NEI International where Mr C. R. Thompson, who joined the Main Board of NEI during the year, has executive responsibility for developing new markets for Group products and guiding trading companies into new territories with unfamiliar trading patterns.

The UK Power Industry

The discussions on inter company restructuring, which had created a climate of uncertainty about the UK power plant industry, have now been discontinued. The boiler and turbine generator businesses remain an integral part of NEI and we are concentrating on developing and exploiting the unique capability of the Group in the power station field.

The UK power station ordering programme now appears to have been settled for the immediate future with the decision to go ahead with the 2,000 MW coal fired station at Drax B and with two nuclear AGR power stations. NEI will be supplying the turbine generators and certain boiler work for Drax B, and design work has already commenced on the steam raising units for the AGR nuclear reactors which are based on Clarke Chapman designs for the units now operating at Hinkley and Hunterston. Tenders have also been submitted and are currently being examined by the Generating Boards for the turbine generators for the new AGR stations.

Our future energy needs in this country can be met only by a strong combination of coal and nuclear power. Even allowing for North Sea supplies, we can expect growing world wide shortages of oil and gas in the coming years. The planned expansion of our coal industry must therefore be pressed ahead vigorously; and we must continue to support the nuclear policy announced by Government in January 1978 with its emphasis on the AGR, to make up the balance of our future requirements. The purpose of these plants is to satisfy the community's desire for energy, but their construction must have regard to public anxiety about the environmental and safety aspects of all modern energy systems, whether conventional or nuclear. I certainly do not see coal as in any way a rival to nuclear energy: both are fundamental to our future.

Turnkey capability for Developing Countries

The turnkey capability of NEI in the design, manufacture and supply of power stations, is of particular significance in connection with exports to developing countries. In this context I am particularly encouraged by the opportunities in China. I was myself a member of the British delegation led by the Trade Secretary in August 1978 and this has been followed by detailed presentations made earlier this year by a very strong NEI team headed by the Group Managing Director and two other Main Board members. The Company has now submitted comprehensive proposals in support of the massive Chinese power station construction programme and I am hopeful that given the necessary Government backing substantial business could result in this important but highly competitive market.

Product Development and Corporate Engineering

Market requirements for engineering products and services continue to change; in particular, developing countries are increasingly anxious to take over on their own account the manufacture of products which fall within their technical capabilities. British industry and in particular the engineering industry must be ready to anticipate and adapt to this changing pattern especially in the development of sophisticated systems and products and so maintain a technological lead or in other cases re-establish that lead.

A substantial amount of product development work is currently being carried out by the individual trading companies and centrally within NEI Mechanical and NEI Electrical. In addition there are the extensive resources of International Research and Development Company Ltd (jointly owned by NEI and Vickers). The product development work is now being co-ordinated and extended on a comprehensive Group basis through a newly established corporate engineering function which will examine critically the Group's existing products and more importantly seek to identify new technologies, plant and systems which will be relevant to the future demands of industry. Co-ordinated programmes are being developed for projects which involve the expertise of several Group companies, effort being directed especially towards energy related projects such as gas and steam turbine plant, coal conversion technology, particularly fluidised bed combustion and coal gasification.

The Company and Employees

I believe that there is now a general recognition of the importance for this country of the wealth creation process to which manufacturing industry contributes, although perhaps the extent of the contribution may not be fully appreciated. What we need is a climate which fosters this process by encouraging enterprise and initiative both for individuals and for companies. At the personal level this involves a pay policy which allows proper reward for skills and effort, and a taxation policy which avoids disincentives. At the company level it involves consistency in Government planning and policy for industry over reasonable periods of time, particularly in relation to the capital programmes for the electricity, steel and transport industries, so that companies can themselves make sensible forward plans for the effective utilisation of resources in terms of capital investment and human skills.

In our industry, it is the human resources which are by far the most important asset. I am myself doubtful about the value of a uniform code of legislation for the purpose of regulating in detail the complex relationships within a company. Indeed there has recently been a surfeit of legislation, which in some instances has imposed serious administrative and financial burdens on companies without any significant countervailing advantages to employees. However I have no doubt at all of the need for clear lines of communication and close consultation between management and employees to secure the success of the business in which they have a common interest. Procedures

should be appropriate to the companies and businesses concerned, and the reality of the collaboration will be much more important than the form of the procedures.

1978 has not been an easy year anywhere in industry, and NEI has had its share of industrial dislocation through pay disputes in certain of its own trading units and through the disruptive effect of industrial action outside the Company. The first quarter of 1979 was also adversely affected by the transport strike and by exceptional weather conditions in the North East at the beginning of the year. However the overall pattern of industrial relations throughout the Group is sound and I should like to express my appreciation for the support and understanding of our employees at all levels in this difficult industrial and economic environment.

The Outlook

Our success in the future is going to depend to an increasing extent on the development of our business in overseas markets. It is in this area in particular that we are now beginning to reap some of the benefits which derive from the merger of complementary activities and from the overall financial strength of the combined Group. In parallel we are ready to take advantage of opportunities which occur for developing and expanding our activities in the UK, as well as overseas, in fields less affected by the capital spending programmes on which heavy engineering relies. Most of the trading activities have a good forward order book, and despite the difficulties at the beginning of this year I believe that the Company is set on the right course to take advantage of the worldwide business opportunities that are available to us.

J. B. WOODESON *Chairman*

Report of the Directors

Report of the Directors of Northern Engineering Industries Limited for the year ended 31st December 1978.

Principal Activities

The principal activities of the Company and its subsidiaries are the manufacture of electrical and mechanical equipment as set out on pages 25 onwards.

Group Structure

The trading structure of the Group is set out on pages 40 and 41 of this report. With certain exceptions assets and trades of the wholly-owned United Kingdom subsidiary companies have been transferred to the Company so that the Trading Companies and Business Units trade as agents of the Company.

In South Africa the interests of the Group in Clarke Chapman Africa Limited and International Combustion Africa Limited have been brought together under Northern Engineering Investments Africa Limited in which the Company has a 64% interest; the greater proportion of remaining capital being held locally.

The wholly owned interests of the Group in Australia and New Zealand are being integrated within a single Australian operating company.

Profit and Loss Account

The consolidated trading profit for the year ended 31st December 1978 was £31,824,000. After taking account of interest, taxation, extraordinary items and minority interests, the available profit attributable to the shareholders of the Company is £22,740,000. As explained in Note 1(g) to the Accounts — Accounting Policies, the accounts reflect a change in accounting policy in relation to deferred taxation and the comparative figures for 1977 have been restated accordingly.

Dividends

Dividends on the preference shares were paid on the due dates.

An interim ordinary dividend for 1978 of 2.5p per share, exclusive of the associated tax credit, was paid on 30th November 1978 and a final dividend for 1978 of 5p per share, exclusive of the associated tax credit, is recommended to be paid on 6th July 1979 to the holders of the ordinary shares of the Company on the register at the close of business on 21st May 1979.

Share Capital

The issued share capital of the Company is shown in notes 15 and 17 on pages 19 and 20 to the Accounts. During 1978 the following issues of ordinary shares were made:

a) 150,000 shares in exchange for a like number of Clarke Chapman Ltd. ordinary shares issued pursuant to the Clarke Chapman Executive Incentive Scheme. The scheme was wound up during the year following the payment in full of the outstanding calls by all the participants.

b) 1,000,000 shares as part consideration for the acquisition of Baldwin & Francis (Holdings) Limited.

c) 400,761 shares upon the conversion of the $6\frac{1}{2}\%$ convertible unsecured loan stock 1989/94.

Loan Capital

In accordance with the terms of issue, the majority of the outstanding $6\frac{1}{2}\%$ convertible unsecured loan stock 1989/94 was converted during the year into ordinary shares and the balance was repaid in cash at par.

The opportunity was taken at various times throughout the year to purchase loan and debenture stocks in the market for redemption.

Acquisitions and Disposals

The acquisition of Baldwin & Francis (Holdings) Limited was completed during the year, the consideration being the issue of 1,000,000 ordinary shares of the Company and the payment of £8.35m in cash.

An announcement was made in February 1979 that agreement in principle had been reached with Ferranti Limited to acquire from them all the issued share capital of Ferranti-Packard Limited their wholly owned Canadian subsidiary at a cost of C$18.0m.

During the year a number of the unlisted investments were disposed of for a total consideration of £7.8m.

Directors

The Directors of the Company are listed on page 3.

In accordance with Article 98 of the Articles of Association, Mr C. R. Thompson who was appointed a Director on 6th July 1978 retires and, being eligible, offers himself for reappointment. The Director retiring by rotation under Article 92 is Mr T. A. Ennis and, being eligible, offers himself for reappointment.

247

Directors' Interests

The interests of the Directors at 1st January 1978, or in the case of Mr C. R. Thompson the date of his appointment, and at 31st December 1978 in the issued capital of the Company, held beneficially except where otherwise stated, were as follows:

Ordinary Shares	1st January 1978	31st December 1978
Sir James Woodeson	32,936	32,936
R. Baker	3,473	3,473
W. H. Bell	3,600	3,600
M. H. Bower	1,844	1,844
G. T. Coughtrie	93,626	93,626
G. T. Coughtrie (as a trustee)	206,435	178,704
T. Harrison	1,000	1,000
T. A. Ennis (non beneficial)	257	—
J. V. Sheffield	1,648	1,648
C. R. Thompson	23,871	23,871
C. R. Thompson (as a trustee with beneficial interest)	10,000	10,000
L. V. D. Tindale	3,000	3,000
Sir John Wrightson	1,920	1,920

8.25% Redeemable Preference Shares

Sir James Woodeson	300	300
W. H. Bell	450	—
G. T. Coughtrie	11,702	11,702
G. T. Coughtrie (as a trustee)	25,803	22,337
Sir John Wrightson	240	240

5.375% Preference shares

D. McDonald	105	105

3% Redeemable Preference Shares

D. McDonald	200	200

Executive shares in Clarke Chapman Ltd.

Sir James Woodeson	10,000	—
R. Baker	10,000	—
T. Harrison	5,000	—

Up to 11th April 1979 there has been no change in the interests of the Directors in the issued capital of the Company compared with their holdings at 31st December 1978.

Mr T. A. Ennis is also a director of Combustion Engineering Inc.

At no time during the year has any Director had any material interest in a contract with the Company, being a contract of significance in relation to the Company's business.

Major Shareholders

At 11th April 1979 the only shareholder known to hold more than 5% of the nominal value of the only class of the issued share capital carrying unrestricted voting rights of the Company was Combustion Engineering Inc., holding 9,094,952 ordinary shares of 25p each representing 12.1 per cent of the ordinary shares then in issue.

Combustion Engineering also has an interest in Northern Engineering Investments Africa Ltd.

Employees

The number of persons employed by the Group at 31st December 1978 was 35,989 of whom 31,595 were employed in the United Kingdom.

The average number of persons employed in the United Kingdom throughout the year was 32,099 and their aggregate remuneration was £136 million.

The South African companies of the Group are operating in accordance with the EEC code of conduct in regard to the employment of African workers and the relevant report has been submitted to the Department of Trade. Copies of the report are available on written request to the Company Secretary.

Geographical Analysis

Turnover and profits of the principal overseas subsidiaries derived from:

	Turnover £'000	Profits before taxation £'000
South Africa	48,108	3,552
Australasia	16,851	1,202

Exports

The exports from the United Kingdom including sales to overseas subsidiaries amounted to approximately £115 million; in addition there were substantial indirect exports.

Fixed Assets

Movements in fixed assets during the year are set out in note 8 to the Accounts on page 16.

Donations

Educational	£10,890
Charitable	£14,280
Political:	
The Northern Industrialists Protection Association	£9,500

'Close' Company

The 'close' company provisions of the Income and Corporation Taxes Act 1970, as amended, do not apply to the Company.

Auditors

A resolution will be proposed that Peat, Marwick, Mitchell & Co. be reappointed auditors to the Company and authorising the Directors to fix their remuneration.

Capitalisation Issue

In order to bring the Company's issued capital more into line with the underlying assets the Directors propose to issue to ordinary shareholders by way of capitalisation of reserves one new ordinary share of 25p credited as fully paid for every one ordinary share of 25p held by members on the register at the close of business on 21st May 1979. Application will be made to the Council of The Stock Exchange for the new shares to be admitted to the official list.

Subject to the capitalisation issue being approved at the Annual General Meeting on 14th June 1979 it is intended to despatch on 15th June 1979 to the holders of ordinary shares renounceable share certificates in respect of the new shares which will be renounceable up to 13th July 1979. The dealings in the new ordinary shares are expected to commence on 18th June 1979. The new shares will not rank for the final dividend payable on 6th July 1979 in respect of 1978 but will rank for all future dividends.

It is necessary to increase the share capital of the Company to permit the proposed capitalisation issue. Accordingly the Directors propose that the authorised capital be increased from £26,181,999 to £56,181,999 by the creation of 120 million new ordinary shares of 25p each of which 75,419,861 ordinary shares will be issued pursuant to the capitalisation issue. The Directors consider it desirable to restore approximately the resources of unissued capital which have reduced by acquisitions since the formation of the Company. They have no intention of issuing any of the unissued ordinary shares and no issue of them will be made which would effectively transfer the control of the Company or substantially change the nature of the Group's business without prior approval of the shareholders in general meeting.

By order of the Board
R. S. Lock
Secretary

Newcastle upon Tyne
19th April 1979

Consolidated Profit and Loss Account *for the year ended 31st December 1978*

	Notes	1978 £'000	1977 £'000
Turnover	1	451,000	387,000
Trading Profit	2	31,824	26,611
Interest on loan capital		1,360	1,454
Profit Before Taxation		30,464	25,157
Taxation	3	6,717	5,896
Profit After Taxation		23,747	19,261
Net profit attributable to minority interests in subsidiaries		984	365
Profit attributable to Shareholders of Northern Engineering Industries Limited		22,763	18,896
Extraordinary items	4	23	750
Profit after Extraordinary Items			
(of which £14,702,000 [1977 £10,514,000] has been dealt with in the accounts of the Company)		22,740	18,146
Dividends	5	6,070	4,004
Profit Retained	6	16,670	14,142
Earnings per 25p Ordinary Share	7	29.63p	28.87p

The comparative figures in respect of 1977 have been restated to reflect the change in accounting policy for deferred taxation (Notes 1(g) and 16).

Balance Sheets *31st December 1978*

	Notes	Consolidated 1978 £'000	Consolidated 1977 £'000	Company 1978 £'000	Company 1977 £'000
Fixed Assets	8	64,388	54,752	40,869	36,518
Interests in Subsidiaries	9	825	825	(28,757)	(18,074)
Investments	10	10,110	16,276	4,663	4,620
Current Assets					
Stocks and work in progress	11	133,064	121,417	85,397	78,104
Debtors	12	142,235	113,526	95,538	75,341
Advance corporation tax recoverable		2,891	1,522	2,891	1,522
Short-term deposits	13	20,074	22,554	12,368	16,736
Bank balances and cash		1,581	1,014	495	357
		299,845	260,033	196,689	172,060
Current Liabilities					
Creditors		144,447	127,575	102,969	89,524
Amounts invoiced in excess of work in progress	11	47,450	39,042	25,534	27,009
Corporation tax		3,594	1,491	795	1,278
Other taxation		5,164	5,914	724	1,539
Bank borrowings	14	9,812	10,987	8,070	10,519
Proposed dividends		3,771	2,955	3,771	2,955
		214,238	187,964	141,863	132,824
Net Current Assets		85,607	72,069	54,826	39,236
Assets Employed		160,930	143,922	71,601	62,300
Representing:					
Ordinary Share Capital	15	18,855	18,468	18,855	18,468
Reserves	16	113,821	99,481	31,428	21,754
Ordinary Shareholders' Interests		132,676	117,949	50,283	40,222
Preference Share Capital	17	6,182	6,182	6,182	6,182
Loan Capital	18	15,553	16,362	15,136	15,896
Minority Interests		6,519	3,429	—	—
		160,930	143,922	71,601	62,300

J. B. WOODESON
D. McDONALD } *Directors*

Consolidated Source and Application of Funds *for the year ended 31st December 1978*

	1978	1977
	£'000	£'000
Sources		
Profit before taxation	30,464	25,157
Extraordinary items before taxation	121	(750)
	30,585	24,407
Depreciation	7,271	5,275
Generated from operations	37,856	29,682
Shares issued	1,463	8,960
Increase in minority interests on acquisition of subsidiaries	2,836	—
Disposal of fixed assets at net book value	1,210	470
Re-alignment of overseas currencies	(1,406)	(1,435)
Goodwill arising on acquisition of subsidiaries	(1,947)	1,031
Miscellaneous items	(428)	(918)
	39,584	37,790
Applications		
Dividends	5,254	3,259
Fixed assets	18,472	12,303
Investments	(6,166)	6,256
Loan capital	810	2,607
Taxation	6,877	1,514
	25,247	25,939
Increase in Working Capital	14,337	11,851
Represented by:		
Increase in stocks and work in progress after taking account of amounts invoiced in excess of work in progress	3,239	25,746
Increase in debtors	28,709	5,929
Increase in creditors	(16,873)	(25,134)
Increase in short-term deposits bank and cash	(738)	5,310
	14,337	11,851

	£000	£000
Summary of the effects of acquisition of subsidiary companies		
Net assets acquired:		
Fixed assets	4,339	1,799
Investments	207	6,256
Stocks and work in progress	6,890	1,630
Debtors	3,518	3,102
Short-term deposits bank and cash	(106)	1,839
Creditors	(2,570)	(2,342)
Taxation	640	(1,005)
Miscellaneous items	130	(171)
	13,048	11,108
Discharged by:		
Shares issued	900	8,576
Increase in creditors	2,237	684
Decrease in short-term deposits bank and cash	6,299	817
Increase in minority interests on acquisition of subsidiaries	2,836	—
Decrease in investments on acquisition of subsidiaries	2,723	—
Goodwill arising on acquisition of subsidiaries	(1,947)	1,031
	13,048	11,108

Notes to the Accounts

1 Accounting Policies

(a) Historical cost convention
The accounts have been prepared under the historical cost convention adjusted for the revaluation of certain freehold and leasehold properties as disclosed in Note 8.

(b) Basis of consolidation
i) Subsidiaries
The consolidated accounts incorporate the accounts of the Company and its subsidiaries the financial years of which end on 31st December. The consolidated accounts exclude the accounts of Anglo Great Lakes Corporation Limited where control is considered to be temporary and those of two subsidiaries incorporated in Rhodesia.
The results of subsidiaries acquired during the year are included in the consolidated profit and loss account from their effective dates of acquisition. The differences between the purchase consideration and the book values of net assets at the dates of acquisition are taken to reserves.
Where completion of the acquisition of subsidiaries takes place at a date subsequent to the effective date of acquisition a notional charge for interest on the cash element of the purchase consideration is deducted in arriving at trading profit with a corresponding credit to reserves.

ii) Associated companies
The attributable shares of the results of the principal associated companies are included on the basis of their latest audited accounts which are made up to the dates specified on page 24; certain other associated companies have been excluded on the grounds that their inclusion would be of no real value in view of the insignificant amounts involved.

(c) Foreign currencies
Assets, liabilities and profit and loss items in foreign currencies are converted into sterling at the exchange rates ruling at the end of each financial year. Exchange differences on trading transactions are dealt with in arriving at the profit before taxation. The net effect of applying year-end exchange rates to the net assets of overseas subsidiary companies at the commencement of the year is dealt with through reserves.

(d) Turnover
Turnover excludes intra group transactions, sales made by associated companies and value added tax, and with the exception of long term contracts represents the invoice value of goods despatched and services rendered. Long term contracts, where the outcome can be assessed with reasonable certainty during the period of the contract, are included in turnover on the basis of the selling value of completed contracts adjusted to reflect the movement between opening and closing work in progress. Other long term contracts are included in turnover at invoice value when they are substantially complete and the final outcome can be reasonably foreseen. Profits are brought to account on the same basis as turnover.

(e) Depreciation
Depreciation is provided at various rates designed to write off the net cost (after deducting government grants) or the revalued amount of fixed assets in equal annual amounts within their anticipated useful lives. No depreciation is provided in respect of freehold land.

(f) Stocks and work in progress
Stocks and work in progress are valued at the lower of cost and net realisable value. The cost of work in progress includes an appropriate proportion of production and administration overheads, substantially all of which are related directly or indirectly to contracts. Full provision is made for estimated losses to completion.
Long term contracts, where the outcome can be assessed with reasonable certainty during the period of the contract, as described in *(d)* above, include a proportion of the estimated profits earned to date, such proportion having regard to the degree of completion of each contract. Progress payments received and receivable are deducted and, to the extent that such payments exceed the value of work in progress on any contract, the excess is included in current liabilities.

(g) Deferred taxation
No provision has been made for deferred taxation arising from timing differences between taxation allowances and the related accounting treatment as the Directors consider that no liability is likely to arise as a result of the reversal of such timing differences within the ensuing three years. The potential full liability is shown in Note 19.
In previous years full provision was made for such timing differences. The comparative figures for 1977 have been restated to reflect this change in accounting policy and the consequent reduction in the deferred taxation account at 31st December 1977 is shown as a restatement of opening reserves.

(h) Research and development
Fixed assets used in research and development are depreciated on the basis described in *(e)* above. All other expenditure on research and development is written off in the year in which it is incurred.

252

2 Trading Profit		1978	1977
		£'000	£'000
Profits of the Company and its subsidiaries		30,566	26,198
Share of profits of associated companies		1,258	413
		31,824	26,611
Trading profit of the Company and its subsidiaries is arrived at after charging:			
Depreciation of fixed assets		7,271	5,275
Hire of machinery and equipment		2,519	2,341
Directors' emoluments *(Note 20)*		315	244
Auditors' remuneration		434	309
Interest on bank and other short-term borrowings		2,922	2,142
and after crediting:			
Income from unlisted investments		32	301
Income from listed investments		350	350
Income from short-term deposits		2,062	1,839
Exceptional exchange gain on overseas contracts		861	1,176

Dividend income from associated companies amounted in the case of unlisted companies to £270,000 (1977 – £248,000) and in the case of listed companies to £281,000 (1977 – £nil).

3 Taxation		1978	1977
		£'000	£'000
The charge is based on the profit of the year and comprises:			
UK corporation tax at 52%		7,945	5,602
Double taxation relief		(1,100)	(1,105)
Overseas taxation		2,046	1,238
Associated companies		354	143
		9,245	5,878
Less: Adjustments in relation to prior years		(2,528)	18
		6,717	5,896

The taxation charge of £6,717,000 (1977 – £5,896,000) has been reduced by £8,237,000 (1977 – £4,686,000) in respect of timing differences between taxation allowances and the related accounting treatment, in respect of which no provision for deferred taxation has been made.

4 Extraordinary Items		1978	1977
		£'000	£'000
Rationalisation costs		2,675	1,001
Surplus on redemption of loan stocks		(97)	(251)
Profit on sale of unlisted investments		(2,699)	—
		(121)	750
UK Corporation tax thereon (net)		144	—
		23	750

5 Dividends

	1978	1977
	£'000	£'000
Ordinary		
Interim 2.5p per share paid (1977 – 2.0p)	1,886	1,280
Final 5p per share proposed (1977 – 4.0p)	3,771	2,955
	5,657	4,235
Less: Final dividend on shares issued in connection with the acquisition of International Combustion (Holdings) Limited	—	394
	5,657	3,841
Preference		
8.25% cumulative redeemable preference shares of £1 each	331	83
5.375% cumulative preference shares of £1 each	38	19
3% cumulative redeemable preference shares of £1 each	44	22
Amounts paid on the preference shares of Clarke Chapman and Reyrolle Parsons prior to their acquisition by the Company	—	39
	413	163
	6,070	4,004

6 Profit Retained

	1978	1977
	£'000	£'000
Company	8,632	6,510
Subsidiaries	7,713	7,530
Associated companies	325	102
	16,670	14,142

7 Earnings Per Share

The earnings per ordinary share are calculated on 75,419,861 ordinary shares (1977 – 64,016,589) and on profits before extraordinary items attributable to ordinary shareholders of £22,350,000 (1977 – £18,483,000).

The profits in 1977 are arrived at after deducting preference dividends of £413,000, being the annual level of dividend on the preference shares of the Company.

8 Fixed Assets

	Land and Buildings			Plant and	
	Freehold	Leasehold		Equipment	Total
		Long	Short		
	£'000	£'000	£'000	£'000	£'000
Consolidated :					
Cost and valuation					
At 31st December 1977	27,382	7,120	662	77,519	112,683
Currency adjustments	(244)	(67)	(3)	(259)	(573)
Additions	1,742	60	540	11,541	13,883
Subsidiaries acquired	1,114	101	135	5,685	7,035
Disposals	(685)	—	(77)	(3,030)	(3,792)
At 31st December 1978	29,309	7,214	1,257	91,456	129,236
Depreciation	7,310	1,793	451	55,294	64,848
Net book value					
At 31st December 1978	21,999	5,421	806	36,162	64,388
At 31st December 1977	20,640	5,387	295	28,430	54,752
Company :					
Cost and valuation					
At 31st December 1977	17,807	4,479	387	54,853	77,526
Additions	1,863	12	461	7,314	9,650
Disposals	(627)	—	(53)	(2,197)	(2,877)
At 31st December 1978	19,043	4,491	795	59,970	84,299
Depreciation	5,205	883	236	37,106	43,430
Net book value					
At 31st December 1978	13,838	3,608	559	22,864	40,869
Net book value					
At 31st December 1977	13,091	3,607	117	19,703	36,518
Depreciation charge for the year					
Consolidated: 1978	730	156	74	6,311	7,271
1977	602	154	23	4,496	5,275
Company: 1978	542	77	16	3,592	4,229
1977	377	76	8	3,362	3,823
Anticipated useful lives	40 years	period of leases		3–20 years	

The net book value of freehold land which is not being depreciated is as follows:

| | 1978 | 1977 |
	£'000	£'000
Company	1,186	930
Subsidiaries	3,153	2,414
	4,339	3,344

| | Consolidated | | Company | |
| | 1978 | 1977 | 1978 | 1977 |
	£'000	£'000	£'000	£'000
Capital expenditure authorised and committed	4,320	5,247	3,428	4,605
Further capital expenditure authorised	1,960	2,660	841	1,708

Capital expenditure authorised is stated before deduction of any government grants.

255

The amounts of land and buildings
included at valuation comprise:

	Freehold £'000	Leasehold Long £'000	Short £'000
At 31st December 1978			
Gross book value			
Company:			
1935	41	—	—
1958	381	—	—
1960	1,763	—	—
1963	153	—	—
1964	927	—	—
1967	2,370	—	—
1968	1,001	—	—
1969	571	—	—
1972	3,990	4,297	250
	11,197	4,297	250
Subsidiaries:			
1959	—	—	5
1967	—	38	—
1972	1,955	550	72
1973	974	—	—
1974	705	—	—
1975	—	296	—
1976	141	—	—
1977	—	282	—
Consolidated	14,972	5,463	327
Net book value	11,174	4,517	60
At 31st December 1977			
Consolidated			
Gross book value	14,902	5,145	324
Net book value	11,520	4,303	81

9 Interests in Subsidiaries

	Consolidated 1978 £'000	1977 £'000	Company 1978 £'000	1977 £'000
Shares at cost	825	825	58,168	48,658
Amounts owing by subsidiaries	—	—	6,052	6,456
Amounts owing to subsidiaries	—	—	(92,977)	(73,188)
	825	825	(28,757)	(18,074)

The principal subsidiaries are set out on
pages 23 and 24.
As stated in Note 1(b) the consolidated
accounts exclude the accounts of the
Anglo Great Lakes Corporation Limited
and those of two subsidiaries incorporated
in Rhodesia. It is considered that to
consolidate the accounts of these would
involve expense and delay out of
proportion to the value to the shareholders
of the Company. The shares in Anglo Great
Lakes Corporation Limited, the investment
in which is considered temporary, are
shown at their estimated net realisable value
and those in the Rhodesian subsidiaries
have been written off.

Notes to the Accounts *continued*

10 Investments	Consolidated		Company	
	1978	1977	1978	1977
	£'000	£'000	£'000	£'000
Unlisted investments:				
Associated companies				
Book value of investments	2,302	1,463	—	—
Attributable post acquisition profits	160	258	—	—
	2,462	1,721	—	—
Other companies	132	4,184	43	—
	2,594	5,905	43	—
Short term loans related thereto	(339)	(229)	—	—
	2,255	5,676	43	—
Listed investments:				
Associated companies				
Listed on overseas exchanges				
Book value of investments				
(market value of £3,738,000				
1977 – £3,269,000)	2,933	5,980	—	—
Attributable post-acquisition profits	302	—	—	—
	3,235	5,980	—	—
Dated gilt edged securities				
(market value £4,063,000				
1977 – £4,521,000)	4,620	4,620	4,620	4,620
	7,855	10,600	4,620	4,620
	10,110	16,276	4,663	4,620

Unlisted investments are valued by the Directors at £2.25 million (1977 – £8.25 million).

Details of the principal associated companies of the Company and its subsidiaries are set out on page 24.

11 Stocks and Work in Progress	Consolidated		Company	
	1978	1977	1978	1977
	£'000	£'000	£'000	£'000
Long term contract work in progress:				
Contracts whic hinclude profits earned to date	344,787	349,054	208,585	172,560
Other contracts	124,455	80,575	94,234	78,816
Other work in progress	83,147	106,786	62,046	74,728
	552,389	536,415	364,865	326,104
Progress payments received and receivable	512,412	497,579	326,698	296,177
	39,977	38,836	38,167	29,927
Amounts invoiced in excess of work in progress transferred to current liabilities	47,450	39,042	25,534	27,009
	87,427	77,878	63,701	56,936
Raw materials and other stocks	45,637	43,539	21,696	21,168
	133,064	121,417	85,397	78,104

12 Debtors

The amounts not due for payment within twelve months are £13,629,000 (1977 – £9,862,000) for the Company and £18,010,000 (1977 – £12,144,000) for the Company and its subsidiaries.

13 Short-Term Deposits

These include amounts on call, short notice and term deposits with banks, finance houses and local governments authorities and certificates of tax deposit.

14 Bank Borrowings

	Consolidated		Company	
	1978	1977	1978	1977
	£'000	£'000	£'000	£'000
Secured	3,427	1,195	88	—
Other	6,385	9,792	7,982	10,519
	9,812	10,987	8,070	10,519

Included in other bank borrowings are £2,629,000 (1977 – £4,783,000) for the Company and £3,213,000 (1977 – £4,966,000) for the Company and its subsidiaries of short-term export finance.

15 Ordinary Share Capital

	1978	1977
	£	£
Authorised: 80,000,000 ordinary shares of 25p each	20,000,000	20,000,000
Issued and fully paid: 75,419,861 (1977 – 64,016,589 issued and 9,855,007 to be issued) ordinary shares of 25p each	18,854,965	18,467,899

The increase in the ordinary shares relates to 1,000,000 shares issued at 90p as part consideration for the acquisition of Baldwin and Francis (Holdings) Limited, 400,761 shares issued on the conversion of the unsecured loan stock (Note 18), 150,000 shares issued for a similar number of Clarke Chapman Limited Executive shares and a decrease of 2,496 in the final number of shares issued to former shareholders of International Combustion (Holdings) Limited.

16 Reserves

	Consolidated		Company	
	1978	1977	1978	1977
	£'000	£'000	£'000	£'000
At 31st December 1977 as reported	84,637	68,782	11,039	—
Deferred taxation no longer required on of change acounting policy	14,844	9,790	10,715	9,132
	99,481	78,572	21,754	9,132
Realignment of overseas currencies	(1,406)	(1,435)	(34)	—
Premium on shares issued in the year	1,076	6,112	1,076	6,112
Movement arising on acquisition of subsidiaries and other changes in the composition of the Group	(2,000)	2,090	—	—
Profit retained	16,670	14,142	8,632	6,510
	113,821	99,481	31,428	21,754

£21 million (1977 – £27 million) of the consolidated reserves and £7,188,000 (1977– £6,112,000) of the Company reserves (of which £7,188,000 (1977 – £6,112,000) is share premium account) are not regarded as distributable. No account has been taken of additional taxation which would be payable should the attributable accumulated reserves of overseas subsidiaries and associated companies available for distribution be remitted to the UK. It is estimated that this additional taxation would amount to some £1.25 million (1977 - £1 million) at 31st December 1978 at the taxation rates then ruling.

17 Preference Share Capital

	1978	1977
	£	£
Authorised, issued and fully paid:		
8.25% cumulative redeemable preference shares of £1 each	4,012,399	4,012,399
5.375% cumulative preference shares of £1 each	709,600	709,600
3% cumulative redeemable preference shares of £1 each	1,460,000	1,460,000
	6,181,999	6,181,999

Both classes of redeemable preference shares are redeemable at the option of the Company on six months' notice – in the case of 8.25% shares, at par, and in the case of the 3% shares, at £1.05 per share. The 8.25% shares are redeemable only in 1982, 1983 and 1984 and are finally redeemable on 31st December 1984.

18 Loan Capital

	Consolidated		Company	
	1978	1977	1978	1977
	£'000	£'000	£'000	£'000
7¾% Debenture stock 1986/91	346	447	346	447
10¼% Debenture stock 1989/94	1,059	1,069	1,059	1,069
Mortgage loans	417	467	—	1
6½% convertible unsecured loan stock 1989/94	—	454	—	454
8¾% unsecured loan stock 1988/93	8,876	8,931	8,876	8,931
9% unsecured loan stock 1990/95	4,445	4,463	4,445	4,463
7% unsecured loan stock 2000/05	410	531	410	531
	15,553	16,362	15,136	15,896

The mortgage loans are repayable over various periods up to 2011 and carry interest at varying rates up to 10% per annum.
During the year £417,459 of the 6½% convertible unsecured loan stock1989/94 was converted on the basis of 96 ordinary shares for each £100 nominal of the stock and the balance was repaid in cash at par.

19 Deferred Taxation

As stated in Note 1(*g*) the Directors consider that there is no need for a provision for deferred taxation. The potential full amount of deferred taxation calculated on the liability method is as follows:

	Consolidated		Company	
	1978	1977	1978	1977
	£'000	£'000	£'000	£'000
Accelerated depreciation allowances	17,393	11,560	11,512	9,302
Stock appreciation relief	13,205	7,053	8,945	5,245
Potential capital gains on revaluation of assets	1,082	1,030	1,030	1,030
Other timing differences	(5,877)	(4,799)	(4,263)	(4,862)
	25,803	14,844	17,224	10,715

20 Directors' and Employees' Emoluments	The aggregate emoluments of the Directors of the Company were:		

The aggregate emoluments of the Directors of the Company were:

		1978	1977
		£'000	£'000
	As Directors	24	13
	Other emoluments	291	231
		315	244

The emoluments, excluding pension contributions were:

	1978		1977
		Net	
	Emoluments	after tax*	
	£	£	£	£
Chairman	55,500	17,800	44,100	14,500

Other Directors	Gross	Net after tax*	1978 Number	1977 Number
	£ £			
* The 'net after tax' figures have been calculated by reference to the higher end of each band (in the case of the Chairman by reference to the actual emoluments shown) and after deducting income tax at the appropriate graduated rates on the assumption that the recipient is a married man without children and with no other source of income.	Nil – 2,500	—	—	1
	2,501 – 5,000	3,900	1	2
	5,001 – 7,500	5,600	3	1
	7,501 – 10,000	7,200	1	—
	20,001 – 22,500		—	1
	22,501 – 25,000		—	2
	25,001 – 27,500		—	1
	30,001 – 32,500	13,900	4	1
	32,501 – 35,000		—	1
	40,001 – 42,500	15,600	1	—
	45,001 – 47,500	16,400	1	—

	Gross	Net after tax*	1978 Number	1977 Number
	£ £			
In addition there were senior employees in the United Kingdom whose emoluments were in excess of £10,000 per annum as follows:	10,000 – 12,500	8,600	52	33
	12,501 – 15,000	9,600	23	7
	15,001 – 17,500	10,500	4	11
	17,501 – 20,000	11,300	13	2
	20,001 – 22,500	11,900	2	1
	22,501 – 25,000	12,500	1	1
	30,001 – 32,500	13,900	1	—

21 Contingent Liabilities

These comprise:

a) Guarantees of export finance, bills discounted etc. entered into in the normal course of business.

b) Uncalled loan capital in an associated company of £320,000 (1977 – £160,000).

c) Guarantees relating to associated companies in respect of loans and bank overdrafts in the sum of £131,000 (1977 – £120,000).

d) The Company has guaranteed bank borrowings of certain subsidiaries which at 31st December 1978 amounted to £1,500,000 (1977 – £800,000).

There are claims outstanding which arise under contracts carried out by the Company and certain subsidiary companies. It is not possible to predict with certainty the results of these claims but the Directors believe, in the light of advice received, and taking into account counter claims, claims against third parties and provisions established in the accounts, that the outcome will not have a material effect on the Group's financial position.

Report of the Auditors

**To The Members of Northern
Engineering Industries Limited.**

We have examined the accounts set out on pages 10 to 21 which have been prepared
under the historical cost convention adjusted by the revaluation of certain properties.
In our opinion they give under the convention stated above a true and fair view of
the state of affairs of the Company and of the Group at the 31st December 1978 and
of the profit and source and application of funds of the Group for the year ended on
that date and comply with the Companies Acts 1948 and 1967.

Peat, Marwick, Mitchell & Co.
Chartered Accountants
London

19th April 1979.

Financial Calendar

Dividends and interest payments
If approved at the annual general meeting, the final ordinary dividend for the year
ended 31st December 1978 will be paid on 6th July 1979 to shareholders on the
register at close of business on 21st May 1979.

Dividend and interest payments are usually made as follows:

Ordinary shares
    Interim dividend   – November
    Final Dividend   – July
    Preference shares – 30th June and 31st December

Loan Capital
$7\frac{3}{4}\%$ Debenture Stock 1986/91
$8\frac{3}{8}\%$ Unsecured Loan Stock 1988/93 } – 31st March and 30th September.

$10\frac{1}{4}\%$ Debenture Stock 1989/94
9% Unsecured Loan Stock 1990/95 } – 30th June and 31st December.
7% Unsecured Loan Stock 2000/05

Principal Subsidiary & Associated Companies

The following were the principal subsidiary and
associated companies of Northern Engineering Industries Limited
during the year ended 31st December 1978.

	Effective Group interest %	Share held by Parent %
Subsidiary Companies		
United Kingdom (a)		
NEI Mechanical Engineering Ltd.	100	100
NEI Thompson Cochran Ltd.	100	100
NEI Clarke Chapman Engineering Ltd.	100	100
NEI International Combustion Ltd.	100	100
NEI John Thompson Ltd.	100	100
NEI Clarke Chapman Cranes Ltd.	100	100
NEI Clarke Chapman Power Engineering Ltd.	100	100
NEI Electrical Engineering Ltd.	100	100
NEI Bruce Peebles Ltd.	100	100
NEI Reyrolle Ltd.	100	100
NEI Parsons Ltd.	100	100
NEI Electronics Ltd.	100	100
NEI Projects Ltd.	100	100
NEI International Ltd.	100	100
NEI Overseas Ltd.	100	100
NEI Overseas Holdings Ltd.	100	100
International Combustion Ltd.	100	—
International Combustion (Holdings) Ltd.	100	100
Bardic Engineering Ltd.	100	—
Butler Jones Nameplates Ltd.	100	—
I. V. Pressure Controllers Ltd.	100	—
Metropole Industries Ltd.	100	—
Power Propeller Co. Ltd.	100	—
W. S. Profiling Co. Ltd.	100	—
Baldwin & Francis (Holdings) Ltd.	100	100
Parsons Peebles Ltd.	100	—
Parsons Peebles Distribution Transformers Ltd.	100	—
The Bushing Company Ltd.	67	—
International Research and Development Co. Ltd.	50	—
Anglo Great Lakes Corporation Ltd. (b)	55	—

Notes

a) All companies are incorporated in England with the exception of Parsons Peebles Ltd. and Parsons Peebles Distribution Transformers Ltd. incorporated in Scotland.

b) As stated in Note 1(b) the accounts of Anglo Great Lakes Corporation Ltd. have not been consolidated.

c) The percentage of shares held refers to the ordinary share capital.

	Notes	Country of incorporation and operation	Effective group interest %	Share held by Parent %

Subsidiary Companies

Overseas

	Notes	Country of incorporation and operation	Effective group interest %	Share held by Parent %
Clarke Chapman (Australia) Pty. Ltd.		Australia	100 100 Preference	— —
John Thompson (Australia) Pty. Ltd.		Australia	100	—
Newcastle Engineering Pty. Ltd.		Australia	100	—
Paklog Controls (Pty.) Ltd.		Australia	52	—
Reyrolle Parsons of Australia Ltd.		Australia	100	—
Reyrolle Pty. Ltd.		Australia	100	—
NEI Canada Ltd.		Canada	100	—
C.A. Parsons of Ireland Ltd.		Eire	100	—
Clarke Chapman (France) S.A.R.L.		France	100	—
Hochdruck Reduziertechnik I.V. Pressure Controllers GmbH & Co. KG		Germany	100	—
NEI Indemnity Ltd.		Guernsey	100	100
NEI (Hong Kong) Ltd.		Hong Kong	100	—
International Combustion HUD Ltd.		Hong Kong	60	—
International Combustion (India) Ltd.		India	50	—
Clarke Chapman (New Zealand) Ltd.		New Zealand	100	—
John Thompson (New Zealand) Ltd.		New Zealand	100	—
Reyrolle Parsons of New Zealand		New Zealand	100	—
Reyrolle Parsons of Singapore Pte. Ltd.		Singapore	100	—
NEI Africa Holdings Pty. Ltd.		South Africa	100	—
Northern Engineering Investments Africa Ltd.		South Africa	64	—
Clarke Chapman Africa Ltd.		South Africa	64	—
International Combustion Africa Ltd.		South Africa	64	—
John Thompson Africa (Pty.) Ltd.		South Africa	64	—
W. S. Thomas & Taylor Ltd.		South Africa	64	—
Cummins Diesel (South Africa) Ltd.		South Africa	64	—
Reyrolle Parsons of South Africa Ltd.		South Africa	100	—
Power Engineers (Proprietary) Ltd.		South Africa	100	—
Reyrolle Africa Ltd.		Zambia	100	—

	Notes	Country of incorporation and operation	Effective group interest %	Accounting year covered
Associated Companies				
Apex International Valves (Pty) Ltd.		South Africa	32	31.12.1978
British Nuclear Associates Ltd.	(a)	England	29	31.12.1978
International Combustion Australia Ltd.		Australia	39	30. 9.1978
La Mont Steam Generator Ltd.		England	46	31. 3.1978
Reyrolle Burn Ltd.		India	50	31. 3.1978
Transformadores de Mexico S.A.		Mexico	49	31.12.1978
Vacuum Interrupters Ltd.		England	20	31.12.1978

Notes

a) The holding in British Nuclear Associates Ltd. represents a 10% interest in National Nuclear Corporation Ltd.

b) Unless otherwise stated the percentage of shares held refers to the ordinary share capital.

CASE STUDY 5:   WHAT REALLY WENT WRONG AT FRANKLIN NATIONAL

by Sanford Rose

The nation's financial system is facing its gravest crisis since the Bank Holiday of 1933. The crisis is one of confidence. The public has become increasingly worried about the solvency of even the most profitable banks. In the past few months, bank-stock prices have fallen far more rapidly than the stock market as a whole—which is saying plenty. The prices of bank stocks are now lower in relation to earnings and book value than they were on Friday, March 3, 1933, the day before the Bank Holiday. Says Morris Schapiro, the dean of American bank analysts: "We don't have a bank holiday yet, but we already have a bank-holiday stock market."

The weakening of public confidence in the banks is traceable, to a considerable extent, to the well-publicized misadventures of the Franklin National Bank of New York. In May, Franklin National, then the twentieth-largest bank in the U.S., with deposits of close to $3 billion, canceled its second-quarter dividend and announced foreign-exchange losses in the neighborhood of $40 million. Many people believed that Franklin, which had been a weak-earning bank for years, would be promptly liquidated by the regulatory authorities and its deposits assumed by a stronger banking institution. Instead, Franklin retained a precarious hold on life during the subsequent months. Aided by a massive loan from the Federal Reserve, the bank was able to meet deposit withdrawals that exceeded $1.5 billion by September.

Franklin's miseries have affected public confidence in two ways. First, the spectacle of a major bank being propped up for months was itself rather unnerving. In addition, the particular ailment that most people associate with Franklin—foreign-exchange losses—seems to have afflicted a fair number of other banks recently. Several small European banks had large foreign-exchange losses and subsequently failed. It seemed reasonable, then, to wonder whether Franklin's problems might be typical of the banking industry.

The answer happens to be no. To be sure, many banks speculate in foreign exchange. But no U.S. bank speculated as heavily or as recklessly as did Franklin. Most banks can make money in much less risky ways. Franklin could not; it is now clear that the bank *had* to speculate in foreign exchange because it could earn virtually nothing on normal operations. Not counting foreign-exchange transactions, Franklin made just about $5 million in 1973. That amounted to about one-tenth of 1 percent of the bank's assets. The average U.S. bank made more than eight times as much on assets during 1973.

The details of Franklin's foreign-exchange operations are lurid enough—as we shall see—but the real story of the bank's downfall has to do with normal banking operations. Franklin's operating performance was deteriorating rapidly after the middle of 1973. Data available to FORTUNE indicate that the bank lost money on a pretax basis from July through September of 1973—not counting foreign exchange. Indeed, were it not for a phony foreign-exchange profit in September, 1973, Franklin might have been forced to cancel its third-quarter dividend—an action that would have terrified its creditors and probably triggered the inevitable crisis eight months earlier. Operating profits reappeared briefly in late 1973. But from February through April, 1974, the bank continued to lose money. And during April its controller's office projected losses of between $5 million and $7 million for the entire second quarter.

Although the total operating shortfall does not equal the foreign-exchange loss—now estimated at about $46 million—it is much more significant. A foreign-exchange loss, even a series of losses, constitutes an extraordinary event. On the other hand, persistent operating deficits betoken fundamental rot. The plain fact is that Franklin could not manage the spread between the yield on loans and bonds and the cost of investable funds, personnel, and occupancy. If Franklin had not received massive assistance from the Federal Reserve, the bank would have been forced to shut its doors sometime in 1974 even if it hadn't lost a dollar in foreign exchange.

The statement seems almost incredible. Most Americans assume banks don't fail unless there is fraud, and that large banks just don't fail at all. Why couldn't Franklin make money doing what other banks do?

PERILS OF A ONE-MAN SHOW

An answer begins with the dearth of professional-caliber management at the bank. It has been run amateurishly for decades. In the 1950s and early 1960s Franklin enjoyed two advantages not given to many other banking institutions. It was located in one of the fastest-growing market areas of the country, Long Island. And it was insulated from serious competition by branching restrictions placed on New York City banks. Embosomed in the soft plush of this uniquely favorable environment, Franklin saw no need to professionalize its management.

Even if it had perceived the need, it is doubtful that anything would have been done about it. The bank was headed in those years by Arthur Roth, a hard-driving autocrat whose favorite homily is "every organization is but the shadow of one man." Roth ran Franklin as a one-man show, surrounding himself with malleable subordinates who had no particular aptitude for banking.

One of these was Harold Gleason, a good public-relations man and a smooth and persuasive talker. Gleason was Roth's faithful subordinate for about a dozen years. Ultimately, though, the two fell out after Roth told Gleason that he didn't measure up and would never be chief executive. Of Gleason, Roth says bitterly: "I treated him like a son. Little did I imagine that the man was just a faker, an egotistical incompetent."

Another of Roth's protégés was John Sadlik, who eventually became the bank's chief financial officer. Sadlik's knowledge of the finer points of finance has always been somewhat sketchy. He would generally approve an investment if its yield was at least one percentage point above the bank's average cost of money. That might sound reasonable to nonbankers. But in a period when demand and savings deposits are declining, average cost can understate the true cost of financing asset growth.

During late 1973, for example, nearly every asset acquired by Franklin had to be financed by borrowings in the money market at rates of between 9 and 11 percent. This *marginal cost* was about 2 to 4 percent above the average cost of Franklin's funds, which, of course, included low-cost demand deposits and passbook-savings accounts. Clinging to the one-percent-above-average standard, Sadlik and others approved the acquisition of many assets on which the bank inevitably lost money.

WAVING ASIDE THE BALANCE SHEET

Despite managerial shortcomings, Roth was able to propel Franklin forward at a frantic pace during the bank's golden age. From 1950 to 1962 Franklin's assets grew from $78 million to over $1 billion. Earnings averaged between 15 and 20 percent of stockholders' equity.

Roth and his epigones could not dispense money fast enough in those early years. The flavor of the bank's lending operations was recalled recently by Roger Elton, a banker who later joined Franklin and rose to become executive vice president. Said Elton: "In the early 1950's the Long Island contractor who built my house needed $25,000. He went to Franklin and they gave him the money before he even showed them his balance sheet. When he produced the statement, they waved it aside."

Clearly, Roth was not averse to risk. Indeed, he often stated that he was willing to take loan losses equal to twice those of the average bank, provided he could earn 0.75 to 1.25 percentage points above the national average on his loan portfolio. But there were years in which loan losses reached three to five times the average.

During the late 1950's and early 1960's, some of the losses grew out of loans made by Franklin in anticipation of public offerings. Small businessmen would come into the bank with letters from underwriters promising to help them raise funds in the capital markets. Franklin would provide the interim financing. But after the stock market collapse of 1962, many of these offerings had to be withdrawn, and a lot of borrowers defaulted. At about the same time, the apartment boom in the metropolitan New York area collapsed, and a number of Franklin's real-estate equity loans went sour.

The alarming rise in loan losses helped change Roth's mind about the kind of assets Franklin should be acquiring. In the early 1960's, the emphasis shifted from loans to municipal bonds. The bank more than doubled the size of its securities portfolio, loading up on 3 to 4 percent Long Island school-district bonds. In buying municipals, Franklin acquired what looked like attractive tax-free assets, while at the same time ingratiating itself with town treasurers, whose deposits—both demand and time—came pouring into the bank.

But Roth overdid it. He bought so many municipals that in later years the bank was stuck with far more of them than were justified by its tax position. Franklin hasn't paid any federal income taxes for most of the last decade. Instead, largely because of its municipal bonds and the slow growth of its taxable revenues, the bank started accumulating a tax-loss carry-forward, which it carried on its balance sheet as an asset.

Without taxable income, it is no fun owning a lot of low-yielding tax-exempt bonds. At the time of the crisis last May, Franklin held close to $300 million in municipal bonds with an average yield of only 4 percent. That yield was about three to 3.5 percentage points below the bank's average cost of money and about seven percentage points below its marginal cost. Just comparing average yield with average cost, the bank was losing about $10 million a year on its municipal-bond holdings.

Most other banks would have shed this albatross a long time ago, even if that meant taking sizable capital losses on the sale of bonds. And there were times in the past when the capital penalty would not have been too onerous. Says Harold Kurtz, a former Franklin vice president: "As late as 1968, we could have disposed of many of those bonds without hurting ourselves too much. But by then our loan losses were so high that we could not afford to take additional losses in the bond account."

Ironically, Franklin's oversized municipal-bond portfolio eventually resulted in the loss of its public deposits. Because Franklin had bought so many municipals in the early and mid-1960's, it was out of the market by the end of the decade. Predictably, the officials of Long Island communities did not at that point dwell on the bank's earlier heavy purchases; instead, they just seemed irritated that Franklin, a local bank, was not now picking up its share of the increase in municipal debt. So they began moving their deposits out of the bank and into competitive institutions like Security National.

HE COULDN'T FIND "21"

By the early 1960's the wall that separated Queens from the rest of Long Island had begun to crumble. The New York City banks had been given the right to branch into Nassau County. Commercial and savings banks alike began pushing into the new territory, poaching on Roth's once inviolate preserve. Roth mapped a counterstrategy. He would go to New York.

Many believe that the decision to enter New York was Roth's most egregious blunder. The bank did not have the ability to compete in the New York market. Says Mike Merkin, the eighty-year-old vice chairman of Franklin: "What business had Roth coming to New York? He didn't even know the way to '21.' "

The move to New York need not have been a mistake, however. Meadowbrook National Bank—now the National Bank of North America—came from Long Island to New York and managed fairly well. It was the way Roth entered New York that hurt him.

First he tried to buy a New York bank, the Federation Bank & Trust. He could not get Federation right away, at least not on terms that satisfied him. Not being one to wait, Roth started branching into the city in 1964. And he arrived traveling first class. Says Jerome Twomey, a former executive vice president at Franklin: "Roth came to New York building monuments—impressive and very costly structures." The move to New York enormously inflated the bank's occupancy expense.

A newcomer to New York City, Franklin could not hope for the choicest bank credits; it had to content itself with shards. The bank fought for small participations in major loans syndicated by the larger New York banks. If the bank won a place in these syndicates at all, it was often because it lacked the nerve to ask for decent compensating balances—i.e., non-interest-bearing funds that must be kept on deposit at all times. Says David Dowd, a former Franklin vice president: "I went directly from Irving Trust to Franklin in the mid-Sixties. At Irving we had a piece of the Woolworth account and we got a compensating balance of between 20 and 30 percent. At Franklin we would not have dared to ask for more than 10 percent. We knew we couldn't get it."

Finding it both difficult and unprofitable to attract national customers, Franklin began to concentrate on a somewhat specialized clientele. The bank soon acquired a reputation as a primary lender to "growth companies"—which usually turned out to mean companies that were promoting their stocks heavily. Says Twomey, who was responsible for a part of the business: "To be perfectly frank, in those years nearly every company that was written up in the *Wall Street Journal* for unusual accounting practices became our customer."

Although this was high-risk business, Franklin did not earn especially high rates. The bank was so committed to rapid growth that its loan officers often shaved rates in order to show volume and remain members in good standing of a go-go shop. When they did reach for yield, it was sometimes in exotic and unproductive forms. For example, a number of loan officers took "shadow warrants," i.e., they included clauses in the loan agreement providing for additional interest payments if the price of the borrower's stock rose above a certain figure. Ordinarily, the stock did not go up enough, and Franklin was left holding a risky loan with a modest yield.

TRIUMPH OF A GENEROUS MAN

In 1967, Franklin finally merged with the Federation Bank & Trust. Roth got the Federation, but in turn the Federation got him. Allying himself with the new directors on Franklin's board, Gleason managed to supplant Roth as chief executive in 1968, and finally pushed him off the board altogether in 1970. Roth retired to the role of gadfly, stinging management, and particularly Gleason, in angry letters to the shareholders.

With Gleason enthroned as chief executive, the bank's fortunes began a serious further declension. An easygoing and generous man, Gleason lacked the disposition to control personnel expenses, and they soared. Under Gleason's guiding hand, the number of employees increased sharply, salaries and bonuses rose, and expense accounts became much more lavish. From 1968 to 1970, the bank's salary expense increased by 50 percent.

At about the same time, Franklin's earnings began to suffer alarmingly from a change in the accounting procedures governing loan losses. Before 1969 banks did not have to show loan losses on their income statements. Instead of reducing reported earnings, the losses were a below-the-line deduction from reserves, in effect a direct charge to capital. Beginning in 1969, however, the supervisory agencies insisted that banks put at least a portion of their losses onto their income statements.

Banks that did not wish to take the full yearly loss against income could choose one of two moving-average procedures. They could compute the ratio of net losses to average loans during the five years ending in the current year (initially 1969), apply that ratio to all current loans, and reduce income by the resulting figure. Alternatively, they could decide that the ratio to be used would be net losses to average loans for 1969–73, or as much of the period as had been completed.

Since Franklin had had a miserable loan-loss experience in the mid-1960's, and a good performance in 1969 it elected the second alternative. That worked out tolerably well until 1971, when losses were horrendous. And with only two other years represented in the average, the 1971 losses had a terrific impact on income; they socked it for a dizzying $7.2 million.

By the early 1970's, Franklin was beginning to show signs of terminal illness. The fall in interest rates from mid-1970 to 1972 reduced loan yields, but the bank's interest expenses did not fall commensurately, in part because the cost of passbook savings—a sizable chunk of Franklin's deposits—remained relatively stable.

Franklin's miseries in this period can be summarized by a comparison of its 1972 operating results with those of a representative group of peer banks—that is, banks of similar deposit size and roughly similar deposit composition.

According to unpublished Federal Reserve data Franklin had a net return in 1972 of less than three quarters of a cent per dollar of investable funds, i.e., deposits and borrowed money. Its peers made more than twice that. Franklin paid more for its money than its peers, and it earned less on its bread and butter, commercial loans, on both a gross and a net basis. Moreover, by 1972 the bank had become almost unbelievably inefficient. Expenses per dollar of commercial-loan volume totaled 50 percent more than at banks of comparable size.

NEW FACES OF THE 1970'S

Since the late 1960's Laurence A. Tisch, head of Loew's Corp., had been quietly buying up Franklin stock. By 1971 he had accumulated a controlling 20 percent, and in mid-1972 he became alarmed at what was happening to his investment. Tisch decided on a major rescue effort. He reached into Bankers Trust and persuaded Paul Luftig, the highly respected head of Banker's metropolitan division, to come aboard as Franklin's president.

An energetic and ambitious man in his early forties, Luftig took the job in May, 1972—fully expecting to succeed Gleason as chief executive officer within a matter of weeks. But in July Tisch undercut Luftig by selling nearly all his stock to Michele Sindona, the Italian financier. Sindona's reasons for buying into the bank remain an enigma, as do many of Sindona's moves. He apparently did not research the acquisition very thoroughly, however; shortly after he bought the bank, he confessed to a reporter that he had never heard of Arthur Roth. When the two men finally met later in 1972, Roth, still a substantial Franklin shareholder, asked Sindona what he was going to do about earnings. Sindona replied: "Don't worry. I'm going to make most of my money in foreign exchange. That's the way I do it in my Italian banks."

Meanwhile, Gleason had been reprieved. He began to cultivate Sindona, traveling to Italy every second weekend for "talks"; he also took Italian lessons. Luftig was isolated, in effect a lame-duck president. Still, he held on tenaciously. He had a five-year contract and he was determined to make a serious effort to get things organized.

Early in 1973, another new face appeared in the top management ranks. Peter Shaddick was recruited by Sindona from the Bank of Montreal to head up the international department. Although Shaddick entered the bank with the title of senior executive vice president, it was clear from the beginning that he intended to function as a sort of co-president. It was also clear that he was going to run the international department as a bank within a Bank. He scorned Franklin's internal auditors and requested his own auditing group. Shaddick was a tiger; and since he was Sindona's man, no one messed with him.

THE SCANDAL IN REAL ESTATE

While Shaddick busied himself with his palatinate, Luftig tried to cut operating costs. He fired some people, although probably not as many as he should have. Overall, Luftig was able to slow down the rate of increase in operating costs, but he was never able to reduce costs absolutely. One of the main reasons was occupancy expense, which increased substantially following the move to 450 Park Avenue in November, 1972.

The bank's real-estate situation had become nothing short of scandalous. Luftig found that Franklin didn't really need about 25 percent of the space it was paying for. In some cases the bank was renting space far above market prices. And at the same time it was charging *less* than market price for the space it subleased to others.

One problem was that the bank had no effective supervision over small leases. In an uncharacteristic effort to save a few pennies on legal fees, the bank had a policy of allowing the other party's lawyer to draw up small leases. The terms of these leases were naturally unfavorable to the bank.

The real-estate problem was aggravated by Franklin's sale-leaseback arrangements. The bank had a continuing, desperate need to show taxable income in order to avoid wasting a portion of its tax-loss carry-forward. In several years, to avoid this waste, Franklin sold a large amount of property and simultaneously leased it back. The bank booked a capital gain, which it used to offset the ordinary income losses of previous years. Unfortunately, these transactions also inflated rental costs: the bank's lease payments exceeded the property taxes it would have paid had it continued to own the buildings.

GAMBLING ON LEVERAGE

Finding it impossible to reduce expenses, Luftig made a procrustean adjustment in his thinking. If the bank's expenses could not be cut down to a level appropriate to its asset size, asset size would have to be expanded. In late 1972 Luftig began borrowing money in order to finance a major expansion of the bank's lending activity. By increasing the bank's already substantial leverage—i.e., the ratio of assets to equity capital—Luftig hoped to raise earnings per share despite the burden of outsize expenses and the handicap of an anemic profit margin. At the time, this seemed a reasonable step, given the bank's predicament. Yet it proved disastrous.

In the first eight months of 1973, Franklin's domestically financed loans grew by nearly 25 percent. But the bank had the bad luck to be expanding its assets in a period when bank lending rates were artificially depressed by Federal Reserve pressure. For a considerable part of 1973, the prime rate remained three-quarters to a full percentage point below the level it would have reached if the Fed had not been trying to hold it down.

Meanwhile, bank borrowing rates were not placed under comparable pressure. The rate on certificates of deposit remained relatively free to rise. The rate on federal funds—the reserve balances that banks borrow from other banks—was artificially held down only until about April, then was more or less allowed to move up.

The behavior of federal funds, which Franklin borrowed heavily, was a special problem. The rate on federal funds eventually rose to higher levels than it otherwise would have precisely because the prime rate was being contained. A bargain prime increases the demand for credit. As more loans are extended, demand deposits also increase, raising the level of required reserves. In turn, the scramble for reserves puts upward pressure on the funds rate. Hence any bank that financed itself with a large amount of federal funds during 1973 faced extraordinary pressure on earnings. At Franklin, profit margins virtually evaporated. At times during the year the bank put assets on its books at a negative earnings spread—i.e., the yield on the asset was less than the cost of financing it.

If Franklin had been able to finance its asset growth by expanding core deposits—demand and passbook-savings money—it would undoubtedly have prospered. Franklin's average monthly prime rate rose from 6 to about 10 percent during 1973. The cost of its demand deposits totaled only about 2¼ percent, and the cost of passbook savings averaged just over 4 percent. But Franklin's demand deposits were actually falling in this period. Passbook savings were also eroding, as savers moved their money into Treasury bills and other money-market instruments. That left Franklin scrambling for funds in the money market, where rates kept rising.

Banks normally strive to hold on to at least enough cheap core money to finance their fixed-rate assets—e.g., bonds, mortgages, consumer loans, and some commercial loans. That way, even if interest rates rise, they are guaranteed a positive earnings spread on a part of the total portfolio. But once the size of the fixed-rate portfolio exceeds the amount of core funds, a bank can end up financing rate-insensitive assets with highly rate-sensitive liabilities.

And that was what happened to Franklin. At the beginning of 1973, the bank's core money just about equaled its fixed-rate portfolio. But during 1973, while the core money eroded, fixed-rate assets increased. At the end of the year the bank was going to the money market for about $500 million to finance the part of its fixed-rate portfolio that was no longer covered by its core deposits. It was also borrowing $1.2 billion to finance its fluctuating-rate loans—i.e., those tied to movements of the prime rate. It made a little money on the spread between the yield and the cost of these loans, but not as much as it lost on the fixed-rate portfolio. On balance, Franklin was losing money on its $1.7 billion in borrowed funds. Luftig's gamble on capital leverage had backfired.

MIRED IN FEDERAL FUNDS

Having become dependent on borrowed funds in a period of rising rates, Franklin might still have effected some substantial economies by lengthening the maturity structure of its borrowings. There were days during 1973 when the bank was borrowing over $1 billion—about 25 percent of total liabilities— in the form of one-day federal funds. At midyear the federal-funds figure was running about $750 million, at a cost of about 8¼ percent. The cost of six-month certificates of deposit was approximately the same. If Franklin had locked up $750 million in six-month money just past midyear, it would not have had to borrow some $930 million in federal funds, at a cost of about 10 percent, during December, 1973. Franklin would have saved about $1 million in interest costs for that one month alone.

But at midyear, 1973, Franklin's management expected interest rates to fall dramatically. And why lock up a lot of expensive money when day-to-day funds would soon be available at much lower rates?

While the bank was playing Russian roulette with its debt structure, it was passing up opportunities to increase the return on its assets. Franklin's overall yield on assets was badly depressed by its huge fixed-rate portfolio, which constituted about half of all domestic earning assets. But even the variable-rate portion of Franklin's portfolio was outrageously underpriced. Loans that other banks made at the prime rate plus 2 percent could be obtained from Franklin at prime plus ½ or 1 percent.

There was nothing irrevocable about these prices. About 45 percent of Franklin's domestic-loan portfolio—over $900 million—matured every three months. The figure includes all the bank's ninety-day discounted loans as well as over $500 million in other loans. The bank could have raised its rates on these maturing assets to competitive levels; alternatively, it could have turned away the business. Eventually, Franklin did some of each but not soon enough to raise earnings in 1973.

EARNING LESS ON MORE

Shaddick was not doing much better abroad. It is true that foreign assets nearly doubled during 1973; by year-end they exceeded a billion dollars, about a quarter of the bank's total earning assets. The only trouble with this growth is that it was totally unprofitable. At the end of 1973 the international department was actually earning fewer dollars on its $1-billion portfolio than it had earned on $600 million the previous December. Profit margins abroad— i.e., the difference between interest earned and interest paid as a proportion of assets—had fallen from about a half cent per dollar of assets in the middle of 1973 to one-tenth of a cent at the end of the year. Adding in the cost of running the overseas branches, Franklin was plainly losing money abroad.

Shaddick's problems mirrored those of the rest of the bank. He was borrowing too short and lending too long at rates of ½ percent to ⅝ percent over his cost of funds. As the cost of day-to-day Eurodollars crept up, margins fell and disaster threatened. Like Luftig, Shaddick had guessed wrong on interest-rate movements.

In July, 1973, Luftig left on vacation, still convinced that interest rates would soon peak. While on vacation he telephoned William Hitchborn, the controller, to ask how the bank was doing. Hitchborn, who worked for John Sadlik, told him not to worry—the bank was having a banner month. Luftig returned to find that the bank had lost nearly $700,000 in July, its worst month in history. Hitchborn had badly miscalculated.

In the latter half of 1973, a deepening sense of gloom pervaded the bank. Luftig now realized that he had to reduce assets, not increase them. Jolted by the Hitchborn incident and others like it, he demanded better and more comprehensive financial data. Luftig also tried to fire Sadlik, but Gleason intervened to save him.

By late summer, the mood in the bank was approaching panic. The third-quarter dividend looked shaky, and this in turn could have jeopardized a plan of Sindona's to help the bank. He had been pushing a merger between Franklin and Talcott National, a factoring and finance company that he also controlled. Since Talcott had profits Franklin would find a use for its tax-loss carry-forward. But if Franklin omitted its third-quarter dividend, the merger would be in trouble.

Suddenly, as if by magic, earnings appeared. Franklin recorded a $2-million profit in foreign exchange during September. Sometime during the month, it is now known, Franklin's foreign-exchange department received a call from a member of senior management. The traders were instructed to arrange offsetting currency transactions with a Swiss bank called Amincor. Franklin bought four or five separate currencies from Amincor and soon thereafter resold them to the Swiss bank at a $2-million profit. But it was later established that the currencies in question had not risen sufficiently in the interim to produce a $2 million gain. The exchange rates placed on the contracts were plainly phony, rigged by agreement with Amincor to guarantee Franklin's profit. At the time, however, no questions were raised. The bank received a check for $2 million from Amincor. The check was addressed to P.R. Shaddick. Buttressed by the bogus foreign exchange profit, Franklin declared its dividend.

During the waning months of 1973, interest rates fell slightly from their September peak, and operating results improved. The bank's earnings were now so sensitive to the movements of the federal-funds rate that a decline of less than a percentage point in October sufficed to raise its gross interest differential by close to $2 million. In November Shaddick added to the good news by coming up with some sizable additional foreign-exchange profits. These appear to have been legitimate.

Beginning in the fourth quarter of 1973, Franklin began gambling heavily in the bond market. Management was convinced that the slight easing of interest rates presaged a sharp further decline. And so the bank authorized its securities department to go long in five- to ten-year government and federal agency bonds. J. Michael Carter, the head of the securities department, ended up buying much more than he was authorized to buy. From late in 1973 until March, 1974, Franklin's bond holdings rose by about $200 million. The yields on these bonds averaged between 7 and 8 percent, which was two to three percentage points less than the cost of the money used to purchase them. Unless interest rates fell substantially in 1974, the bank was obviously headed for further sizable operating deficits.

ONCE MORE WITH AMINCOR

By early 1974, the bank was almost a complete hostage to the vagaries of the federal-funds rate. When the rate fell in January, the bank remained marginally profitable. When it started to rise strongly in April, the bank's monthly operating deficit soared to $3 million.

Well aware of the bank's precarious operating position, Shaddick redoubled his efforts to make extraordinary gain in foreign exchange. There were profits of $3.8 million in January, but losses of $2.5 million in February. By March it was time for another Amincor deal. On March 28, the bank arranged a transaction in future foreign exchange (currencies bought and sold for future delivery), and these netted a phony unrealized profit of another $2 million. As a result, a prospective March foreign-exchange loss of $1 million was converted into a $1-million profit. The following month, Shaddick cracked up under the strain and spent two weeks in a hospital.

By April, Luftig was spending about half his time on the telephone trying to persuade other banks to continue selling Franklin federal funds. Morgan, then Franklin's major correspondent bank, had stopped selling it funds in the fall of 1973. Now Bank of America was cutting back its allotment, from $50 million to $30 million. Gradually, as word spread through the banking business that Franklin might fail, a growing number of banks either reduced or suspended sales.

Despite enormous difficulties, Franklin was still able to buy more than $500 million a day in federal funds during the first week of May. But it was clear that, within a short period of time, the bank would simply be unable to finance itself. Given the continued high level of the federal-funds rate, the bank was sure to continue losing money throughout the second quarter. By the end of the quarter, it would very probably face a massive run on its deposits.

LURCHING TOWARD MERGER

On May 6, Luftig told the bank's executive committee that Franklin had to be merged. By the end of the day the committee voted unanimously to authorize him to seek a merger. Luftig informed the Federal Reserve of the bank's predicament on the following day and started talks immediately with John McGillicuddy, president of Manufacturers Hanover. McGillicuddy liked the idea of a merger, but he had some conditions. He wanted antitrust clearance from the Justice Department. He wanted a guarantee that he would not have to bring any of Franklin's top executives into Manufacturers' senior management. In addition, McGillicuddy had a record of earnings growth at Manufacturers that he cherished. If he took on Franklin's losses, the record would surely be tarnished. And so some form of subsidy from the Federal Deposit Insurance Corporation would be required.

During the week of May 6, progress was made on at least two of the three issues raised by McGillicuddy. The Fed agreed to intercede with the Justice Department on the antitrust issue. And Franklin's executive committee agreed to the personnel condition. There was, moreover, some reason to expect a favorable response from the FDIC. It had provided a subsidy to the Crocker National Bank when it absorbed U.S. National in October, 1973. It would probably do the same in this case. In any event, on Friday Luftig called McGillicuddy and said: "I think we've got a deal." But then a bombshell exploded.

During the week, Franklin's top management had been getting intimations that the bank had suffered additional foreign-exchange losses—losses not recorded on the bank's books. But it wasn't until Friday night, May 10, that some idea of the magnitude of the losses emerged. That night, Luftig apprehensively passed the news to Manufacturers that Franklin had apparently sustained a huge loss in foreign-exchange trading. To his relief, Manufacturers indicated it was still willing to negotiate. On the weekend teams from both banks sat down to work out merger arrangements.

But on Sunday, May 12, Sindona moved to quash the effort. He managed to set up a remarkable high-level meeting at the Federal Reserve Bank of New York with representatives of the Fed, the Securities and Exchange Commission, and the Comptroller of the Currency. Representing Franklin were Sindona; his personal lawyer, Randolph Guthrie, of Mudge Rose Guthrie & Alexander; Carlo Bordoni, a close Sindona associate who was also a member of Franklin's board; Harold Gleason; and the bank's public-relations man, Arthur Perfall. Of this group, the only one who could conceivably claim a nodding acquaintance with Franklin's operating problems was Gleason.

Sindona had excluded from the meeting all the bank's top operating executives. And while he brought along his own personal lawyer, he did not invite the bank's longtime law firm, Kaye, Scholer, Fierman, Hays & Handler. It is little wonder, then, that the regulatory authorities received a badly garbled account of the bank's situation at the meeting. What is puzzling is that the regulators accepted this account without too much question.

After presumably pondering the condition of the bank, the regulators approved a Sindona plan to salvage Franklin by raising $50 million in additional capital from the bank's shareholders. Then a most astounding press release was prepared. The release, which was distributed by the Federal Reserve as well as by Franklin, implied that the entire $39-million or $40-million foreign-exchange loss had occurred during the second quarter; whereas at least $14 million had plainly occurred during the first quarter. The release also stated that Franklin believed it was insured "for a substantial portion of the loss." Some of the bank's top executives knew that wasn't true. In fact, Kaye, Scholer had just reported that the bank was probably not insured for any part of the loss.

The release further stated that the Comptroller of the Currency had assured the Federal Reserve that Franklin was a solvent institution and therefore eligible for loans at the Fed's discount window. It is hard to see how the Comptroller could have offered any such assurance. When Luftig was informed by telephone of the contents of the release, he called in Edward Lake, the bank examiner from the Comptroller's office who had been assigned to the Franklin account. Asked Luftig: "Are we solvent?" Replied Lake: "No."

A SPECIAL KIND OF INSOLVENCY

Considering only its liquidation value, Franklin was obviously insolvent on May 12. It could be argued that, in one sense, most other banks were also insolvent. After years of rising interest rates, the market value of their bond portfolios and their fixed-rate loans is appreciably below their liabilities.

But most other banks are going concerns that earn profits and pay dividends; it is reasonable to ignore their technical insolvency. Franklin was not at all a going concern on May 12. The bank had no prospects of making money then or in the foreseeable future.

The bank had no very good way of dealing with its central problem: its dependence on fixed-rate assets. As of May 12, Franklin had about $1.6 billion in fixed-rate assets—$900 million in bonds and another $700 million in loans. The bank had unrealized depreciation of about $100 billion in the bond account alone. If Franklin had tried to cut its fixed-rate portfolio to manageable proportions, it would have had to take huge losses—in addition that is, to its operating losses and those already sustained on foreign-exchange transactions. Sindona's plan for a $50-million capital increase would not have helped much.

It is, in fact, hard to see what merit the regulators saw in Sindona's rescue plan. Why didn't they reject it and push hard to get Franklin merged with Manufacturers? With any encouragement from the regulators, a merger would have been speedily arranged, Manufacturers would have quietly assumed Franklin's deposit obligations, and there would have been no mass withdrawals. Franklin's troubles would not have remained in the headlines for many months.

LUFTIG CALLS HIS LAWYER

After the session at the Fed broke up, Gleason returned for an emergency meeting of Franklin's executive committee later that evening. He confirmed that merger talks were suspended. Then Luftig told Gleason that his press release was inaccurate. Gleason said nothing, except that certain management changes would be discussed the next day. Whereupon Gleason left the meeting and Luftig called his lawyer.

The following day, Shaddick resigned and Luftig was fired. Gleason was named president as well as chairman. Five weeks later, on June 20, the bank revised that press release. It raised the figure for foreign-exchange losses from about $39 million to $45.8 million and assigned $26.7 million of this amount to the first quarter. The second release said that the first-quarter loss had resulted from falsified or unauthorized foreign-exchange contracts.

There is still very little known about those mysterious foreign-exchange transactions. At the end of June, however, it was learned that Sindona had had previous dealings with the Amincor Bank of Switzerland and had used the bank in his acquisition of Interphoto Corp. in 1970. Moreover, Carlo Bordoni, who continued on Franklin's board unitl late June, 1974, had also seen service on Amincor's board from 1969 to early 1973.

Sources in the SEC now confirm that the $4 million in foreign-exchange profits realized in September, 1973 and in March, 1974, was the result of self-dealing transactions. But what about the huge losses? Did they result from legitimate gambles that did not pay off? Or did Sindona give up on his attempt to prop up the bank after the two Amincor incidents? Did he instead decide that, since Franklin was in any case lost, it was now time to recoup his $10-million stock investment by sticking the bank with some foreign-exchange losses? Both the FBI and the SEC are still pursuing the answers.

To be sure, some of the circumstances surrounding the foreign-exchange losses are highly suspicious. A big chunk of these losses was attributed to a single trader, Donald Emrich, who had been hired by Shaddick in July, 1973. He was scarcely what one would call a topflight candidate for a trading job. He had previously been fired by Continental Illinois for the precise offense he committed at Franklin—unauthorized trading in foreign exchange. Before that he had been fired from Marine Midland Bank for irregularities pertaining to petty cash.

Perhaps Shaddick did not bother to inquire closely into Emrich's background. And since Shaddick was a law unto himself at Franklin, perhaps nobody bothered to check up on his choice. But there are other possibilities too. Shaddick himself had previously worked at Continental Illinois and had many contacts in the foreign-exchange department. It is conceivable that Shaddick may have known all about Emrich and decided that he might be just the right man to have around.

It is also conceivable that the foreign-exchange losses were simply the result of some desperate gambles. There is no doubt that, during much of the second half of 1973 and early 1974, Shaddick was putting enormous pressure on the foreign-exchange department to show profits. In that sort of atmosphere, a trader like Emrich might conceivably have felt justified in taking some fairly wild gambles—and then hiding the results from management if they proved unfavorable.

BARR GOES SHOPPING

On the same day that the bank revised its figures on foreign exchange, Gleason resigned as chairman and president, turning over both jobs to Joseph Barr, a former Secretary of the Treasury in the Johnson Administration. Barr spent most of his time attempting to sell the bank. He asked bank analyst Morris Schapiro to try to persuade would-be foreign and out-of-state acquirers that it was worthwhile paying a substantial premium to get a foot into the New York market.

Schapiro and Barr shopped around for buyers during the rest of June. But as Franklin continued to lose deposits, live prospects became increasingly scarce. Finally, on July 2, the Comptroller of the Currency asked Frank Wille, Chairman of the FDIC, to try to arrange a government-assisted purchase of Franklin. For the last three months Wille has been trying to dispose of Franklin by offering what amounts to a huge subsidy. Under one plan, the FDIC would assume all of Franklin's debt to the Federal Reserve.

As this article went to press, the best guess about Franklin's fate was that it would disappear as an independent banking entity sometime in late September or October. There is a plan to preserve Franklin as a purely Long Island bank, but, in mid-September, the regulators did not seem convinced that the plan was viable. It seems likely that Franklin's assets will shortly be auctioned off to one or more big banks. Wille will then have done essentially what Luftig tried to do four or five months earlier: merge Franklin into a stronger institution. In the interim, Franklin will have lost a minimum of 50 percent of its deposits, its stockholders will have lost most, if not all, of their investment, and the country's financial system will have received its worst scare since the Depression.

The Franklin tale reads like a modern-dress Greek tragedy. Error begat error, and events moved inexorably to a denouement that the bank's management feared, but seemed powerless to prevent. Roth started it all by making a lot of risky loans. When the loans went bad, Roth turned to bonds. When the bonds fell in value, they could not be sold because of the loan losses. And so the bank ended up trapped with a wad of low-yielding assets that had to be financed with progressively higher-cost money. Meanwhile, non-interest expense was increasing sharply because of reckless branching and the inflation of personnel costs.

By 1972 the only way to raise earnings to tolerable levels was by vastly increasing capital leverage. But there never was a more opportune time to leverage a bank than in late 1972 and 1973. The cost of borrowed money increased much more rapidly than the return on assets. Profit margins were nearly obliterated,and the stage was set for a final desperate gamble. Hoping for a drop in interest rates, the bank bought still more bonds.But interest rates rose even higher. By then the bank was mortally wounded. The foreign-exchange losses were merely the proverbial coup de grace.

In one respect, certainly, Franklin's problems were not at all typical of U.S. banking. Just about every big-league bank in the country has had better management. But in another respect, Franklin does fairly represent a powerful new current in the banking industry: a zeal for endless growth is shared by many other banks, including some big ones. It might ultimately prove to be a problem for some of them too.

Appendix 2 Solution to Northern Engineering Industries Problem

The following solution to the problem posed in Case Study 4 is suggested, but readers should note that it is based on certain assumptions explained in the notes to the transaction analysis. However, only two "plug" numbers are used, and both are quite small.

Sources of Cash (thousands of pounds)		Uses of Cash (thousands of pounds)	
Cash from Operations	19,432	Capital Expenditure	13,883
Sale of Investments	6,751	Acquisitions for Cash	6,299
Investment Income	2,444	Loan Stock Repaid	150
Dividends from Associates	502	Rationalization Costs	2,675
Assets Sold	742	Short-Term Debt Repaid	1,281
Net Decline in Cash	1,914	Payment to Minority Holders	730
		Dividends	5,254
		Advance Corporation Tax	1,369
		Tax on Exceptional Items	144
	31,785		31,785

NOTES TO THE TRANSACTION ANALYSIS SHEET

Begin with p. 10 of the annual report, then work through notes to financial statements.

Line 4. Tax expense is 6,717 of which 354 is attributed to associate companies (see note 3).

Line 6. Great care must be taken to deal separately with each extraordinary item to see its cash effect. Since rationalization costs are non-

Northern Engineering Industries Transaction Analysis Sheet

	Cash	Net Working Assets	Accounts Receivable	Fixed Assets	Subsidiaries and Investments	Goodwill	STD	Proposed Dividend	Loan Capital	Minority Interest	Preference Stock and Owner's Equity
1 31 Dec. 77	23,568	60,921	1,522	52,752	17,101	0	10,987	2,955	16,362	3,429	124,131
2 Trading Profit		+31,824									31,824
3 Interest		(6,363)									(1,360)
4 Tax					(354)						(6,717)
5 Minority Share										+984	(984)
6 Rationalization Cost	(2,675)										(2,675)
7 Surplus on Loan Stock	+97										+97
8 Profit on Investment	+6,751				(4,052)						+2,699
9 Tax on Exceptional Items	(144)										(144)
10 Divs. Proposed								+6,070			(6,070)
11 Divs. Paid	(5,254)							(5,254)			
12 Advance Corp. Tax	(1,369)		+1,369								
13 Associates Income		(1,258)			+1,258						
14 Depreciation		+7,271		(7,271)							
15 Investment Income	+2,444	(2,444)									
16 Dividends from Associates	+502				(502)						
17 Acquisitions	(6,299)	+6,371		+4,339	(2,516)	+1,947	+106			+2,836	+900
18 Paid to Minority Interest	(730)									(730)	
19 Loan Stock Repaid	(247)								(810)		563
20 Short-Term Debt Repaid	(1,281)						(1,281)				
21 Foreign Exchange Movements		(833)		(573)							(1,406)
22 Disposals	+742			(742)							
23 Capital Expenditure	(13,883)			+13,883							
24 Goodwill		(53)				+53					
25 Cash from Operations	+19,432	(19,432)									
31 Dec. 78	21,655	74,644	2,891	64,388	10,935	2,000	9,812	3,771	15,553	6,519	140,858

operating and nonrepeating, they are treated as a cash expense (see note 4).

Line 7. Although 97 is a gain, it represents a cash saving in payments to redeem loan stocks: Thus, loan stocks must have been redeemed below par value. This must be summarized with line 19 "Loan stock repaid or converted" (see note 4).

Line 8. Before dealing with profit on sale of unlisted investments entirely, we must establish original cost. This is found by subtracting 132 from 4,184 being the "other companies" line in note 10.

Line 9. From note 4 on p. 14.

Line 12. Advanced corporation tax is due on payment in cash of a dividend. Until it is offset against the company's current taxes it becomes a recoverable asset.

Line 13. From note 2 on p. 14. As we had already taken 31, 824 into net working assets, we must reverse out the 1,258 that is noncash income (accounting basis income).

Line 14. From note 2 on p. 14.

Line 15. All of the investment income is nonoperating income (note 2, p. 14), but 861 is a realized transaction gain and so is operating income.

Line 16. Dividends from associates from note 2 should be 551 not 502, but 502 will balance the column. Possibly some foreign exchange losses should be assigned to investments from net working assets, but then cash from operations would need adjustment. The missing figure is 49. Possibly a connection with the missing 53 in goodwill.

Line 17. This is difficult despite p. 12. The cash consideration of £6,299,000 is not the same as the amount in the directors' report (p. 8). Maybe cash balances were acquired. But if so, why 106 negative in the funds flow statement against "short-term deposits to cash"? Investments decrease by 2,723 as an investment becomes a subsidiary and is then consolidated. However, 207 appears to have been investments acquired in the transaction: hence, negative 2,516 to investments. Net working assets increases by 6,371 (6,890 + 3,518 − 2,570 + 640 + 130 − 2,237). And if goodwill goes up by 1,947, where is the remaining 53 to bring it to an end-year figure of 2,000? Is this related to the 106 negative—that is, an increase in short-term debt?

Line 19. From note 18, we know that loan capital decreased by 810, of which £417,569 was convertible loan stock. Other loans were repaid too in cash.

Line 21. From note 16, we know that 1,406 was charged against reserves of which 573 was for fixed assets (see note 8), so the balance must have been in net working assets, absent any foreign currency debt.

Line 22.   In the absence of a reliable figure, we have to use the "plug"
           figure for disposals of fixed assets. This is 742. Any loss against
           book value might be hidden as a cost in capital expenditure. The
           figure of 1,210 for disposals (p. 12) is the net book value, not the
           cash received.

Line 24.   See comments on line 17.

Appendix 3 Glossary of Financial Terms

ACCELERATE. (as in to accelerate a loan) To bring forward the date of re-payment from some future date to the immediate present. This arises typically because of an Event of Default (see below). See also CROSS-ACCELERATION.

ACCEPTANCE. A type of Bill of Exchange. By accepting (or adding his ac-ceptance to) a bill of exchange, the drawee undertakes to pay it on the maturity date. Accepted bills are often called acceptances. Acceptance can also be by endorsement. Bankers' acceptances are those where a bank has endorsed the bill and thus guarantees payment.

ACCEPTING HOUSE. Bank or financial organization whose specialty is add-ing its acceptance to its customer's bills so that they can be discounted in the discount market at favorable rates.

ACCOMMODATION PAPER. A note, trade acceptance, or draft endorsed by a person solely for the purpose of inducing a bank to lend money to a borrower when the latter's credit is not substantial enough to warrant a loan.

ACCOUNT PAYABLE. Money owed to creditors, usually suppliers.

ACCOUNT RECEIVABLE. Debtor. Money owed to the business.

ACCOUNTING PERIOD. Period of time from one balance sheet to the next. Period of the income statement, usually one year.

ACCOUNTING REPORTS. Balance sheet and income statement (profit and loss account).

ACCOUNTS RECEIVABLE FINANCING. Procedure whereby a specialized fi-nancial institution or bank makes loans against the pledge of accounts receivable.

ACCRUAL LIABILITY. Creditor, accounts payable, current liability. Ac-counting concept: income and expense for the accounting period must be included whether for cash or credit.

ACCUMULATED DEPRECIATION. Extent to which the fixed asset cost has been allocated to depreciate expense, since the asset was originally acquired. "Reserve" for depreciation. "Provision" for depreciation. Deducted from fixed assets.

ACCUMULATED PROFIT.   Retained earnings. Balance of profit retained in the business. Increase in owner's equity due to profit earned but not paid out in dividends. Profit and loss account balance carried forward. Profit for more than one year.

ACQUISITION.   The purchase of a company by another company

ADMINISTRATIVE EXPENSE.   Cost of directing and controlling a business. Includes such expenses as director's fees, office salaries, office rent, lighting, heating, legal fees, auditor's fees, and accounting services, but not research, manufacturing, sales, or distribution expenses.

ADVANCE.   A generic term for the ways in which a bank lends money, whether loan, overdraft, or discount.

ADVICE.   Note telling a customer how much his or her account has been debited or credited for a transaction.

ADVISE A CREDIT.   A letter of credit is opened when the importer's bankers mail it to their correspondent. It is advised when the correspondent passes it on to the exporter.

ADVISING BANK.   The correspondent in the exporter's country that advises the credit.

AFFILIATE.   A corporation or other organization related to another by being partly owned (not more than 50%). See also ASSOCIATE.

AMENDMENT.   Alteration of the terms of a credit on the opener's instructions with the beneficiaries concerned.

AMORTIZATION.   Depreciation, especially of intangible assets.

APPROPRIATION ACCOUNT.   Statement of accumulated profit.

ARBITRAGE.   Simultaneous purchase and sale of the same or equivalent items, to take advantage of a price discrepancy. The purchase of a security traded on two or more markets at the same time; also, occurs in the foreign exchange, commodity and money markets.

ARRANGEMENTS.   Arrangements between correspondents about reimbursement for payments made on each other's behalf and about reciprocal business.

ASSET.   Something owned that has a measurable cost. Fixed, current, or other assets. Includes claims on other persons.

ASSOCIATE.   An associate is a partly owned company (less than 50% but more than 5%).

AT SIGHT.   Payable on demand, like a check, as distinct from payable at a fixed period after acceptance.

AUTHORIZED CAPITAL.   Amount of capital shareholders authorize a company to raise when a company starts business. Published in the memorandum and articles of association. Authorized capital can be increased after formation.

AUTHORIZED POSITIONS.   The extent of the position in any currency that has been approved by management.

BAD DEBT.   Debtor who fails to pay. Amount written off the expense.

BALANCE SHEET.   A statement of the assets and liabilities of a company drawn up so as to give a fair view of the state of its affairs at a certain date.

BANKER'S ACCEPTANCE.   See ACCEPTANCE.

BANKER'S PAYMENT.   A payment instruction from one U.K. bank to another that is cleared like a check.

BC.   Bill for collection. Most commonly the shipping documents will be released to the drawee against payment of a sight draft or acceptance of a time draft.

BENEFICIARY.   Most commonly the exporter, the party who benefits from the credit by being able to negotiate documents for cash.

BILL COLLECTOR.   The bank's representative who collects payment from drawees in exchange for bills of exchange drawn on them.

BILL OF EXCHANGE.   A written instruction to a debtor to pay money on demand or in some cases at a determinable future data. A check is a type of bill of exchange. Defined in the U.K. under the Bills of Exchange Act 1882.

BILL OF LADING.   A receipt given by a carrier to a shipper for goods received stating that the goods have been accepted for shipment and detailing the terms and conditions under which they will be transported. The original copy carries title to the goods, is negotiable, and is attached to the draft which is used to effect payment for shipment.

BILL PAYABLE.   A bill of exchange which has to be paid; the opposite of a bill receivable.

BILLS DEPARTMENT.   The department concerned with imports and exports. So called because it is common practice for an exporter to have a bill for the value of his goods collected from the importer by a bank in the importer's country.

BOND.   Credit instrument that contains a promise to pay a specified amount of money at a fixed date or dates, usually more than 10 years after issuance, and a promise to pay interest periodically at stated dates.

BOOK VALUE.   Two meanings: (1) value of assets in the books, or, (2) value of ordinary shares in the books.
(Computed: owner's equity less preference shares, divided by the number of ordinary shares.)

BORROWING LONG.   Borrowing money for long periods.

BORROWING SHORT.   Borrowing money for short periods, as distinct from borrowing long.

BULLET LOANS.   These are term loans with repayment in full at the end of the period; there are no part payments along the way.

BUYING RATE.   The rate at which the bank will buy foreign exchange from customers, paying them the equivalent in local currency.

CALL DEPOSITS.   Deposits which are repayable on the demand either of the bank or of the depositor.

CAPITAL EQUIPMENT.   Premises and plant, as distinct from current assets, such as stock.

CAPITAL RESERVE.   Capital surplus. Capital profit. Not available for normal dividend. Not accumulated profit. Includes share premium. Not cash.

CAPITAL STOCK.   Share capital in units of money.

CAPITAL SURPLUS.   Capital reserve.

CAPITALIZATION.   The summation of long-term debt, capital stock, and surplus. Also, "market capitalization" means total number of common shares multiplied by current share price.

CASH.   Money assets of a business. Includes both cash in hand and cash at bank. Balance sheet current assets.

CASHFLOW.   Cashflow normally means the cash resulting from sales minus operating expenses other than depreciation.

CASH DISCOUNT.   Discount allowed to a debtor for early payment of a debt. Terms might be for payment within 10 days or net (not discount) for payment within one month.

CD.   A certificate of deposit, usually negotiable by delivery, representing funds deposited at a bank.

CEILING.   A limit imposed on something; for example, regulatory authorities may impose a ceiling on loans.

CHARGE.   To take a charge is to take a mortgage or pledge over an asset.

CHARGE OFF.   To reduce a loan by treating it as an accounting expense. Loans are charged off when considered uncollectible.

CIF.   Cost, insurance, and freight, all of which are paid by the exporter and included in the invoice total. The main alternatives are C and F (cost and freight), where the importer looks after the insurance and is therefore not invoiced for it, and FOB (free on board), where the importer looks after both freight and insurance and is invoiced for neither.

CLEAN.   Clean bills of lading bear no clauses. Shipping companies add clauses to bills of lading to protect themselves when cargo or packing appears defective.

CLEANUP.   Describes the payment of all outstanding debts by a company to a bank. On occasion, a bank may require a cleanup (30–90 days) in order for the company to continue borrowing.

CLOSE.   The legal process when the buyer's lawyer pays the purchase price to the seller's lawyer in exchange for the documents of title.

CLOSING.   The procedure for signing a mortgage, or a syndicated loan or a bond issue. Also known as "signing."

CLOSING STOCK.   Inventory at the end of the accounting period. Part of the computation of cost of goods sold.

COLLATERAL.   Anything pledged or deposited in support of a loan over which the lender has taken a charge.

CO-MAKER.   A person who signs a note in addition to the borrower to give extra security to the loan because of weakness of the borrower as an individual credit risk. A co-maker is distinguished in U.S. law from an endorser or guarantor in that, in a legal sense, the co-maker is jointly liable with the borrower for repayment. Whereas an endorser or guarantor is required to make good the loan only after certain legal technicalities have been fulfilled.

COMMERCIAL PAPER.   Consists of promissory notes of large business concerns of high credit standing, usually maturing in 30, 60, or 90 days, which are bought and sold in the open market.

COMMITMENT.   Any extension of credit to which the bank is committed, whether advance, letter of credit, guarantee, loan or overdraft.

COMMON STOCK.   Ordinary shares.

CONFIRM A CREDIT.   A bank which opens a credit is liable under it; a bank which advises a credit is not liable under that credit unless it confirms it, thereby guaranteeing payment whether the opening bank pays or not.

CONFIRMATION COMMISSION.   A bank's charge for confirming a credit.

CONTINGENT LIABILITY.   A liability not generally recorded on the balance sheet. May or may not become an actual liability. Liabilities to make payments if certain things happen—for example, if an exporter presents documents under a credit. Different from direct liabilities, such as liabilities to repay debts. A guarantee is often a contingent liability.

CONTRA.   A vital term of double-entry bookkeeping. Books are a record of transactions between debtors and creditors; every entry to the credit of a creditor's account for money or value owed to the creditor must be matched by equal and opposite contra entries to the debit of the debtor's account for money or value owed by the debtor.

CONVENTION.   Assumption made in accounting. Many accounting concepts arise from assumptions that have proven to be practicable.

CONVERTIBLE BONDS.   Bonds issued by a corporation which may be converted by the holder into stock of the corporation within a specified time period and a specified price.

CORPORATE RESOLUTION.   A document given to a bank by a corporation defining the authority vested in each of its officers who may sign for and otherwise conduct the business of the corporation with the bank. These powers are granted by the Board of Directors of the firm.

CORRESPONDENT.   A bank in another place which performs services, particularly making and receiving payments to the debit or credit of a nostro account in their books.

COUNTERPARTY.   The party with whom a bank makes a contract covering its contract with a customer, when it squares its position.

COVENANT.   A promise made by a borrower in a term loan agreement.

COVER.   When a bank instructs its correspondent to pay out more than it has in its account, it has to put the account in funds again (or cover) by instructing another bank to pay the correspondent. A very important part of foreign exchange activity.

COVERED FORWARD.   A Trader, who is to receive foreign currency and will want to exchange it for his own, covers himself forward against the risk of loss in exchange by selling the foreign currency immediately to his bankers, so that he knows how much of his own currency they will receive, whatever happens to the exchange rates since he fixes the future rate at the time of the deal. See also FORWARD CONTRACTS.

CREDIT LIMIT/CREDIT LINES.   The limits up to which a bank is prepared to lend money or grant credit to a customer. A line of credit is not normally a legal commitment, only a willingness to do business.

CREDIT TRANSACTION.   Transaction that incurs (accrues) liability. No cash is paid or received until later.

CREDITOR.   Payable, account payable, liability. Money owed to other parties. Current or long-term liability.

CREDITOR'S CLAIMS.   Liabilities.

CROSS ACCELERATION.   The process of making a term credit immediately payable because another term credit has become capable of being made immediately payable.

CROSS DEFAULT.   The right to call an Event of Default under a loan agreement when another lender in another agreement has called an Event of Default. This right is frustrated if the other lender grants a waiver.

CURRENT ACCOUNT.   The most common form of bank account, against which one can write checks. Commercial current accounts—between companies or between companies and their directors, for instance, are accounts that may be settled on demand, as distinct from loan accounts that are not settled before due.

CURRENT ASSETS.   Assets which are normally realized in cash or used up in operations during one operating period (normally one year). Includes cash, debtors, inventory, and prepaid expenses.

CURRENT LIABILITY.   Liability due for payment within one operating cycle (usually but not always one year).

CURRENT RATIO.   Ratio of current assets to current liabilities. Measure of liquidity.

D/A. Documents against acceptance, as distinct from D/P, when the documents are released only against payment.

DEBENTURE. An obligation, a bond. Long-term debt. May be secured or unsecured.

DEBT SERVICE COVERAGE RATIO. See interest coverage ratio. Sometimes also includes required payments with interest payments (see Chapter 6).

DEFERRED INCOME. Income received in advance of being earned and recognized. Normally left as a current liability on the balance sheet until the sale is made and the income recognized.

DEFERRED SHARES. Shares of a company, ranking for dividend after preference or preferred and ordinary shares.

DEFERRED STOCK. Deferred shares.

DEMURRAGE. Charges incurred as a result of delay in clearing goods at a port.

DEPRECIATION. The amount by which the assets of a business are judged to have diminished during the year. Tax authorities limit the amount of depreciation which may be allowed to diminish a company's profits. Allocation of the cost of a fixed asset to expense over its working life. Measure of the cost of using the fixed asset.

DEPRECIATION EXPENSE. Depreciation (at cost) during the accounting period. Not the same as accumulated depreciation except in the first year of the fixed asset.

DIRECTORS' LOANS. In small companies, the directors are often the main shareholders. They cannot withdraw their capital from the company without complicated legal procedure, and therefore they often finance its growth by loans rather than capital.

DOCUMENTARY CREDIT LINE. The maximum value of documentary credits which a bank will have outstanding for a customer at one time.

DOCUMENTARY CREDITS. Documentary credits are banker's promises to pay for specified shipping documents covering shipments on certain items.

DRAFT. Bill of exchange. Often used in banks in a restricted sense to mean bills or checks drawn by a bank on its branch or correspondent.

ENDORSE. To sign one's name, and usually on the back of a check or draft.

ENDORSED IN BLANK. Cargo is delivered in accordance with the orders endorsed on the bill of lading. If it is endorsed in blank, the cargo may be delivered in acccordance with the collecting bank's order.

ENDORSEMENT. A person transfers his right to receive an amount of money. The endorser accepts the liability of making payment on the instrument of the original maker if prior endorsers fail to do so.

ENDOWMENT POLICY. A type of life insurance policy under which the insurance company promises to pay on a certain date or at death, whichever is earlier.

ENTITY.   Accounting concept: accounting reports are prepared for a specific entity.

ENTRIES.   Transactions in a bank are entered in the books. Hence, transactions passing through the books are described as book entries or simply, entries. You pass entries when you make out vouchers; you post entries when you enter them in a ledger.

EQUIPMENT.   Fixed asset if acquired for long-term use and not for resale. Recorded in the balance sheet at cost less depreciation, not at market value.

EQUITY.   The shareholders' stake in a business.

EURODOLLARS.   Dollars owned by nonresidents of the United States and held in bank accounts outside the United States.

EVENT OF DEFAULT.   A covenant, term or a condition of a long term loan which when broken by the borrower causes the loan to become immediately due and payable. See also ACCELERATE.

EXCESS.   The amount by which an overdraft or other credit exceeds its authorized limits.

EXCHANGE CONTRACT.   Contract between a bank and a company to exchange one currency for another, generally either at a fixed future date or spot (for example, two business days after the deal is made).

EXCHANGE POSITION.   A bank's spot or forward assets or liabilities in foreign currency.

EXPIRY DATES.   Letters of credit have two expiry dates—the last date for shipment and the last date for negotiation of the documents.

FACE VALUE.   Nominal value of shares. Not the book (owner's equity) value or market value.

FACTORING.   Procedure whereby a specialized finance company or bank purchases the accounts receivable of a firm without recourse.

FEDERAL FUNDS.   Sight claims on Federal Reserve banks or the U.S. Treasury. A method whereby member banks may adjust their reserve balance with the Federal Reserve bank. Generally borrowed for one day.

FIDUCIARY.   An individual, corporation, or association, such as a bank or trust company, to whom certain assets are given to hold in trust, according to a trust agreement.

FIRST PRESENTATION.   The drawee of a sight bill (that is, a bill of exchange payable at once) is expected to require a day or two to arrange funds to pay it, and payment of first presentation is unusual. A usance bill, on the other hand, must be paid on the due date. By deferring acceptance, a drawee defers eventual payment.

FISCAL STATEMENT.   A statement for a yearly period at the end of which a firm determines its financial condition without regard to the calendar year.

FIXED ASSETS. Such assets as land, plant, and equipment acquired for long-term use in the business and not for resale. Charged to overhead expense periodically as depreciation. Recorded in the balance sheet at cost less depreciation, not market value. Sometimes revalued periodically if accounting principles permit (GAAP does not).

FIXED EXPENSES. Fixed expenses occur whatever volume is produced. Compare variable expenses.

FLOATING CHARGE. Charge over a debtor's fluctuating assets, such as the inventory which the debtor undertakes to convert into a charge for a fixed amount if the creditor demands that the debtor do so.

FOB. Free on board. The importer arranges and pays for freight and insurance and is therefore invoiced for neither. See also CIF.

FORWARD CONTRACTS. You may buy or sell a currency for future delivery fixing the future exchange rate today. This is a forward contract. Forward rates reflect the cost of interest on the money to be used.

GOODWILL. Value of the name, reputation, or intangible assets of the business. In accounting, this is only recorded when the business is purchased, and it is wholly amortized. Represents the excess of price paid over the value of the net assets acquired.

GROSS PROFIT. Difference between sales and cost of goods sold. Profit computed before charging for selling and administrative expenses, and other expenses.

GROSS PROFIT PERCENTAGE. Measure of profitability computed as:

$$\frac{\text{Gross profit}}{\text{Net sales}} \times 100\%$$

INCOME. Earnings, profit, revenue. Sometimes used to mean sales and all forms of income benefits, not necessarily in cash.

INDEMNITY. Generally, a form letter in which a bank undertakes to do something and to refund any cost or loss the beneficiary may suffer from some specified event.

INFLATION ACCOUNTING. A set of rules which attempts to adjust historic cost accounts to allow for the changes in values arising from rates of inflation. Assumes that accounting should record "value."

INTANGIBLE ASSET. Asset which cannot actually be touched, for example copyrights and goodwill.

INTERBANK MARKET. Where banks deal extensively with each other, covering their positions in local currency and foreign exchange.

INTEREST COVERAGE RATIO. Earnings before interest and taxes divided by interest expense.

INVENTORY. Stock of goods on hand for resale. It includes stores and supplies, and is valued at the lower of cost or market value, not selling price.

It is increased by purchases and decreased by cost of goods sold. Also, a balance sheet current asset.

IRREVOCABLE CREDIT.   Bankers' promise to pay in exchange for shipping documents covering shipment on certain terms that can not be revoked by the bank that opens it (issues it) without the permission of the beneficiary.

ISSUED CAPITAL.   Share capital actually issued by a company. See also AUTHORIZED CAPITAL. Price at which a share is first sold by a company; normally the nominal value plus share premium or less share discount. May be ordinary, preference or deferred shares, not bonds or debentures.

LETTER OF CREDIT.   Bankers' promise to pay in exchange for shipping documents covering shipment on certain terms.

LIMITED COMPANY.   Company whose shareholders have limited their liability to the amounts that they subscribe to the shares which they hold.

LINE OF CREDIT.   An indication of willingness by a lender to do business by way of extending credit to the borrower up to the figure specified. Not a commitment to lend. Normally reviewed annually but subject to cancellation without notice.

LIQUID.   The liquid assets of a company are those which can easily be realized, such as cash and marketable securities.

LONG.   A position in which assets exceed liabilities; for example, a bank whose contracts to buy dollars for sterling exceed its contract to sell dollars for sterling is long in dollars and short in sterling. Also called "overbought."

LONG-TERM LIABILITY.   Liability not due for payment within one year. Bonds, debentures, or loans. Holders are creditors and receive interest; they are not shareholders.

MANAGEMENT CONTROL RETURNS.   A class of accounting returns whose object is to enable management to control the business more effectively.

MARGIN COLLATERAL.   A bank lends only a proportion of the quoted value of any security, in case the market value diminishes. The margin is the difference between the value of the collateral and the amount lent.

MARGIN (PROFIT).   The element of profit in sales after deducting sales costs, usually measured as a percentage of sales.

MARKETABLE STOCK.   Shares and bonds which are traded on stock exchanges and are correspondingly easy to market. Because of marketing difficulties, banks are usually not keen on unquoted stocks or bonds as collateral.

MATERIALS.   Directors' valuation of these in a balance sheet is generally at cost or present market value, whichever is lower. The trading profit is affected by this valuation.

MATURITY.   The date on which a loan or deposit is due to be repaid.

MEMORANDUM AND ARTICLES OF ASSOCIATION. The documents setting out a company constitution.

MONEY MARKET. The market in which banks, finance houses, and major companies lend each other their surplus funds.

MORTGAGE. Long-term loan normally secured on a fixed asset. Long-term liability.

NET CURRENT ASSETS. The amount by which a company's current assets exceed its current liabilities.

NET WORTH. The amount which would be divided among the shareholders if a company were to liquidate. It is the sum of the paid-up capital and all the reserves. Tangible net worth is the amount less any intangible assets.

NOMINAL VALUE. Face value of shares. Authorized and issued share capital in the balance sheet shows the nominal value of the shares separately from any premium or discount. Not the book value or market value of shares.

NOSTRO ACCOUNT. An account belonging to our bank at another bank (that is, our own operating account). See also VOSTRO ACCOUNT.

ON DEMAND. The paying bank will pay as soon as the draft is presented to it by another bank or reaches it by mail.

OPEN A CREDIT. A credit is opened when the importer's bank issues it, as distinct from being advised by the bank in the exporter's country. The importer is sometimes referred to as the opener of the credit, though this is not correct.

OPENING STOCK. Inventory at the beginning of the accounting period.

ORDINARY SHARES. Share capital. Part of owner's equity in the balance sheet. Holders are entitled to dividends recommended by the directors. Net preference shares. Possible values: face or nominal value, market value, issue price (including any premium), book value (total owner's equity less the nominal value of preference shares).

OVERDRAFT LIMIT. Customers may draw up to a certain limit more than they have in their accounts, and interest is charged on the actual day-to-day debit balance in the account that results.

OVERHEADS. The administrative expenses of a business, often fixed costs, such as rent.

OWNER'S EQUITY. Net worth. Amount due to owners of the business. Increased by profits. Reduced by losses, and dividends. Assets minus liabilities equals owner's equity.

P&L. Profit and loss account. Also income statement.

PATENT. Legal right to exploit an invention. Asset in the balance sheet. Recorded at cost less depreciation under the heading "Other Assets."

PLANT. Manufacturing equipment and machinery. Fixed asset if acquired for use and not for resale. Often used to describe both a factory and the equipment in it.

PLOUGH BACK PROFIT. Retain net profit in the business by carrying it forward in the profit and loss account instead of distributing it in dividends.

PORTFOLIO. A group term for assets, including securities, acceptances, discounts, loans, and overdrafts. One also talks in a more detailed sense of a portfolio of acceptances.

POST. Enter transactions in the bank's books, either by hand or by machine.

PREFERRED STOCK. Also known in some countries as preference share.

PREFERENCE SHARE. Share which entitles the holder to fixed dividends (only) in preference to the dividends for ordinary shares. On liquidation, normally entitled only to the nominal value. No right to share in profits, except where specified.

PREMIUM. Sum paid periodically to an insurance company for insuring one's life or property. In the case of forward currency, the amount which it costs more than spot currency. For instance, if spot U.S. $ dollars cost 2.3950 per British pound and the one-month premium is 12 points, you get only $2.3938 in exchange for £1 if you fix a contract for delivery one month ahead.

PREPAYMENTS. Items, such as rent, which have to be paid in advance.

PRICE/EARNINGS RATIO. The ratio between the price to be paid for a company and its net earnings or profit. Multiply the number of shares issued by the official quoted price, and compare this figure with the last published net profit.

PROFIT AND LOSS ACCCOUNT. The account in which companies record the amount of profit they retain or the amount of loss they have not yet recovered. Income statement. Statement showing sales, costs, expenses, and profit for an acccounting period.

PROVISION. Strictly means liability, but often has several different meanings: reserve (for example, future income tax liability), accumulation, (accumulated depreciation), expense (for example, depreciation expense), accrual (for example, accrued expense, liability).

PUBLISHED FINANCIAL STATEMENTS. Balance sheet, profit and loss account, and statement of accumulated profit, with comparative figures and notes disclosing information.

RECOGNITION OF PROFIT. As accounting concept: Profit is not recognized and recorded until realized (in cash or accounts receivable). By contrast, losses are often recognized when goods are shipped to the customer, not when the order is received or when the customer pays for the goods.

RECONCILIATION. Proving an account is right by comparing it in detail with a statement of the same account in someone else's books.

REDEEMABLE PREFERENCE SHARES. Preference shares which may be repurchased by the company from the shareholders. Part of owner's equity. Not ordinary shares.

RESERVE. Strictly means accumulated profit. Used more vaguely. See REVENUE RESERVE, PROVISION.

RETIRE. Collections of shipping documents are retired by being paid for and released. Debt is retired by being paid.

RETAINED EARNINGS. Accumulated profits, available for dividend. Part of owner's equity.

REVALUATION. Sometimes fixed assets are revalued from historic cost to current values. The difference is credited to reserves.

REVENUE. Earnings, income, profit; sometimes also used to mean sales.

REVENUE RESERVE. Profit available for dividends. Accumulated profit and general reserve. Retained earnings.

SCHEDULES. Collection schedules give details of the documents being handled and instructions on how to handle them. Accounting schedules, on the other hand, usually give tabulated information about particular aspects of the business.

SECURED LOAN. A loan against security in which the lender can realize an asset if the borrower fails to pay, as opposed to an unsecured loan which gives the lender no claim over any asset.

SECURITIES. Documents of title to investments, such as share certificates and bonds.

SECURITY. Collateral such as property (real or personal), goods, or documents of title.

SHARE. Document certifying ownership of shares in a company.

SHARE PREMIUM. Excess of original sales price of a share over its face or nominal value. Not available for dividend.

SHORT. A position in which liabilities exceed assets. For example, if contracts to sell marks for sterling exceed contracts to buy, one is short in marks and long in sterling. Also called "oversold."

SIGHT CREDITS. Letters of credit calling for sight drafts, as distinct from usance credits calling for usance drafts.

SIGHT DRAFTS. Drafts payable on demand (at sight), as distinct from usance drafts payable a certain period after acceptance or date.

SPOT. For payment two business days ahead: this gives everyone time to handle all the paperwork conveniently. The normal term for dealings in the foreign exchange market.

SQUARE. A position in which asset and liabilities are matched. One sometimes talks of a square position if it is matched overall, even if it is oversold one month and overbought six. Also called "matched."

STOCK.   Inventory. Supply of finished goods, raw material, or both. Valued at the lower of manufacturing cost or market value.

STOCKHOLDER.   Shareholder.

STRAIGHT-LINE DEPRECIATION.   Depreciation method charging off the cost of a fixed asset equally over the years of its working life. See also DEPRECIATION.

SUBORDINATION.   An agreement between a company and some of its creditors not to repay them before it repays the bank.

SUM OF THE YEAR'S DIGITS.   This is a method of depreciation with emphasis on early years. If the life of an asset is five years, depreciation in the first year will be 5/15 (15 being the sum of $5 + 4 + 3 + 2 + 1$), hence the name. In the second year it will be $\frac{4}{15}$ and so on.

TANGIBLE ASSET.   Asset that can be physically identified or touched. Sometimes means only those assets that have a definite value—that is, excludes intangible assets, goodwill, and research and development expenditures or other expenditures that have been capitalized.

TANGIBLE NET WORTH.   This is the sum of all reserves and capital funds less any intangible assets. It is "true" owners' equity, as far as that can be determined.

TIME DEPOSITS.   Deposits placed with the bank for a fixed period, as distinct from call deposits. Interest is normally payable at maturity.

TERM LOANS.   Loans made by the bank for a fixed period, as distinct from demand loans and from overdrafts, which fluctuate in amount. The time for interest payment varies from loan to loan.

TRADE CREDITORS AND TRADE DEBTORS.   Many manufacturers have to allow their customers time to pay for goods purchased and correspondingly demand credit from their own suppliers, without which they are unable to buy from them. You owe to a trade creditor; a trade debtor owes to you.

TRADE INVESTMENT.   Investment in shares or debentures of another company in the same trade or industry. Long-term investment. "Other asset" in the balance sheet. Valued at cost, unless there is a substantial loss.

TRADING PROFIT.   The difference between the value of sales and the total cost of goods sold. Carried into profit and loss account.

TRANSACTION.   Change in two items in the balance sheet. Cash or credit transaction. May be sale, purchase, cash receipt, cash payment, or accounting adjustment.

TRANSFER DEED.   An instruction signed by both the seller and the buyer of shares and bonds, or their agents, to the registrar of a company to transfer the shares or bonds into the buyer's name.

TRUE AND FAIR.   Accounting concept. Balance sheet and income statement show a "true and fair view" of the business, in accordance with generally accepted accounting principles.

TRUST RECEIPT.   Receipt given by a customer to a bank for documents released to him before payment of the bill. He holds the goods in trust for the bank to whom he undertakes to pay the sale proceeds, to meet the bill in due course. Not normally a legal claim, it may help a bank establish a legal right over the goods against another party with a claim.

TURNOVER.   Total sales.

UNCERTAINTY.   Limitation of accounting. Uncertainty at the end of each accounting period makes it difficult to determine the "true and fair" position. Uncertainty arises from incomplete transactions, market value of inventory, working life of fixed assets for depreciation calculations, realizable values of current assets, and contingent liabilities not yet known or calculable.

UNREALIZED.   Profit is realized only when it is actually received—in the case of exchange position, when the forward contracts have matured.

UNWIND.   Square the position by buying to cover an oversold position or selling to cover an overbought position.

USANCE CREDIT.   Letter of credit calling for bills maturing at a determinable future date, as distinct from a sight credit calling for bills payable at sight.

USANCE DRAFT.   A draft payable on a specified date.

VALUE.   Several meanings:
1. Accounting value—value according to accounting concepts, appropriate to the particular asset. Fixed assets valued at cost less depreciation. Current assets generally valued at cost or lower realizable value.
2. Market value—realizable value of inventory in the normal course of business (not in liquidation).
3. Real value—not known in accounting.

VARIABLE EXPENSES.   Expenses that vary with the volume produced, as distinct from fixed expenses, which do not.

VOSTRO ACCOUNT.   An account at our bank belonging to another bank.

VOUCHERS.   Each book entry in a bank arises from a voucher—that is, either a check or deposit slip prepared by a customer, or a slip prepared by bank staff on customer's instructions.

WAIVER.   An agreement by a lender to forgive a broken condition or covenant in a term loan (usually for a short period) which would otherwise give rise to an Event of Default.

WASTE.   An old banking term which in accounting language would be a journal. A large sheet on which the waste clerk analyzes and adds up all the different types of bank book entries during the day. The various totals balance with corresponding totals in the other parts of the bank, which

proves the accuracy of the entries. That is, for every credit, there mus
be a corresponding debit.

WORKING CAPITAL.   Current assets less current liabilities.

WORKING CAPITAL RATIO.   Ratio of current assets to current liabilities. In
dicates the liquidity of the business.

WOUND UP.   A company is dissolved by being wound up with the court'
permission.

WRITE DOWN.   To decrease; an asset when it is written down is decrease
in its recorded value.

WRITE OFF.   When a loan is written off, it is reduced to zero on the book
of the lender. See also CHARGE OFF.

Index

Accounting, creative, 146
Accounting principles, 16
Accounts payable, 46, 95
Accounts receivable, aging, 110
  days of, 46, 95, 110
Adler, Frederick R., 147
AEG Telefunken, 148
Altman, Edward I., 135-138
American Express Company, 77-78
Argenti, John, 135, 140-149
Assets, efficiency of, 97
  quality of, 103, 111
Auditors, change of, 16
Auditors opinion, 12, 13, 15

Banco Intercambio, 177
Bank analysis, 167-189
Bank of England, 180-184
Banks, ratios for, 179-181
Barriers to entry, 127
Baruch, Bernard M., 79
Beaver, W. H., 63, 91, 113, 137
Bond ratings, 105
Boston Consulting Group, 123
Braniff Airways, 138, 142
Breakup analysis, 115
British Printing Corporation, 148
Buyer power, 132

Capital markets, 105, 211
Capital Structure, 114
Cash, sources and uses, 62
  cycle, 47, 111
Cash from operations, 5, 19
  negative, 63, 135
Cashflow, basis for debt, 1, 89
  growth rate and, 95
  not affected by accounting, 17, 18
  projections, 161
  total liabilities and, 91, 113

Cashflow analysis, 3, 60-62
  assumptions in, 61
  how to do, 39
Change, adapting to, 82, 121, 143
Character, 214
Charge off, 9
Chrysler Corp., 21, 145
Collateral, 1, 216
Comfort letters, 74-76
Comparative analysis, 7, 8
Consolidated statements, 21, 65
Consolidating statements, 69, 72
Contingent liabilities, 174
Contracts, long term, 20
Corporate collapse, 135-139
Corporate structure, 65
Cost of capital, 114
Covenants, 155-156
Credit analysis, 1, 207-208
Credit function, 8

Darwin, Charles, 82, 121, 143
Debt, subordinated, 119
Debt capacity, 4, 5, 89
Debt/equity ratio, 87, 116
Debt priority, 69, 117
Debt ratios, 90
Debt service coverage, 4, 93, 113, 137
Deferred taxes, 87, 118
Depreciation, 18-19
Dewing, A. S., 2, 3
Disraeli, Benjamin, 151, 154
Diversification, 153
Donaldson, Gordon, 4
Drucker, Peter F., 121

EBIT/TA, 84-86, 137
Events of default, 159

Fairness, 12

Finance companies, 190-198
Financial condition, 103-105
Financial ratios, 79
Financial statements, 11, 22-29
Fog factor, 205
Foreign exchange, 31, 144, 175-176
Fowler, H. W., 204
Franklin National Bank, 167
Free capital ratio, 181-182
Freeport Sulphur, 77
Funds flow, 60

GAAP, 14, 17, 65, 136
General Motors, 21
Goodwill, 65
Government relations, 126
Grant, W. T. Company, 63, 105, 142
GTI Corporation, 139, 140
Guarantees, use of, 218

Hallmark Cards, 12
Herstatt, Bankhaus I. D., 167, 176
Holding companies, 69, 211
Howard B. B. & Upton, M., 3

Industry, dynamics, 127
  identification, 99
Innovation, 124
Inventory, accounting for, 17, 104
  concealment of, 106
  costs of, 21
  days of, 46, 95, 105
  quality of, 103, 105

Kipling, Rudyard, 11

Lafleur, James K., 139
Laker Airways, 144
Largay J. A., & Strickney, C. P., 63
Lawrence, H. L., 142
Leverage, financial, 86-94, 145, 169
  operating, 92
Liabilities, 112
Liquidity, 94, 137
Loans, purpose of, 215
  portfolios, 213
Locke, John, 1

Management, 141
Management Today, 84
Market share, 122-123
Massey Ferguson, 145
Meccano, 124

Michelin, 12
Minority Interest, 65, 67, 68, 89
Mitchell Construction, 145
Moore, Peter G., 203

N. L. Industries, 200-202
Napoleon, 206
Net asset value, 115
Net interest income, 169
Net working assests, 40, 45, 123, 163
Nondisclosure, 11, 12
Nonoperating items, 47

One man rule, 141
Overtrading, 145

Penn Central, 140, 148
Pension liabilities, 15, 21
Pertamina, 145
Porter, Michael E., 127
Preferred Creditors, 72, 118
Present value, 91, 92
Profitability, 80, 82, 122
Projections, 163
Public responsibility, 126

Ratios, 79, 81, 94-97, 112, 115
Resources, Human, 125
Return on equity, 81-85, 122
Revenue recognition, 20, 193
Risk, 6, 7, 207, 213
Rolls Royce, 140, 141, 145

Salter, M. S. and Weinhold, W. A., 153
Slatter, S. St. P., 123
Solvency, 94
Spreading, 22-29, 180
Standard & Poor's Corporation, 105
Statement of changes, 60
Stauffer Chemical, 14-17, 23-29, 47-59
Strunk, William, Jr., 199
Subsidiaries, 21, 68, 74-76
Supplier power, 133

Teleflex, 202
Term loans, 151-155
Thomson Brandt, 72
Transacrion analysis, 47, 60

Working capital, 2, 40, 42,
  107

Z Scores, 136-139